Pastor M[illegible]

B.C.

Sermon Texts

SERMON TEXTS

Sermon Texts

Ernst H. Wendland, *Editor*

NORTHWESTERN PUBLISHING HOUSE
Milwaukee, Wisconsin

Library of Congress Card 84-62030

Northwestern Publishing House
3624 W. North Ave., Milwaukee, WI 53208-0902

Published 1984

Printed in the United States of America

ISBN 0-8100-0186-1

CONTENTS

PREFACE

Within recent years two helpful books for the busy preacher's library are no longer in print. They are Paul W. Nesper's *Biblical Texts* (Augsburg Publishing House) and Frederic H. K. Soll's *Pericopes and Selections*. They served as a ready reference for the various pericopic selections developed through many centuries of preaching on the church year as well as offering suggestions for sermon texts for special occasions.

The editorial staff of the Northwestern Publishing House extended an appeal to the homiletics department of Wisconsin Lutheran Seminary to assist in replacing these important tools for the ministry. The result is this book, *Sermon Texts*, in which the seminary faculty participated. Seminary students also helped in preparing the index.

After the listing of each text the thought which identifies the text is given in summary form. It should be mentioned that these text summaries are not intended to be sermon themes.

This book is offered in the hope that it will provide a useful aid in the all important work of proclaiming God's word.

PART ONE

TEXTS ACCORDING TO PERICOPIC SERIES FOR THE CHURCH YEAR

The word pericope means "a circumscribed portion." The use of this term to refer to the appointed Scripture readings has been traced to late sixteenth century Protestantism. The practice of assigning certain Gospel and Epistle readings to the various Sundays, festivals and saints' days, however, has been followed from at least the time of Jerome (fl. 400). His lectionary may have provided the basis for the Roman *Ordo*, the selections used by Gregory the Great (590-604), whose writing include forty homilies on the ancient Gospel selections. This Roman series, with some modification, came into general use in the western church at the time of Charlemagne (d. 814).

With slight modification, these Gospels and Epistles were used during the Middle Ages. They were taken over by Luther with minor adjustments, and he used these pericopes as texts for his *Kirchenpostille*, a model sermon book for evangelical preachers. A disadvantage of this ancient series is that it includes only a few Old Testament selections which are used as Epistle readings.

In modern times a number of other series have been developed. These offer Gospel and Epistle selections which relate to the ancient pericopes while affording variety. Seven of these have been included in this volume. All of them include Old Testament selections.

The inclusion of Old Testament texts is a distinct advantage in these modern arrangements. The gradual working out of God's plan of salvation, the Messianic promises and prophecies, the significance of the various names of God, the portions which are interpreted by Jesus and his Apostles in the New Testament all provide important gospel content and insight into what God has done and is doing for our salvation. The Old Testament, like the New, focuses on Christ.

Usually pericopic selections offer a manageable portion of Scripture for treatment in a given sermon. They contain a complete unit of thought which the preacher can expound and apply in a unified way. The use of pericopic texts makes it possible for a preacher to accept an assignment and carry it out in a disciplined way. It relieves him of the task of searching for suitable texts week by week. It helps him avoid any tendency to concentrate on a pet subject. It keeps him from selecting favorite or easy or motto texts. It provides him with texts that are rich in doctrinal and practical content. Pericopic texts challenge a preacher to do solid exegetical work. They help him and the congregation grow in the knowledge of Scripture.

To recommend the use of pericopic series is not to urge the use of a contrived system or pattern which exists for its own sake. We are speaking of a plan for the annual review of Christ's work for us and Christ's work in us. The church year is an aid to proclaiming the saving acts of the triune God and teaching his will for our lives.

The pericopic series are helpful tools to be used rather than a burden to be borne. That is, we use them in freedom because they provide a nutritious and varied diet of food from God's Word. Yet we are not bound to them. We will surely depart from them when a special occasion or the needs of the congregation call for something more specific.

1. THE HISTORIC PERICOPES

With a few changes, Luther and the sixteenth-century reformers adopted the Christian year of the medieval western church, using the prescribed Epistle and Gospel selections. These readings usually provided the text for the day's sermon. The Old Testament selections which are included here were chosen by the Joint Commission on a Common Liturgy of the church bodies which later constituted the Lutheran Church in America and the American Lutheran Church. They were chosen to complement the "ancient" Epistles and Gospels, and the preacher may expect to find in them points of contact with the Epistles and Gospels.

In listing the Sundays according to the seasons of the church year, the sequence will be designated as follows:

Advent 1 — First Sunday in Advent
Christmas 1 — First Sunday after Christmas
Epiphany 1 — First Sunday after Epiphany
Lent 1 — First Sunday in Lent
Easter 1 — First Sunday after Easter
Trinity 1 — First Sunday after Trinity

These designations apply to the Eisenach, Thomasius, Synodical Conference and Soll selections as well. The ILCW selections follow a different pattern.

Advent 1

O.T.:	Jr 31:31-34	The New Covenant Offers Forgiveness
Ep.:	Ro 13:11-14	The Hour Has Come to Awake from Slumber
Gosp.:	Mt 21:1-9	Jesus Enters Jerusalem

Advent 2

O.T.:	Mal 4:1-6	The Day of the Lord Is Coming
Ep.:	Ro 15:4-13	The Gentiles Will Come to Faith in Christ
Gosp.:	Lk 21:25-36	Watch for the Lord's Second Advent

Advent 3

O.T.:	Is 40:1-8	God Comforts His People

Ep.:	1 Cor 4:1-5	The Lord Judges His Servants
Gosp.:	Mt 11:2-10	Jesus Testifies That He Is the Christ

Advent 4

O.T.:	Dt 18:15-19	God Will Raise Up a Prophet Like Moses
Ep.:	Php 4:4-7	Rejoice in the Lord Always
Gosp.:	Jn 1:19-28	John the Baptist Testifies That He Is Not the Christ

Christmas — The Nativity Of Our Lord

O.T.:	Is 9:2-7	To Us a Child Is Born
Ep.:	Tt 2:11-14	God's Saving Grace Has Appeared to All
Gosp.:	Lk 2:1-14	Jesus, the Savior, Is Born

Sunday after Christmas

O.T.:	Is 63:7-16	You, O Lord, Are Our Father
Ep.:	Ga 4:1-7	When the Right Time Came, God Sent His Son
Gosp.:	Lk 2:33-40	Simeon And Anna Rejoice in Their Savior

New Year's Day

O.T.:	Jos 24:14-18	We Will Serve the Lord
Ep.:	Ga 3:23-29	You Are All One in Christ Jesus
Gosp.:	Lk 2:21	Jesus Receives His Name

Sunday after New Year

O.T.:	1 Sm 2:1-10	Hannah Thanks the Lord
Ep.:	1 Pe 4:12-19	Rejoice When You Suffer for Being a Christian
Gosp.:	Mt 2:13-23	God Protects the Christ Child

Epiphany

O.T.:	Is 2:2-5	The Gospel Goes Out from Zion
Ep.:	Is 60:1-6	The Nations Come to Zion's Light
Gosp.:	Mt 2:1-12	Wise Men Worship the Christ Child

Epiphany 1

O.T.:	Ec 12:1-7	Remember Your Creator in the Days of Your Youth
Ep.:	Ro 12:1-5	Offer Your Bodies As Living Sacrifices
Gosp.:	Lk 2:41-52	As a Twelve Year Old Boy Jesus Visits the Temple

Epiphany 2

O.T.:	Is 61:1-6	The Spirit of the Lord Equips Christ for His Work
Ep.:	Ro 12:6-16	Serve One Another in Christian Love
Gosp.:	Jn 2:1-11	Jesus Reveals His Glory at the Wedding in Cana

Epiphany 3

O.T.:	2 Kgs 5:1-19	Naaman Is Healed of Leprosy
Ep.:	Ro 12:17-21	Overcome Evil with Good
Gosp.:	Mt 8:1-13	Jesus Heals a Leper and the Centurion's Servant

Epiphany 4

O.T.:	Ex 14:21-31	Israel Passes through the Red Sea
Ep.:	Ro 13:8-10	Love Is the Fulfillment of the Law
Gosp.:	Mt 8:23-27	Jesus Calms the Sea

Epiphany 5

O.T.:	Eze 33:10-16	Turn from Your Evil Ways
Ep.:	Col 3:12-17	Love Binds All Together in Perfect Unity
Gosp.:	Mt 13:24-30	The Parable of the Weeds in the Wheat Field

Transfiguration

O.T.:	Ex 3:1-6	God Appears to Moses in the Burning Bush
Ep.:	2 Pe 1:16-21	God's Word Is Our Guiding Light
Gosp.:	Mt 17:1-9	Jesus in His Transfiguration

Septuagesima

O.T.:	Jr 9:23,24	Knowledge of the Lord Is the True Cause for Boasting
Ep.:	1 Cor 9:24—10:5	Run To Win the Prize
Gosp.:	Mt 20:1-16	The Parable of the Workers in the Vineyard

Sexagesima

O.T.:	Am 8:11,12	The Lord Will Send a Famine of His Word
Ep.:	2 Cor 11:19—12:9	My Grace Is All You Need
Gosp.:	Lk 8:4-15	The Parable of the Sower

Quinquagesima

O.T.:	Jr 8:4-9	God's People Have Rejected His Word
Ep.:	1 Cor 13	Love Is the Greatest Gift
Gosp.:	Lk 18:31-43	Jesus Starts Out for Jerusalem

Ash Wednesday

Ep.:	Jl 2:12-19	Rend Your Heart And Not Your Garments
Gosp.:	Mt 6:16-21	Store Up for Yourselves Treasures in Heaven

Lent 1

O.T.:	Gn 22:1-14	God Commands Abraham To Offer Isaac
Ep.:	2 Cor 6:1-10	Do Not Receive God's Grace in Vain
Gosp.:	Mt 4:1-11	Jesus Overcomes the Devil's Temptations

Lent 2

O.T.:	Ex 33:17-25	Moses Asks To See God's Glory
Ep.:	1 Th 4:1-7	God Called Us To Live a Holy Life
Gosp.:	Mt 15:21-28	Jesus Heals the Canaanite Woman's Daughter

Lent 3

O.T.:	Jr 26:1-15	Jeremiah's Call to Repentance Is Rejected
Ep.:	Eph 5:1-9	Live as Children of Light
Gosp.:	Lk 11:14-28	Jesus Is Stronger Than Beelzebub

Lent 4

O.T.:	Is 52:7-10	How Beautiful Are the Feet of Those Who Preach the Gospel
Ep.:	Ga 4:21-31	Hagar and Sarah Represent Two Covenants
Gosp.:	Jn 6:1-15	Jesus Feeds Five Thousand Men

Passion Sunday (Lent 5)

O.T.:	Nu 21:4-9	Moses Puts Up a Bronze Snake
Ep.:	He 9:11-15	Christ Is the Mediator of a New Covenant
Gosp.:	Jn 8:46-59	Before Abraham Was Born, I Am

Palm Sunday

O.T.:	Zch 9:8-12	Rejoice, Your King Is Coming to You
Ep.:	Php 2:5-11	Imitate Christ's Humility
Gosp.:	Mt 21:1-9	Jesus Enters Jerusalem

Maundy Thursday

O.T.:	Ex 12:1-14	God Institutes the Passover
Ep.:	1 Cor 11:23-32	Examine Yourselves before Eating the Lord's Supper
Gosp.:	Jn 13:1-15	Jesus Washes His Disciples' Feet

Good Friday

O.T.:	Is 53:1-7	The Lord's Servant Is Led Like a Lamb to the Slaughter
Ep.:	Is 52:13—53:12	The Lord's Suffering Servant Triumphs through His Death
Gosp.:	Jn 18:1—19:42	Jesus Suffers, Dies And Is Buried

Easter — The Resurrection Of Our Lord

O.T.:	Is 25:1-8	The Lord Prepares a Banquet for All Nations
Ep.:	1 Cor 5:6-8	Christ, Our Passover Lamb, Has Been Sacrificed
Gosp.:	Mk 16:1-8	An Angel Announces the Lord's Resurrection

Easter 1

O.T.:	Gn 32:22-31	Jacob Wrestles with God
Ep.:	1 Jn 5:4-12	Faith Wins the Victory over the World
Gosp.:	Jn 20:19-31	Jesus Appears to Thomas

Easter 2

O.T.:	Eze 34:11-16	The Lord Promises To Shepherd His Flock
Ep.:	1 Pe 2:21-25	Follow Christ's Example in Suffering
Gosp.:	Jn 10:11-16	I Am the Good Shepherd

Easter 3

O.T.:	Is 40:26-31	Those Who Trust in the Lord Will Soar on Wings Like Eagles
Ep.:	1 Pe 2:11-20	Live As Aliens And Strangers in the World
Gosp.:	Jn 16:16-23	The Sorrow of Jesus' Disciples Will Be Turned into Joy

Easter 4

O.T.:	Is 49:1-15	Rejoice in the Lord's Comfort
Ep.:	Jas 1:16-21	Every Good Gift Comes from God
Gosp.:	Jn 16:5-15	Jesus Promises To Send the Holy Spirit

Easter 5

O.T.:	Is 55:6-11	My Word Will Do Everything I Send It To Do
Ep.:	Jas 1:22-27	Do What the Word Says; Don't Just Listen to It
Gosp.:	Jn 16:23-30	The Father Will Give You Whatever You Ask in My Name

Ascension

O.T.:	Gn 5:21-24	Enoch Is Translated
Ep.:	Ac 1:1-11	Jesus Is Taken Up into Heaven
Gosp.:	Mk 16:14-20	Jesus Commissions His Disciples To Preach the Gospel

Sunday after Ascension

O.T.:	Is 32:14-20	The Spirit Is Poured upon Us from on High
Ep.:	1 Pe 4:7-11	Be Good Managers of God's Gifts
Gosp.:	Jn 15:26—16:4	Jesus Promises To Send the Spirit of Truth

Pentecost

O.T.:	Eze 36:22-28	I Will Put My Spirit in You
Ep.:	Ac 2:1-13	The Holy Spirit Comes at Pentecost
Gosp.:	Jn 14:23-31	The Holy Spirit Will Teach You

Trinity Sunday

O.T.:	Is 6:1-6	God Calls Isaiah To Be a Prophet
Ep.:	Ro 11:33-36	Paul Praises God's Wisdom And Knowledge
Gosp.:	Jn 3:1-15	Jesus Instructs Nicodemus

Trinity 1

O.T.:	Dt 6:4-13	Love the Lord with All Your Heart
Ep.:	1 Jn 4:16-21	God Is Love
Gosp.:	Lk 16:19-31	Jesus Compares the Rich Man with Lazarus

Trinity 2

O.T.:	Pr 9:1-10	The Fear of the Lord Is the Beginning of Wisdom
Ep.:	1 Jn 3:13-18	True Love Shows Itself in Deeds
Gosp.:	Lk 14:16-24	The Parable of the Great Banquet

Trinity 3

O.T.:	Is 12:1-6	You Will Draw Water from the Wells of Salvation
Ep.:	1 Pe 5:6-11	God Cares for You
Gosp.:	Lk 15:1-10	There Is Joy in Heaven over One Sinner Who Repents

Trinity 4

O.T.:	Is 65:17-19,24,25	I Will Create New Heavens And a New Earth
Ep.:	Ro 8:18-23	Our Present Sufferings And Our Future Glory
Gosp.:	Lk 6:36-42	Do Not Hypocritically Judge Others

Trinity 5

O.T.:	Lm 3:22-32	The Lord's Compassion Never Fails
Ep.:	1 Pe 3:8-15	You Were Called To Inherit a Blessing
Gosp.:	Lk 5:1-11	Jesus Calls His First Disciples

Trinity 6

O.T.:	Ru 1:1-17	Your God Will be My God
Ep.:	Ro 6:3-11	We Are Dead to Sin But Alive to God
Gosp.:	Mt 5:20-26	Jesus Explains the Fifth Commandment

Trinity 7

O.T.:	Is 62:6-12	Zion Will Be Called the City No Longer Deserted
Ep.:	Ro 6:19-23	The Gift of God Is Eternal Life
Gosp.:	Mk 8:1-9	Jesus Feeds Four Thousand Men

Trinity 8

O.T.:	Jr 23:16-29	Let the One Who Has My Word Speak It Faithfully
Ep.:	Ro 8:12-17	Those Led by God's Spirit Are God's Sons
Gosp.:	Mt 7:15-23	Be on Guard against False Prophets

Trinity 9

O.T.:	Pr 16:1-9	Ask the Lord To Bless Your Plans
Ep.:	1 Cor 10:6-13	God Gives Us Strength To Withstand Temptation
Gosp.:	Lk 16:1-9	The Parable of the Shrewd Manager

Trinity 10

O.T.:	Jr 7:1-11	Change Your Evil Ways
Ep.:	1 Cor 12:1-11	The Spirit Gives Various Spiritual Gifts
Gosp.:	Lk 19:41-48	Jesus Weeps over Jerusalem

Trinity 11

O.T.:	Dn 9:15-18	Our Requests Appeal to God's Mercy
Ep.:	1 Cor 15:1-10	By God's Grace I Am What I Am
Gosp.:	Lk 18:9-14	The Parable of the Pharisee And the Tax Collector

Trinity 12

O.T.:	Is 29:18-21	The Deaf Will Hear And the Blind Will See
Ep.:	2 Cor 3:4-11	The Ministry of the New Covenant Has Greater Glory
Gosp.:	Mk 7:31-37	Jesus Heals a Deaf And Dumb Man

Trinity 13

O.T.:	Zch 7:4-10	Show Kindness And Mercy to One Another
Ep.:	Ga 3:15-22	The Law Did Not Set Aside the Promise Given to Abraham
Gosp.:	Lk 10:23-37	The Parable of the Good Samaritan

Trinity 14

O.T.:	Pr 4:14-23	Guard Your Heart, the Well-Spring of Life
Ep.:	Ga 5:16-24	Live According to Your New Nature
Gosp.:	Lk 17:11-19	Jesus Heals Ten Men of Leprosy

Trinity 15

O.T.:	1 Kgs 17:8-16	God Miraculously Provides for Elijah And the Widow
Ep.:	Ga 5:25—6:10	Let Us Not Become Weary of Doing Good
Gosp.:	Mt 6:24-34	Let God's Kingdom Be Your First Concern

Trinity 16

O.T.:	Job 5:17-26	Blessed Is the Person Whom God Corrects
Ep.:	Eph 3:13-21	May Christ Dwell in Your Hearts through Faith
Gosp.:	Lk 7:11-17	Jesus Restores the Widow's Son to Life

Trinity 17

O.T.:	Pr 25:6-13	Practice the Virtue of Humility
Ep.:	Eph 4:1-6	Do Your Best To Preserve the Unity of the Spirit
Gosp.:	Lk 14:1-11	Jesus Teaches Humility

Trinity 18

O.T.:	2 Chr 1:7-12	Solomon Prays for Wisdom
Ep.:	1 Cor 1:4-9	God Will Keep You Strong to the End
Gosp.:	Mt 22:34-46	The Law Requires a Loving Heart

Trinity 19

O.T.:	Gn 28:10-17	Jacob Dreams of a Ladder Reaching to Heaven
Ep.:	Eph 4:22-28	Put On the New Man
Gosp.:	Mt 9:1-8	Jesus Forgives And Heals a Paralytic

Trinity 20

O.T.:	Pr 2:1-8	The Lord Gives Wisdom
Ep.:	Eph 5:15-21	Be Very Careful How You Live
Gosp.:	Mt 22:1-14	The Parable of the Wedding Banquet

Trinity 21

O.T.:	2 Sm 7:17-29	David Thanks the Lord for His Promises
Ep.:	Eph 6:10-17	Put On the Full Armor of God
Gosp.:	Jn 4:46-54	Jesus Heals an Official's Son

Trinity 22

O.T.:	Pr 24:14-20	Wisdom Is Good for the Soul
Ep.:	Php 1:3-11	Paul Prays for the Philippians
Gosp.:	Mt 18:23-35	The Parable of the Unforgiving Servant

Trinity 23

O.T.:	2 Kgs 23:1-3	Josiah Renews the Covenant with the Lord
Ep.:	Php 3:17-21	Our Citizenship Is in Heaven
Gosp.:	Mt 22:15-22	Jesus Answers a Question about Paying Taxes

Trinity 24

O.T.:	1 Kgs 17:17-24	Elijah Restores the Widow's Son to Life
Ep.:	Col 1:9-14	You Will Share in the Inheritance of the Saints
Gosp.:	Mt 9:18-26	Jesus Raises the Daughter of Jairus

Trinity 25

O.T.:	Job 14:1-5	Man's Life Is Short And Full of Trouble
Ep.:	1 Th 4:13-18	Do Not Grieve Like Those Who Have No Hope
Gosp.:	Mt 24:15-28	The Son of Man Will Come Like the Lightning

Trinity 26

O.T.:	Dn 7:9-14	The Kingdom of the Son of Man Will Never End
Ep.:	2 Pe 3:3-14	The Day of the Lord Will Come Like a Thief
Gosp.:	Mt 25:31-46	The Son of Man Will Judge All Nations

Trinity 27

O.T.:	Is 35:3-10	The Redeemed Will Walk on the Way of Holiness
Ep.:	1 Th 5:1-11	Be Ready for the Lord's Coming
Gosp.:	Mt 25:1-13	The Parable of the Ten Virgins

Festival Of The Reformation

O.T.:	1 Sm 3:19—4:1	Israel Recognized Samuel As a Prophet of the Lord
Ep.:	Re 14:6,7	An Angel Proclaims the Eternal Gospel
Gosp.:	Jn 8:31-36	The Truth Will Set You Free

Festival Of Harvest

O.T.:	Dt 11:8-17	If You Obey My Commands, I Will Bless Your Land
Ep.:	2 Cor 9:6-11	God Loves a Cheerful Giver
Gosp.:	Lk 12:15-21	The Parable of the Rich Fool

Thanksgiving

O.T.:	Dt 8:1-20	Do Not Forget the Lord our God
Ep.:	1 Tm 2:1-8	Offer Prayers And Thanksgiving
Gosp.:	Mt 6:25-34	Let God's Kingdom Be Your First Concern

2. THE EISENACH SELECTIONS

The Evangelische-Kirchliche Konferenz was the group which, in the 19th century, became a sort of forum and coordinating agency for the Lutheran, Reformed and Union state churches of Germany. In 1896 this group, more popularly known as the Eisenach Conference, published a selection of texts which was to supplement the Historic Pericopes. Epistles and Gospels were intended to parallel the "ancient" readings; Old Testament selections were added. The texts chosen were to emphasize the atoning work of Christ. The sermon studies of Dr. R.C.H. Lenski did much to popularize this series among Lutheran preachers in the United States.

Advent 1

O.T.:	Jr 31:31-34	I Will Make a New Covenant with Israel
Ep.:	He 10:19-25	Let Us Hold Firmly to the Hope We Profess
Gosp.:	Lk 1:68-79	Zechariah Sings a Hymn of Praise

Advent 2

O.T.:	Mal 4:1-6	The Day of the Lord Is Surely Coming
Ep.:	2 Pe 1:3-11	Make Your Calling And Election Sure
Gosp.:	Lk 17:20-30	The Kingdom of God Does Not Come Visibly

Advent 3

O.T.:	Is 40:1-8	Comfort, Comfort My People
Ep.:	2 Tm 4:5-8	I Have Fought a Good Fight
Gosp.:	Mt 3:1-11	John the Baptist Preaches Repentance

Advent 4

O.T.:	Dt 18:15-19	The Lord Promises To Send a Prophet Like Moses
Ep.:	1 Jn 1:1-4	The Word of Life Has Appeared to Us
Gosp.:	Jn 1:15-18	Grace And Truth Came through Jesus Christ

Christmas — The Nativity Of Our Lord

O.T.:	Is 9:6,7	To Us a Child Is Born
Ep.:	1 Jn 3:1-5	How Great Is the Father's Love for Us
Gosp.:	Mt 1:18-23	He Will Be Called Immanuel

Sunday after Christmas

O.T.:	Is 63:7-16	You, O Lord, Are Our Father
Ep.:	2 Cor 5:1-9	We Live by Faith, Not by Sight
Gosp.:	Lk 2:25-32	Simeon Praises God for the Christ Child

New Year's Day

O.T.:	Ps 90	Lord, You Have Always Been Our Dwelling Place
Ep.:	Ro 8:24-32	All Things Work Together for Good to Those Who Love God
Gosp.:	Lk 4:16-21	The Time of the Lord's Favor Has Come

Sunday after New Year

O.T.:	Ps 73:23-28	Whom Have I in Heaven But You?
Ep.:	Jas 4:13-17	What Is Your Life?
Gosp.:	Mt 16:1-4	The Only Sign You Will Be Given Is the Sign of Jonah

Epiphany

O.T.:	Is 2:2-5	The Word of the Lord Will Go Out from Jerusalem
Ep.:	2 Cor 4:3-6	God Made His Light Shine in Our Hearts
Gosp.:	Mt 3:13-17	John Baptizes Jesus

Epiphany 1

O.T.:	Ps 122	Let Us Go to the House of the Lord
Ep.:	2 Cor 6:14—7:1	Do Not be Yoked Together with Unbelievers
Gosp.:	Jn 1:35-42	Jesus Gains His First Disciples

Epiphany 2

O.T.:	Is 61:1-6	The Spirit of the Sovereign Lord Is on Me
Ep.:	1 Cor 2:6-16	We Proclaim God's Secret Wisdom
Gosp.:	Jn 1:43-51	Jesus Calls Philip And Nathanael

Epiphany 3

O.T.:	2 Kgs 5:1-19	Naaman Is Healed of Leprosy
Ep.:	Ro 1:13-20	The Gospel Is God's Power To Save All Who Believe
Gosp.:	Jn 4:5-14	Jesus Offers Living Water

Epiphany 4

O.T.:	Ps 93	The Lord Reigns in Majesty
Ep.:	Ro 7:7-16	The Law Is Holy
Gosp.:	Jn 4:31-42	The Fields Are Ripe for Harvest

Epiphany 5

O.T.:	Eze 33:10-16	Turn from Your Evil Ways
Ep.:	Ro 8:1-9	There Is No Condemnation for Those in Christ Jesus
Gosp.:	Mt 7:24-29	The Wise and Foolish House Builders

Transfiguration

O.T.:	Ex 3:1-6	God Appears to Moses in the Burning Bush
Ep.:	2 Cor 3:12-18	We Reflect the Lord's Glory
Gosp.:	Jn 5:39-47	The Scriptures Testify about Christ

Septuagesima

O.T.:	Jr 9:23,24	Let Him Who Boasts Boast about Knowing the Lord
Ep.:	Php 1:27—2:4	Conduct Yourselves in a Manner Worthy of the Gospel
Gosp.:	Lk 10:38-42	Jesus Visits Martha And Mary

Sexagesima

O.T.:	Am 8:11,12	God Threatens To Send a Famine of His Word
Ep.:	Php 1:12-21	For Me, To Live Is Christ And To Die Is Gain
Gosp.:	Jn 11:20-27	I Am the Resurrection And the Life

Quinquagesima

O.T.:	Jr 8:4-9	Jeremiah's Call to Repentance
Ep.:	1 Cor 1:21-31	We Preach Christ Crucified
Gosp.:	Jn 11:47-57	The Sanhedrin Plots To Kill Jesus

Lent 1

O.T.:	Gn 22:1-14	God Commands Abraham To Offer Isaac
Ep.:	He 4:15,16	Jesus Is Our Great High Priest
Gosp.:	Mt 16:21-26	Jesus Predicts His Suffering And Death

Lent 2

O.T.:	Ex 33:17-23	Moses Asks To See God's Glory
Ep.:	1 Jn 2:12-17	Do Not Love the World
Gosp.:	Lk 10:17-20	Rejoice That Your Names Are Written in Heaven

Lent 3

O.T.:	Jr 26:1-15	Jeremiah Preaches Repentance
Ep.:	1 Pe 1:13-16	Be Holy As God Is Holy
Gosp.:	Lk 9:51-56	A Samaritan Village Refuses To Welcome Jesus

Lent 4

O.T.:	Is 52:7-10	How Beautiful Are the Feet of Those Who Bring Good News
Ep.:	2 Cor 7:4-10	Godly Sorrow Brings Repentance That Leads to Salvation
Gosp.:	Jn 6:47-57	I Am the Bread of Life

Passion Sunday (Lent 5)

O.T.:	Nu 21:4-9	Moses Puts Up a Bronze Snake
Ep.:	1 Pe 1:17-25	You Were Redeemed with the Precious Blood of Christ
Gosp.:	Jn 13:31-35	A New Commandment I Give You

Palm Sunday

O.T.:	Zch 9:8-12	Rejoice, Your King Is Coming to You
Ep.:	He 12:1-6	Jesus Is the Author And Perfecter of Our Faith
Gosp.:	Jn 12:1-8	Mary Anoints Jesus' Feet

Maundy Thursday

O.T.:	Ps 111	Great Are the Works of the Lord
Ep.:	1 Cor 10:16,17	The Lord's Supper Is a Sharing in Christ's Body And Blood
Gosp.:	Lk 22:14-20	Jesus Institutes the Lord's Supper

Good Friday

O.T.:	Ps 22:1-11	My God, My God, Why Have You Forsaken Me?
Ep.:	2 Cor 5:14-21	God Reconciled Us to Himself through Christ
Gosp.:	Lk 23:39-46	Jesus Dies on the Cross

Easter — The Resurrection Of Our Lord

O.T.:	Ps 118:14-24	This Is the Day the Lord Has Made
Ep.:	1 Cor 15:12-20	Christ Has Indeed Been Raised from the Dead
Gosp.:	Mt 28:1-10	He Has Risen, Just As He Said

Easter 1

O.T.:	Gn 32:22-31	Jacob Wrestles with God
Ep.:	1 Pe 1:3-9	Praise to God for a Living Hope
Gosp.:	Jn 21:15-19	Jesus Reinstates Penitent Peter

Easter 2

O.T.:	Ps 23	The Lord Is My Shepherd
Ep.:	Eph 2:4-10	By Grace You Have Been Saved through Faith
Gosp.:	Jn 14:1-6	I Am the Way, the Truth And the Life

Easter 3

O.T.:	Is 40:26-31	Those Who Hope in the Lord Will Soar on Wings Like Eagles
Ep.:	1 Jn 4:9-14	The Father Has Sent His Son To Be the Savior of the World
Gosp.:	Jn 12:20-26	Some Greeks Want To See Jesus

Easter 4

O.T.:	Ps 98	Sing to the Lord a New Song
Ep.:	2 Tm 2:8-13	Remember Jesus Christ, Who Was Raised from the Dead
Gosp.:	Jn 6:60-69	Lord, You Have the Words of Eternal Life

Easter 5

O.T.:	Is 55:6-11	My Word Will Do Everything I Send It To Do
Ep.:	1 Tm 2:1-6	God Wants All Men To Be Saved
Gosp.:	Lk 11:5-13	Ask, And It Will Be Given to You

Ascension

O.T.:	Ps 110	Sit at My Right Hand
Ep.:	Col 3:1-4	Set Your Hearts on Things Above
Gosp.:	Lk 24:50-53	Jesus Ascends into Heaven

Sunday after Ascension

O.T.:	Ps 42	My Soul Thirsts for God
Ep.:	Eph 1:15-23	God Seated Christ at His Right Hand in the Heavenly Realms
Gosp.:	Jn 7:33-39	Whoever Is Thirsty Should Come to Me And Drink

Pentecost

O.T.:	Eze 36:22-28	I Will Put My Spirit in You
Ep.:	Eph 2:10-22	You Are Now Fellow Citizens with God's People
Gosp.:	Jn 14:15-21	Jesus Promises To Send the Holy Spirit

Trinity Sunday

O.T.:	Is 6:1-8	Holy, Holy, Holy Is the Lord of Hosts
	Nu 6:22-27	The Aaronic Benediction
Ep.:	Eph 1:3-14	God Has Blessed Us with Every Spiritual Blessing in Christ
	2 Cor 13:11-14	The New Testament Benediction
Gosp.:	Mt 28:16-20	Go And Make Disciples of All Nations

Trinity 1

O.T.:	Dt 6:4-13	Love the Lord with All Your Heart
Ep.:	Ac 4:32-35	The Believers Share Their Possessions
Gosp.:	Mt 13:31-35	The Kingdom of Heaven Is Like Mustard Seed And Like Yeast

Trinity 2		
O.T.:	Pr 9:1-10	The Fear of the Lord Is the Beginning of Wisdom
Ep.:	Ro 10:1-15	How Can They Believe in Christ If They Have Not Heard of Him?
Gosp.:	Mt 9:9-13	Jesus Calls Matthew
Trinity 3		
O.T.:	Is 12:1-6	With Joy You Will Draw Water from the Wells of Salvation
Ep.:	Ac 3:1-16	Peter Heals the Crippled Beggar
Gosp.:	Lk 15:11-32	The Parable of the Lost Son
Trinity 4		
O.T.:	Is 65:17-19;24,25	I Will Create New Heavens And a New Earth
Ep.:	Ac 4:1-12	Peter And John Are Brought before the Sanhedrin
Gosp.:	Mt 5:13-16	Believers Are Like Salt And Light
Trinity 5		
O.T.:	Lm 3:22-32	The Lord's Compassions Never Fail
Ep.:	Ac 5:34-42	Gamaliel Gives the Sanhedrin Foolish Advice
Gosp.:	Lk 9:18-26	Following Jesus Involves Cross-Bearing
Trinity 6		
O.T.:	Ps 1	The Righteous Are Compared with the Wicked
Ep.:	Ac 8:26-39	Philip Tells the Ethiopian Eunuch about Jesus
Gosp.:	Mt 21:28-32	The Parable of the Two Sons
Trinity 7		
O.T.:	Is 62:6-12	Daughter of Zion, Your Savior Comes
Ep.:	1 Tm 6:6-12	Godliness with Contentment Is Great Gain
Gosp.:	Mk 4:26-29	The Kingdom of God Is Like Growing Seed
Trinity 8		
O.T.:	Jr 23:16-29	The One Who Has My Word Should Speak It Faithfully
Ep.:	Ac 16:16-32	The Jailer of Philippi Comes to Faith
Gosp.:	Mt 12:46-50	Jesus' Relatives Are Those Who Do What His Father Wants
Trinity 9		
O.T.:	Pr 16:1-9	Man Plans His Course, But the Lord Determines His Steps
Ep.:	Ac 17:16-34	Paul Preaches in Athens
Gosp.:	Mt 13:44-46	The Parables of the Hidden Treasure And the Pearl

Trinity 10

O.T.:	Jr 7:1-11	Change Your Ways And Your Actions
Ep.:	Ac 20:17-38	Paul Bids Farewell to the Ephesian Elders
Gosp.:	Mt 23:34-39	Jesus Laments over Jerusalem

Trinity 11

O.T.:	Dn 9:15-19	David Pleads with the Lord To Forgive His People
Ep.:	Ro 8:33-39	We Are More Than Conquerors
Gosp.:	Lk 7:36-50	Jesus Forgives a Sinful Woman

Trinity 12

O.T.:	Is 29:18-21	In That Day the Deaf Will Hear And the Blind See
Ep.:	Ac 16:9-15	Come Over to Macedonia And Help Us
Gosp.:	Jn 8:31-36	The Truth Will Set You Free

Trinity 13

O.T.:	Zch 7:4-10	Show Mercy And Compassion to One Another
Ep.:	1 Pe 2:1-10	You Are a Chosen People
Gosp.:	Mk 12:41-44	Jesus Is Pleased with the Widow's Offering

Trinity 14

O.T.:	Ps 50:14-23	God Delights in Obedience
Ep.:	1 Tm 1:12-17	Christ Jesus Came into the World To Save Sinners
Gosp.:	Jn 5:1-14	Jesus Heals the Invalid at the Pool of Bethesda

Trinity 15

O.T.:	1 Kgs 17:8-16	God Provides for Elijah And the Widow
Ep.:	2 Th 3:6-13	Whoever Refuses To Work Shall Not Eat
Gosp.:	Jn 11:1-11	Jesus Is Told That Lazarus Is Sick

Trinity 16

O.T.:	Job 5:17-26	Blessed Is the Man Whom God Corrects
Ep.:	He 12:18-24	You Have Come to the Heavenly Jerusalem
Gosp.:	Mt 11:25-30	Come to Me, And I Will Give You Rest

Trinity 17

O.T.:	Ps 75:4-7	It Is God Who Judges
Ep.:	He 4:9-13	There Remains a Sabbath-Rest for the People of God
Gosp.:	Mt 12:1-8	The Son of Man Is Lord of the Sabbath

Trinity 18

O.T.:	2 Chr 1:7-12	Solomon Asks for Wisdom
Ep.:	Jas 2:10-17	Faith Not Accompanied by Action Is Dead
Gosp.:	Mk 10:17-27	A Rich Young Man Declines Jesus' Call

Trinity 19

O.T.:	Ps 32:1-7	Blessed Is He Whose Transgressions Are Forgiven
Ep.:	Jas 5:13-20	The Prayer of a Righteous Man Is Effective
Gosp.:	Jn 9:24-41	The Man Born Blind Confesses His Faith

Trinity 20

O.T.:	Pr 2:1-8	The Lord Gives Wisdom
Ep.:	Ro 14:1-9	None of Us Lives for Himself Only
Gosp.:	Jn 15:1-8	I Am the Vine; You Are the Branches

Trinity 21

O.T.:	2 Sm 7:17-29	David Thanks the Lord for His Promise
Ep.:	Eph 6:1-9	God Holds Us Accountable
Gosp.:	Mk 10:13-16	Let the Little Children Come to Me

Trinity 22

O.T.:	Pr 24:14-20	Wisdom Is Sweet to the Soul
Ep.:	He 13:1-9	Our Hearts Are Strengthened for Christian Living
Gosp.:	Lk 9:57-62	Count the Cost of Following Jesus

Trinity 23

O.T.:	Ps 85:6-13	Salvation Is Near for Those Who Fear the Lord
Ep.:	1 Tm 4:4-11	Paul Urges Timothy To Be a Good Minister of Jesus Christ
Gosp.:	Mt 10:24-33	Do Not Be Afraid of Those Who Kill the Body

Trinity 24

O.T.:	Ps 39	Each Man's Life Is But a Breath
Ep.:	1 Th 5:14-24	May God Make You Holy in Every Way
Gosp.:	Jn 10:23-30	My Sheep Listen to My Voice

Trinity 25

O.T.:	Job 14:1-5	Man, Born of Woman, Is of Few Days
Ep.:	He 10:32-39	Do Not Throw Away Your Confidence
Gosp.:	Jn 5:19-29	The Son Has Authority To Judge

Trinity 26

O.T.:	Ps 126	Those Who Sow in Tears Will Reap with Joy
Ep.:	Re 2:8-11	Be Faithful Till You Die
Gosp.:	Lk 19:11-27	God Requires Faithfulness of His Servants

Trinity 27

O.T.:	Is 35:3-10	The Ransomed of the Lord Enter Zion
Ep.:	Re 7:9-17	The Great Multitude in White Robes
Gosp.:	Lk 12:35-43	Be Ready for the Coming of the Son of Man

Festival Of The Reformation

O.T.:	Ps 46	God Is Our Refuge And Strength
Ep.:	1 Cor 3:11-23	No One Can Lay Any Other Foundation
Gosp.:	Jn 2:13-17	Jesus Drives the Merchants Out of the Temple

Festival Of Harvest

O.T.:	Ps 34:1-9	Taste And See That the Lord Is Good
Ep.:	2 Cor 9:6-11	God Loves A Cheerful Giver
Gosp.:	Jn 6:24-29	Work for the Food that Endures

3. THE THOMASIUS SELECTIONS

Gottfried Thomasius served in the parish ministry for seventeen years, first as a village pastor and then as a popular preacher in Nuremberg. During his years in Nuremberg he also distinguished himself as an instructor in the local *Gymnasium*. In 1842 he became professor of dogmatics in the University of Erlangen, where he continued for 33 years. During 30 of those years he was also the university preacher. In 1865 the General Synod of Bavaria recommended his selections for use in the churches of Bavaria, and from there they became more widely circulated.

Advent 1

O.T.:	Is 61:1-3	Christ Is God's Anointed One
Ep.:	Re 1:4-8	The Lord Who Is To Come
Gosp.:	Lk 1:68-79	John, the Prophet of the Most High

Advent 2

O.T.:	Mal 4:1-6	The Healing Sun of Righteousness
Ep.:	1 Tm 6:11-16	Fight the Good Fight of Faith
Gosp.:	Lk 17:20-30	The Kingdom of God Is within You

Advent 3

O.T.:	Is 40:1-10	God Comforts His People
Ep.:	Ro 2:12-16	Judgment by the Law
Gosp.:	Mt 3:1-12	John the Baptist's Call to Repentance

Advent 4

O.T.:	Is 2:2-5	The Kingdom of the Lord Will Be Established
Ep.:	1 Cor 1:26-29	What God Has Chosen
Gosp.:	Lk 1:46-55	The Magnificat of Mary

Christmas — The Nativity Of Our Lord

O.T.:	Is 9:6,7	To Us a Child Is Born
Ep.:	He 1:1-6	God Has Spoken to Us by His Son
Gosp.:	Lk 2:1-20	The Savior Is Born

Second Christmas Day

O.T.:	Mic 5:1-3	The Birth of Christ Foretold
Ep.:	1 Jn 1:1-4	Our Fellowship with the Father
Gosp.:	Jn 1:1-14	The Word Became Flesh

Sunday after Christmas

O.T.:	Is 63:7-17	The Kindness of the Lord
Ep.:	2 Tm 4:3-8	A Crown of Righteousness
Gosp.:	Lk 2:22-32	Adoration And Prophecy of Simeon

New Year's Day

O.T.:	Lm 3:22-32	The Greatness of God's Love
Ep.:	He 13:8	The Changeless Christ
Gosp.:	Lk 13:6-9	The Parable of the Fig Tree

Sunday after New Year

O.T.:	Ps 73:23-28	Whom Have I in Heaven But You?
Ep.:	Ac 19:1-7	The Ephesians Receive the Spirit
Gosp.:	Mk 6:20-29	The Death of John the Baptist

Epiphany

O.T.:	Is 49:1-9	A Light for the Gentiles
Ep.:	1 Jn 3:1-6	Now Are We the Children of God
Gosp.:	Mt 3:13-17	This Is My Son Whom I Love

Epiphany 1

O.T.:	Dt 6:1-9	Fear And Love the Lord Your God
Ep.:	Ro 10:12-21	The Universality of the Gospel
Gosp.:	Jn 1:36-51	John's Disciples Follow Jesus

Epiphany 2

O.T.:	Is 8:20-22	To the Law And to the Testimony
Ep.:	Ro 10:1-12	Necessity for the Gospel
Gosp.:	Lk 4:14-22	The Year of the Lord's Favor

Epiphany 3

O.T.:	Nu 24:10-17	A Scepter Will Rise Out of Israel
Ep.:	Ro 5:1-5	The Blessings of Justification
Gosp.:	Mt 11:25-30	Come to Me

Epiphany 4

O.T.:	Is 51:1-12	God Will Comfort His Church
Ep.:	1 Jn 1:5-10	Purified by the Blood of Christ
Gosp.:	Jn 8:12-16	I Am the Light of the World

Epiphany 5

O.T.:	Jr 18:1-10	The Parable of the Potter
Ep.:	1 Jn 4:7-17	The Atoning Sacrifice for Our Sins
Gosp.:	Jn 6:26-35	Food That Endures to Eternal Life

Transfiguration

O.T.:	Ex 3:1-6	God Calls Moses at the Burning Bush
Ep.:	1 Pe 1:3-21	The Cost of Our Redemption
Gosp.:	Lk 7:1-10	Jesus Heals the Centurion's Servant

Septuagesima

O.T.:	Dn 5:17-30	The Handwriting on the Wall
	Dn 4:31-34	Nebuchadnezzar Glorifies God
Ep.:	2 Pe 1:3-11	Make Your Calling And Election Sure
Gosp.:	Jn 7:14-17	Jesus Teaches in the Temple

Sexagesima

O.T.:	Is 25:1-9	Joy in the Salvation of God
Ep.:	2 Pe 1:16-21	The Light of the Prophetic Word
	2 Cor 3:12-18	The Veil of Moses
Gosp.:	Mt 17:1-9	The Transfiguration of Our Lord

Quinquagesima

O.T.:	Jr 8:19-22	Is There No Balm in Gilead?
Ep.:	1 Cor 1:18-24	The Preaching of the Cross
Gosp.:	Mk 10:32-45	Whoever Wants To Become Great
	Mk 8:27-38	Jesus Foretells His Suffering

Lent 1

O.T.:	Jr 2:17-19	Backsliding Israel Rebuked
	Jr 3:22,23	Israel Invited To Return
Ep.:	He 12:14-17	Live in Peace with All Men
Gosp.:	Mt 11:20-24	Jesus Denounces the Cities

Lent 2

O.T.:	Ex 14:13-21	The Lord Rescues Israel
	Is 52:7-17	Good Tidings of Salvation
Ep.:	He 2:10-15	Jesus Made Perfect through Suffering
Gosp.:	Jn 8:21-30	When the Son of Man Is Lifted Up

Lent 3

O.T.:	Gn 22:1-19	Abraham Commanded To Offer His Son Isaac
Ep.:	He 5:1-10	The Source of Eternal Salvation
Gosp.:	Jn 10:24-33	The Gift of Eternal Life

Lent 4

O.T.:	Is 42:1-8	The Messiah Is the Servant of the Lord
Ep.:	He 10:1-14	One Sacrifice for Sins Forever
Gosp.:	Jn 11:47-57	The Prophecy of Caiaphas

Passion Sunday (Lent 5)

O.T.:	Nu 21:4-9	Moses And the Bronze Snake
Ep.:	He 7:24-27	The Permanent Priesthood of Christ
	He 4:14-16	Our Great High Priest
Gosp.:	Jn 12:23-33	If I Am Lifted Up

Palm Sunday

O.T.:	Zch 9:8-12	Your King Comes to You
Ep.:	He 12:1-6	Fixing Our Eyes on Jesus
Gosp.:	Jn 12:1-19	Jesus Enters Jerusalem

Maundy Thursday

O.T.:	Ex 12:1-14	The Passover Instituted
Ep.:	1 Cor 10:16,17	The Cup of Thanksgiving
	1 Cor 11:28-32	A Man Ought To Examine Himself
Gosp.:	Jn 13:1-17	Jesus Washes the Disciples' Feet
	Lk 22:14-23	The Institution of the Holy Communion

Good Friday

O.T.:	Is 53:1-7	Christ's Suffering Foretold
Ep.:	He 10:19-23	By a New And Living Way
	2 Cor 5:14-21	Reconciliation through Christ
Gosp.:	Mt 27:29-56	Crucifixion And Death of Jesus

Easter — The Resurrection Of Our Lord

O.T.:	Is 53:8-12	Christ's Life Poured Out unto Death
	Job 19:22-27	I Know That My Redeemer Lives
Ep.:	1 Pe 1:3-9	Born Anew to a Living Hope
Gosp.:	Mt 28:1-8	The Women at the Sepulcher

Easter 1

O.T.:	Gn 32:22-31	Jacob Wrestles with the Angel
Ep.:	1 Jn 4:1-6	How To Test the Spirits
	1 Pe 1:22-25	Born Again of Imperishable Seed
Gosp.:	Jn 21:15-24	Jesus Restores the Penitent Peter
	Jn 6:65-71	To Whom Shall We Go?

Easter 2

O.T.:	Eze 34:11-16	A Shepherd in Israel Promised
	Eze 34:23-31	A Covenant of Peace
Ep.:	Re 2:1-5	The Letter to the Church in Ephesus
Gosp.:	Jn 21:1-14	A Morning Meal with the Risen Christ

Easter 3

O.T.:	Is 61:10,11	The Robe of Righteousness
Ep.:	Re 3:1-6	The Letter to the Church in Sardis
Gosp.:	Jn 10:1-11	I Am the Good Shepherd

Easter 4

O.T.:	Is 5:1-7	The Vineyard of the Lord
Ep.:	Re 3:7-11	The Letter to the Church in Philadelphia
Gosp.:	Jn 15:1-11	I Am the True Vine

Easter 5

O.T.:	Is 54:7-13	God's Unfailing Love
Ep.:	Re 3:14-22	The Letter to the Church of the Laodiceans
Gosp.:	Jn 14:13-21	The Promised Counselor

Ascension

O.T.:	Ps 110	Sit at My Right Hand
Ep.:	Eph 1:15-23	Christ, the Head of the Church
Gosp.:	Lk 24:50-53	The Ascension of Christ

Sunday after Ascension

O.T.:	Is 64:1,2	Prayer for the Demonstration of God's Power
Ep.:	1 Jn 3:19-24	The Assurance of Salvation
Gosp.:	Jn 14:1-12	The Way, the Truth, the Life

Pentecost

O.T.:	Is 44:1-6	Apart from Me There Is No God
Ep.:	He 8:8-11	The Promise of a New Covenant
Gosp.:	Jn 7:37-39	Streams of Living Water

Trinity Sunday

O.T.:	Is 6:3-7	The Prophet's Vision of the Lord's Glory
	Nu 6:22-27	The Aaronic Blessing

Ep.: 1 Cor 12:4-13 The Gifts of the Spirit
Gosp.: Mt 28:18-20 The Great Commission

Trinity 1

O.T.: Gn 12:1-4 The Call of Abram
Ep.: Ac 2:42-47 Life in the Apostolic Church
Gosp.: Mk 4:26-29 The Growth of the Seed

Trinity 2

O.T.: Gn 15:1-6 God Promises Abram a Son
Ep.: Ac 3:1-10 The Crippled Man Healed
Gosp.: Mt 9:9-13 The Calling of Matthew

Trinity 3

O.T.: Gn 17:1-9 God Renews His Covenant with Abraham
Ep.: Ac 4:1-12 Peter and John before the Rulers
Gosp.: Mt 5:1-6 The Beatitudes I

Trinity 4

O.T.: Gn 18:20-33 Abraham Pleads for Sodom
Ep.: Ac 8:26-38 Philip And the Ethiopian
Gosp.: Mt 5:7-12 The Beatitudes II

Trinity 5

O.T.: Gn 19:15-26 Sodom And Gomorrah Destroyed
Ep.: Ac 9:1-19 The Conversion of Saul
Gosp.: Mt 7:24-29 Rock Or Sand?

Trinity 6

O.T.: Gn 25:7-10 Death And Burial of Abraham
Ep.: Ac 14:8-18 Paul And Barnabas Called Gods
Gosp.: Mt 19:16-26 The Rich Young Man

Trinity 7

O.T.: Gn 28:10-22 Jacob's Dream at Bethel
Ep.: Ac 16:22-33 Conversion of the Jailer at Philippi
Gosp.: Mt 13:44-46 The Parable of the Treasure And the Pearl

Trinity 8

O.T.: Ex 3:1-14 Moses' Call at the Burning Bush
Ep.: Ac 16:12-15 The Conversion of Lydia
Gosp.: Mk 8:34-38 What Can a Man Give in Exchange for His Soul?

Trinity 9

O.T.: Ex 17:1-7 Water from the Rock in Horeb
Ep.: Ac 24:22-26 Paul's Second Hearing before Felix
Gosp.: Mt 14:22-34 Jesus Walks on the Water

Trinity 10

O.T.:	Dt 32:1-9	The Song of Moses
Ep.:	Ac 7:54-59	Stephen Stoned to Death
Gosp.:	Mt 23:34-39	Jesus Laments over Jerusalem

Trinity 11

O.T.:	1 Sm 7:5-12	The Philistines Are Subdued
Ep.:	Ac 17:15-34	Paul at Athens
Gosp.:	Mt 16:13-20	Peter's Confession of Faith

Trinity 12

O.T.:	1 Sm 16:1-13	Samuel Anoints David
Ep.:	Ac 19:23-40	The Silversmiths at Ephesus
Gosp.:	Mt 13:31-35	The Parable of the Mustard Seed And Leaven

Trinity 13

O.T.:	2 Sm 12:1-10	Nathan's Parable
Ep.:	Ac 20:17-38	Charge to the Ephesian Elders
Gosp.:	Mt 5:13-19	The Salt And the Light

Trinity 14

O.T.:	Pr 4:14-23	The Righteous Contrasted with the Wicked
Ep.:	Eph 2:19-22	Fellow Citizens with God's People
Gosp.:	Mt 10:16-22	The Twelve Instructed And Sent Out

Trinity 15

O.T.:	1 Kgs 17:1-16	Elijah And the Widow
Ep.:	Eph 4:8-16	Christ, the Head of the Church
Gosp.:	Lk 11:5-13	Encouragement to Prayer
	Lk 18:1-8	The Persistent Widow

Trinity 16

O.T.:	1 Kgs 17:17-24	Elijah Restores the Widow's Son
Ep.:	1 Th 5:14-24	The Blameless Christian Life
Gosp.:	Mt 25:14-30	The Parable of the Talents

Trinity 17

O.T.:	Pr 16:1-9	God's Mind And Man's Mind
Ep.:	Jas 3:13-18	Worldly And Heavenly Wisdom
Gosp.:	Lk 10:38-42	Jesus Commends Mary

Trinity 18

O.T.:	Jr 17:5-10	The Deceitfulness of Man's Heart
Ep.:	2 Cor 7:6-10	Repentance That Leads to Salvation
Gosp.:	Lk 7:36-50	Jesus Anointed by a Sinful Woman

Trinity 19

O.T.:	1 Kgs 19:1-18	God's Voice Comes to Elijah
Ep.:	2 Th 3:5-12	Never Tire of Doing What Is Right
Gosp.:	Mt 12:1-13	Lord of the Sabbath

Trinity 20

O.T.:	1 Kgs 21:17-25	Elijah Denounces King Ahab
Ep.:	Eph 6:1-9	Domestic Duties
Gosp.:	Lk 19:1-5	Jesus And Zacchaeus

Trinity 21

O.T.:	Is 30:15-19	Blessed Are All Who Wait for the Lord
Ep.:	2 Cor 8:1-12	The Grace of Liberal Giving
	1 Tm 6:3-12	The Gain of Godliness
Gosp.:	Lk 12:15-21	The Rich Man's Folly

Trinity 22

O.T.:	Zph 3:14-20	Restoration of Israel
Ep.:	Jas 5:7-11	Patient Waiting for the Lord
Gosp.:	Lk 10:17-22	The Return of the Seventy

Trinity 23

O.T.:	Hg 2:1-10	The Glory of the Second Temple
Ep.:	Col 3:1-4	Set Your Hearts on Things Above
	He 4:9-13	A Rest for the People of God
Gosp.:	Lk 13:23-30	The Narrow Door of the Kingdom

Trinity 24

O.T.:	Is 63:1-9	The Year of My Redemption Has Come
Ep.:	1 Th 5:1-11	Sons of Light And of the Day
Gosp.:	Mt 24:1-14	Jesus Teaches Concerning His Coming

Trinity 25

O.T.:	Is 35:4-10	The Return of the Ransomed of the Lord
Ep.:	2 Th 2:1-12	The Man of Lawlessness
Gosp.:	Jn 11:21-27	I Am the Resurrection And the Life

Trinity 26

Ep.:	Re 7:9-17	The Multitude before the Throne
	He 12:18-24	The Heavenly Jerusalem
Gosp.:	Jn 5:19-29	The Righteous Judge

Trinity 27

Ep.:	Re 21:1-7	A New Heaven And a New Earth
Gosp.:	Lk 12:35-46	Be Ready

Festival Of The Reformation

O.T.:	Ps 87:1-3	The Great Glory of God's City
	2 Chr 29:12-19	Hezekiah Purifies the Temple
Ep.:	He 13:7-9	The Changeless Christ
Gosp.:	Jn 2:15-17	Jesus Cleanses the Temple
	Jn 8:30-36	The Truth Will Set You Free

Festival Of Harvest

O.T.:	Ps 145:15-21	The Eyes of All Look to You
	Dt 26:1-11	The Offering of Firstfruits
Ep.:	2 Cor 9:6-15	God Loves a Cheerful Giver
Gosp.:	Mt 15:29-39	Jesus Feeds the Four Thousand
	Lk 12:15-21	The Rich Man's Folly

Mission Festival

O.T.:	Ps 69	God Will Save Zion
Ep.:	Ac 13:44-49	We Turn to the Gentiles
	Ac 16:8-10	The Macedonian Call
Gosp.:	Mt 9:35-38	The Harvest Is Plenteous

4. THE SYNODICAL CONFERENCE SELECTIONS

These texts were selected by a Committee on Revision from a larger system devised by Frederic H. K. Soll, a pastor of the Wisconsin Synod. Two Gospel, an Epistle and an Old Testament text for each Sunday and holiday were recommended to the Evangelical Lutheran Synodical Conference of North America, which adopted them in 1912. Paul W. Nesper valued them highly: "The freshness of approach and the new insights into the vital truths of faith and life which they offer have established these selections as one of the richest and fullest of the pericope systems."

Advent 1

O.T.:	Ps 24	Preparing the King's Highway
Ep.:	Ro 1:16-20	The Gospel Is God's Power To Save
Gosp.:	Mt 11:25-30	Come to Me
	Lk 17:20-25	The Kingdom of God Is within You

Advent 2

O.T.:	Dt 18:15-22	A Prophet from Their Own Brothers
Ep.:	2 Tm 3:10-17	The Value of the Holy Scriptures
Gosp.:	Lk 17:26-37	The Coming of the Son of Man
	Lk 1:67-80	Zechariah's Hymn of Praise

Advent 3

O.T.:	Is 61	The Work of the Promised Messiah
Ep.:	1 Cor 9:16-23	All Things to All Men
Gosp.:	Mt 3:1-12	John the Baptist Calls to Repentance
	Lk 3:3-14	John Preaches And Baptizes

Advent 4

O.T.:	Hg 2:7-10	The Glory of the Second Temple
Ep.:	1 Tm 2:1-6	One Mediator between God And Men
Gosp.:	Mk 6:17-29	The Death of John the Baptist
	Jn 1:29-34	This Is the Son of God

Christmas — The Nativity Of Our Lord

O.T.:	Is 9:2-7	To Us a Child Is Born
Ep.:	He 1:1-12	God Has Spoken to Us by His Son
Gosp.:	Mt 1:18-25	Immanuel, God with Us
	Jn 1:1-14	The Word Became Flesh

Christmas 2

O.T.:	Zch 2:10-13	Be Glad, O Daughter of Zion
Ep.:	1 Jn 4:9-16	The Atoning Sacrifice for Our Sins
Gosp.:	Lk 1:46-55	The Magnificat of Mary
	Jn 1:15-18	Grace And Truth Came through Jesus Christ

Sunday after Christmas

O.T.:	Is 28:14-19	Christ, the Sure Foundation
Ep.:	1 Pe 2:1-10	You Are a Chosen People
Gosp.:	Lk 2:22-32	Adoration And Prophecy of Simeon
	Lk 9:57-62	Fitness for Service in the Kingdom

New Year's Day

O.T.:	Ps 121	God's Help And Protection
Ep.:	Col 2:6-15	Rooted And Built Up in Jesus
Gosp.:	Lk 13:1-9	Parable of the Fig Tree
	Lk 12:4-9	Confessing Christ before Men

Sunday after New Year

O.T.:	Lm 3:22-32	The Faithfulness of God's Mercies
Ep.:	Ro 3:21-26	Justification by Grace
Gosp.:	Mt 9:9-13	The Calling of Matthew
	Lk 13:18-24	The Parable of the Mustard Seed, the Leaven And the Narrow Door

Epiphany

O.T.:	Is 60:1-11	Arise, Shine, For Your Light Has Come
Ep.:	Ac 8:26-39	Philip And the Ethiopian
Gosp.:	Lk 4:16-21	The Year of the Lord's Favor
	Mt 4:12-17	Jesus Preaches Repentance

Epiphany 1

O.T.:	Ps 78:1-7	Declaring God's Teaching
Ep.:	Ro 10:8-18	The Universality of the Gospel
Gosp.:	Jn 6:28-40	The Will of Him Who Sent Me
	Mt 10:32-39	Conditions of Discipleship

Epiphany 2

O.T.:	Ps 104:24-35	The Providence of the Lord
Ep.:	Eph 5:22-33	Christ the Head of the Church in Christian Marriage
Gosp.:	Mt 12:46-50	Who Are My Brothers?
	Jn 1:35-42	Look, the Lamb of God

Epiphany 3

O.T.:	Dn 6:10-23	Daniel in the Lions' Den
Ep.:	Ro 8:24-30	God Works for the Good of Those Who Love Him
Gosp.:	Lk 4:38-44	The Great Physician
	Jn 4:1-14	The Living Water Christ Offers

Epiphany 4

O.T.:	1 Kgs 19:9-18	God's Voice Comes to Elijah
Ep.:	1 Cor 3:1-11	Jesus Christ, the True Foundation
Gosp.:	Mt 14:22-33	Jesus Walks on the Water
	Jn 4:15-26	Worship in Spirit And in Truth

Epiphany 5

O.T.:	Gn 11:1-9	The Confusion of Tongues at Babel
Ep.:	Col 2:16-23	A Shadow of Things To Come
Gosp.:	Mt 13:31-35	The Parable of the Mustard Seed And the Leaven
	Mk 4:26-32	The Growth of the Seed

Transfiguration

O.T.:	Gn 28:10-22	Jacob's Vision of the Stairway Reaching to Heaven
Ep.:	2 Pe 3:14-18	Grow in Grace And Knowledge
Gosp.:	Mk 9:2-13	The Transfiguration of Christ
	Jn 4:27-42	Christ, the Savior of the World

Septuagesima

O.T.:	Jr 31:31-34	The New Covenant
Ep.:	Eph 1:3-14	Blessed with Every Spiritual Blessing
Gosp.:	Mt 5:17-29	The Righteousness Which God Looks For
	Lk 10:38-42	Only One Thing Is Needed

Sexagesima

O.T.:	1 Sm 17:42-51	David And Goliath
Ep.:	Ac 16:24-35	Conversion of the Jailer at Philippi
Gosp.:	Jn 8:25-36	The Truth Will Set You Free
	Mt 16:13-20	Peter Confesses Christ

Quinquagesima

O.T.:	Jon 3:10—4:11	The Lord Reproves Jonah
Ep.:	He 13:12-21	Offer God the Sacrifice of Praise
Gosp.:	Mt 20:17-28	The Son of Man Came To Serve
	Mt 16:21-23	Jesus Foretells His Suffering

Lent 1

O.T.:	Gn 3:1-15	The Fall of Adam And Eve
Ep.:	Ro 3:27-31	Justification by Faith
Gosp.:	Lk 4:1-15	The Temptation of Christ
	Jn 15:9-17	Remain in My Love

Lent 2

O.T.:	Gn 22:1-9	Abraham Offers His Son Isaac
Ep.:	1 Cor 1:18-25	The Preaching of the Cross
Gosp.:	Jn 12:20-26	We Would Like To See Jesus
	Jn 15:18-25	The Unbelieving World Hates Christ's Disciples

Lent 3

O.T.:	Ps 25	O Lord, Remember Your Great Mercy
Ep.:	Ga 2:17-21	Justification by Faith
Gosp.:	Jn 2:13-25	Jesus Cleanses the Temple
	Mk 10:35-45	The Son of Man Came To Serve

Lent 4

O.T.:	Dt 7:6-11	God Is a Faithful God
Ep.:	Re 5:8-14	Worthy Is the Lamb Who Was Slain
Gosp.:	Jn 11:46-57	Caiaphas Prophesies Jesus' Death
	Jn 17:1-16	Christ Prays for His Disciples

Passion Sunday (Lent 5)

O.T.:	Gn 14:8-20	Abram And Melchizedek
Ep.:	Eph 2:1-10	God Is Rich in Mercy
Gosp.:	Jn 12:27-36	When I Am Lifted Up
	Mt 23:34-39	Jesus Laments over Jerusalem

Palm Sunday

O.T.:	Ps 8	God's Great Love for Man
Ep.:	Php 2:12-18	God's Children Shine Like Stars in the World
Gosp.:	Jn 3:22-36	John's Witness of Christ
	Jn 12:1-11	Mary Anoints the Feet of Jesus
	Jn 12:12-19	Jesus Enters Jerusalem

Maundy Thursday

O.T.:	Ex 12:1-14	The Passover Instituted
Ep.:	1 Cor 10:14-21	The Cup of Thanksgiving
Gosp.:	Mt 26:17-30	The Institution of the Lord's Supper
	Lk 22:7-20	The Institution of the Lord's Supper

Good Friday

O.T.:	Is 53	Christ's Suffering Foretold
Ep.:	2 Cor 5:14-21	Reconciliation through Christ
Gosp.:	Lk 23:39-53	Jesus Dies on the Cross
	Jn 19:17-30	The Crucifixion And Death of Christ

Easter — Resurrection Of Our Lord

O.T.:	Job 19:23-27	I Know That My Redeemer Lives
Ep.:	Ac 13:26-39	Paul Preaches the Risen Christ
Gosp.:	Lk 24:1-12	The Resurrection of the Lord
	Mt 28:1-10	The Women at Christ's Grave

Easter 1

O.T.:	2 Sm 12:1-10	Nathan's Parable
Ep.:	Eph 2:11-18	Christ Jesus Is Our Peace
Gosp.:	Mt 12:38-42	The Sign of the Prophet Jonah
	Jn 21:1-14	A Morning Meal with the Risen Christ

Easter 2

O.T.:	Ps 23	The Lord Is My Shepherd
Ep.:	He 4:1-13	A Rest for the People of God
Gosp.:	Jn 10:1-11	I Am the Good Shepherd
	Jn 10:17-21	Christ Lays Down His Life

Easter 3

O.T.:	Ps 100	Shout for Joy to the Lord
Ep.:	1 Jn 2:3-11	Love Is Made Complete in Obedience
Gosp.:	Mk 2:18-22	Parables of the Cloth And the Wineskins
	Jn 11:1-16	Jesus And His Friends in Bethany

Easter 4

O.T.:	Jr 15:15-21	God's Promise To Save
Ep.:	Eph 2:19-22	Fellow Citizens with God's People
Gosp.:	Jn 5:19-29	The Righteous Judge
	Jn 11:17-27	I Am the Resurrection And the Life

Easter 5

O.T.:	Gn 18:16-33	Abraham Pleads for Sodom
Ep.:	1 Jn 3:19-24	We Have Confidence before God
Gosp.:	Lk 18:1-8	The Parable of the Persistent Widow
	Jn 11:28-45	Jesus Raises Lazarus to Life

Ascension

O.T.:	Ps 47	God Has Ascended Amid Shouts of Joy
Ep.:	Eph 4:7-16	The Variety of Spiritual Gifts
Gosp.:	Lk 24:50-53	The Ascension of Christ
	Jn 17:17-26	Christ Prays for the Believers

Sunday after Ascension

O.T.:	Is 55	A Call to Faith And Repentance
Ep.:	2 Cor 5:1-10	We Live by Faith, Not by Sight
Gosp.:	Jn 8:12-20	I Am the Light of the World
	Lk 11:5-13	Ask, And It Will Be Given to You

Pentecost

O.T.:	Eze 36:22-28	God's Promise of a New Spirit
Ep.:	1 Cor 2:6-16	The Hidden Wisdom of God
Gosp.:	Jn 14:15-21	The Promised Counselor
	Jn 6:60-71	The Confession of Peter

Trinity Sunday

O.T.:	Nu 6:22-27	The Blessing of Aaron
Ep.:	1 Pe 1:1-9	God Has Given Us New Birth into a Living Hope
Gosp.:	Mt 3:13-17	This Is My Son Whom I Love
	Mt 28:16-20	The Great Commission

Trinity 1

O.T.:	Pr 11:23-31	God Promises To Bless Generosity
Ep.:	Ro 8:1-11	Free from Condemnation
Gosp.:	Mt 19:16-26	The Rich Young Man
	Jn 15:1-8	I Am the True Vine

Trinity 2

O.T.:	Jdg 2:1-12	The Angel of the Lord at Bokim
Ep.:	He 13:1-9	Exhortations to Love And Purity
Gosp.:	Jn 8:1-11	Christ Forgives the Adulterous Woman
	Mt 11:16-24	Jesus Denounces Certain Cities

Trinity 3

O.T.:	2 Chr 33:9-16	God Restores King Manasseh
Ep.:	1 Tm 1:8-17	Christ Came To Save Sinners
Gosp.:	Lk 15:11-32	The Parable of the Lost Son
	Mk 10:13-16	Jesus Blesses Little Children

Trinity 4

O.T.:	Is 12:1-6	The Lord Has Become My Salvation
Ep.:	Ac 7:54—8:3	Stephen Stoned to Death
Gosp.:	Mt 7:1-6	Do Not Judge, Or You Too Will Be Judged
	Lk 17:1-10	Faith Working through Love

Trinity 5

O.T.:	Ex 3:1-15	Moses at the Burning Bush
Ep.:	Ac 9:1-22	The Conversion of Saul
Gosp.:	Jn 1:43-51	Philip And Nathanael
	Jn 21:15-19	Jesus Restores the Penitent Peter

Trinity 6

O.T.:	Gn 4:3-16	Cain Murders His Brother Abel
Ep.:	Ro 6:12-18	Slaves to Righteousness
Gosp.:	Mt 18:1-14	The Greatest in the Kingdom of Heaven
	Mt 15:1-9	God's Commandments And Men's Traditions

Trinity 7

O.T.:	1 Kgs 17:1-16	Elijah And the Widow
Ep.:	Eph 4:29-32	Do Not Grieve the Holy Spirit

Gosp.:	Mt 18:15-22	Forgiving a Brother
	Mt 15:10-20	What Makes a Person Unclean

Trinity 8

O.T.:	Jr 23:21-32	Judgment against False Prophets
Ep.:	1 Jn 4:1-6	How To Test the Spirits
Gosp.:	Jn 7:14-24	Jesus Teaches in the Temple
	Jn 5:30-38	Greater Testimony Than John's

Trinity 9

O.T.:	Ex 32:1-14	Worship of the Golden Calf
Ep.:	1 Tm 6:6-10	Godliness with Contentment
Gosp.:	Mk 12:38-44	Jesus And the Widow's Mite
	Jn 5:39-47	The Scriptures Testify of Christ

Trinity 10

O.T.:	Dt 4:23-31	Dispersion of Israel Prophesied
Ep.:	Ac 4:8-20	Boldness of Peter And John
Gosp.:	Mt 21:33-46	Parable of the Wicked Tenant Farmers
	Mt 21:12-22	Jesus' Second Temple Cleansing

Trinity 11

O.T.:	Mic 2:7-13	God Promises Judgment And Restoration for His People
Ep.:	2 Tm 4:1-8	Paul's Charge to Timothy
Gosp.:	Mk 2:13-17	Jesus Calls Matthew
	Jn 9:1-7	Jesus Heals the Man Born Blind

Trinity 12

O.T.:	Ex 34:29-35	Moses' Shining Face
Ep.:	2 Cor 3:12-18	The Veil of Moses
Gosp.:	Mt 9:27-34	Jesus Heals Two Blind Men
	Jn 9:24-41	The Testimony of the Man Born Blind

Trinity 13

O.T.:	Ex 20:18-24	The Lord Commands an Altar To Be Built
Ep.:	Jas 1:2-12	The Worth And Work of Trials
Gosp.:	Jn 7:25-31	Christ's Deity Challenged
	Mk 12:28-37	Jesus Refutes the Teachers of the Law

Trinity 14

O.T.:	Nu 21:4-9	The Bronze Snake
Ep.:	Ro 7:14-25	The Law of Sin at Work in My Members
Gosp.:	Lk 7:36-50	The Woman Who Was a Sinner
	Mt 12:9-21	Jesus Heals the Man with the Shriveled Hand

Trinity 15

O.T.:	1 Kgs 18:21-40	Elijah Slays the Prophets of Baal
Ep.:	2 Cor 9:6-11	God Loves a Cheerful Giver
Gosp.:	Jn 14:7-14	Lord, Show Us the Father
	Lk 14:12-15	Admonition To Love Selflessly

Trinity 16

O.T.:	2 Kgs 5:8-19	Elisha Heals Naaman the Leper
Ep.:	1 Jn 3:1-9	God's Great Love toward Us
Gosp.:	Mt 22:23-33	No Marriage at the Resurrection
	Lk 20:27-40	The Resurrection And Marriage

Trinity 17

O.T.:	1 Sm 15:13-26	The Lord Rejects King Saul
Ep.:	Ac 6:1-7	The Seven Deacons Chosen
Gosp.:	Lk 13:10-17	Jesus Heals a Woman on the Sabbath
	Mt 12:1-8	Lord Even of the Sabbath

Trinity 18

O.T.:	Eze 3:17-21	God's Instructions to the Prophet
Ep.:	2 Th 3:1-5	Paul Requests the Prayers of the Brothers
Gosp.:	Mt 5:1-12	The Beatitudes
	Mt 6:5-15	The Lord's Prayer

Trinity 19

O.T.:	Ps 37:25-40	Inheritance of the Righteous
Ep.:	Col 3:1-10	Set Your Heart on Things Above
Gosp.:	Mt 10:40-42	God Rewards Kindness Shown to His Servants
	Mt 6:19-23	Store Up Treasures in Heaven

Trinity 20

O.T.:	2 Kgs 2:6-18	Elijah Taken Up to Heaven
Ep.:	1 Jn 1:5—2:2	Walk in the Light
Gosp.:	Lk 6:43-49	The Wise And Foolish Builders
	Mt 7:24-29	Rock Or Sand?

Trinity 21

O.T.:	Dn 3:19-30	The Three Men in the Fiery Furnace
Ep.:	Ro 14:4-12	Judging One's Brother
Gosp.:	Mk 10:46-52	Jesus Heals Blind Bartimaeus
	Jn 5:1-9	Jesus at the Pool of Bethesda

Trinity 22

O.T.:	Gn 50:15-23	Joseph Reassures His Brothers
Ep.:	Ro 4:1-8	Abraham Justified by Faith

Gosp.:	Lk 14:25-35	Counting the Cost
	Lk 8:27-39	Jesus Heals the Demon-Possessed Man

Trinity 23

O.T.:	1 Sm 20:27-42	Jonathan's Loyalty to David
Ep.:	Ac 20:26-32	Paul's Farewell to the Ephesian Elders
Gosp.:	Mt 17:24-27	Jesus Pays the Temple Tax
	Jn 7:1-13	My Time Has Not Yet Come

Trinity 24

O.T.:	Is 54:7-13	God's Kindness Shall Not Depart
Ep.:	Re 3:7-13	The Letter to the Church in Philadelphia
Gosp.:	Mk 8:34-38	Losing One's Life for Christ
	Jn 10:22-30	The Gift of Eternal Life

Trinity 25

O.T.:	Ex 33:11-17	God Promises Moses His Presence
Ep.:	Ro 8:31-39	We Are More Than Conquerors
Gosp.:	Mt 13:44-52	Parable of the Pearl And the Net
	Mt 16:1-12	The Yeast of the Pharisees And Sadducees

Trinity 26

O.T.:	Gn 19:15-29	Sodom And Gomorrah Destroyed
Ep.:	He 4:14-16	Our Great High Priest
Gosp.:	Lk 19:11-27	Blessed Is the Faithful Servant
	Lk 16:10-17	You Cannot Serve Both God And Money

Trinity 27

O.T.:	Ps 126	Those Who Sow in Tears Will Reap in Joy
Ep.:	Re 22:12-21	I Am Coming Soon
Gosp.:	Mt 25:13-30	The Parable of the Talents
	Lk 22:24-30	Greatness in the Kingdom

Reformation Festival

O.T.:	Ps 46	God Is Our Refuge And Strength
	2 Kgs 23:21-27	The Lord Rejects Jerusalem
Ep.:	2 Th 2:7-17	The Coming of the Lawless One
Gosp.:	Mt 23:1-12	Whoever Exalts Himself Will Be Humbled
	Lk 7:27-35	Christ's Testimony Concerning John

Harvest Festival

O.T.:	Gn 8:15-22	God's Promise to Noah
Ep.:	Ac 14:11-17	The Heathen Consider Paul And Barnabas Gods
Gosp.:	Lk 12:24-34	God's Faithful Providence
	Mt 6:1-4	Piety That Pleases God

Mission Festival

O.T.:	Zph 3:8-17	Restoration of Israel
Ep.:	Ac 16:9-15	Paul's Macedonian Call
Gosp.:	Mt 9:35-38	The Harvest Is Plentiful
	Mt 5:13-16	Christians Are Salt And Light

Thanksgiving Day

O.T.:	Dt 8:16-18	Remember the Lord Your God
Ep.:	Ac 17:22-31	Paul's Sermon in Athens
Gosp.:	Lk 12:15-21	The Rich Fool
	Mt 5:42-48	God's Providence Is Impartial

5. THE SOLL SELECTIONS

For many years seniors at Wisconsin Lutheran Seminary were presented with a copy of *Pericopes and Selections*, prepared and published by the Rev. Frederic H. K. Soll. This pamphlet included many texts which Soll had proposed for The Synodical Conference Selections but which had not been included in that series. The texts listed here are those which, for the most part, are not included in the other pericopic systems published in this volume.

Advent 1

O.T.:	Is 62:10-12	See, Your Savior Comes
Ep.:	Eph 5:6-14	Walk as Children of Light
Gosp.:	Lk 19:29-40	Blessed Is the King Who Comes

Advent 2

O.T.:	Zph 1:7-18	The Day of the Lord Is Near
Ep.:	2 Cor 10:7-18	Boasting in the Lord
Gosp.:	Mk 13:1-8	Signs at the End of the Age

Advent 3

O.T.:	Is 56:1-7	A House of Prayer for All People
Ep.:	2 Tm 2:3-15	Show Yourself Approved unto God
Gosp.:	Lk 7:18-26	Are You the One Who Was To Come?

Advent 4

O.T.:	Zch 6:12-15	The Branch Will Build the Temple
Ep.:	1 Pe 4:3-7	The End of All Things Is Near
Gosp.:	Lk 1:56-66	John the Baptist Named

Christmas Day — The Nativity Of Our Lord

O.T.:	Eze 17:22-24	I Will Plant a Tender Sprig
Ep.:	1 Tm 3:16	The Mystery of Godliness Is Great
Gosp.:	Lk 1:26-38	The Annunication

Sunday after Christmas

O.T.:	Is 43:16-20	I Am Doing a New Thing
Ep.:	Ac 18:24-28	Apollos Instructed
Gosp.:	Jn 10:31-42	The Scripture Cannot Be Broken

New Year's Day

O.T.:	Is 60:17-22	The Lord Will Be Your Everlasting Light
Ep.:	Php 4:8-17	I Can Do All Things through Christ
Gosp.:	Lk 12:1-3	Warnings of Jesus

Sunday after New Year

O.T.:	Gn 27:22-46	Isaac's Blessings
Ep.:	Ro 9:1-8	Children of the Promise
Gosp.:	Lk 5:27-32	The Calling of Levi

Epiphany

O.T.:	Zch 14:8-11	The Lord Will Be King over All
Ep.:	3 Jn 1-12	Imitate What Is Good
Gosp.:	Mt 13:10-17	Why Speak in Parables?

Epiphany 1

O.T.:	Mal 1:6-11	My Name Will Be Great among the Nations
Ep.:	Ro 14:13-23	The Weak And the Strong
Gosp.:	Lk 12:51-59	Not Peace, But Division

Epiphany 2

O.T.:	Gn 46:28-34	Jacob And Joseph Reunited
Ep.:	Tt 2:1-10	Directions for Doctrine And Life
Gosp.:	Mt 8:19-22	The Cost of Discipleship

Epiphany 3

O.T.:	Job 1:1-22	Job's First Test
Ep.:	1 Pe 3:15-17	Be Ready To Answer
Gosp.:	Mk 1:40-45	Jesus Cleanses the Leper

Epiphany 4

O.T.:	Job 2:1-13	Job's Second Test
Ep.:	1 Cor 1:10-17	Is Christ Divided?
Gosp.:	Mk 6:45-56	Jesus Walks on the Water

Epiphany 5

O.T.:	Hg 1:2-14	A Call To Build the Lord's House
Ep.:	Ga 3:5-14	Abraham, Father of the Faithful
Gosp.:	Mk 6:1-6	Jesus Rejected at Nazareth

Transfiguration

O.T.:	Ex 40:34-38	The Glory of the Lord
Ep.:	2 Cor 4:1-10	Heavenly Treasure in Jars of Clay
Gosp.:	Lk 9:28-36	The Transfiguration of Christ

Septuagesima

O.T.:	Dt 34:1-12	Death And Burial of Moses
Ep.:	2 Cor 13:5-14	Examine Yourselves
Gosp.:	Lk 6:20-35	Jesus Pronounces Blessings And Woes

Sexagesima

O.T.:	Ex 32:15-35	The Golden Calf And Moses
Ep.:	2 Cor 1:3-7	The God of All Comfort
Gosp.:	Mt 13:1-9; 18-23	The Parable of the Sower

Quinquagesima

O.T.:	Jon 3:1-9	The Repentance of the Ninevites
Ep.:	Heb 12:18-29	The Church of the Firstborn
Gosp.:	Mk 9:30-32	Jesus Foretells His Death

Lent 1

O.T.:	Nu 20:1-13	Water out of the Rock
Ep.:	He 1:13—2:10	Jesus Made Perfect through Suffering
Gosp.:	Mt 26:36-46	Jesus in Gethsemane

Lent 2

O.T.:	Lv 20:6-8	I Am the Lord Your God
Ep.:	Col 2:1-5	The Mystery of God — Christ
Gosp.:	Mk 7:24-30	Jesus Casts Out a Demon

Lent 3

O.T.:	Is 49:22-26	I, the Lord, Am Your Savior
Ep.:	Ro 5:17—6:2	Dead to Sin, Alive in Christ
Gosp.:	Mt 12:22-29	Jesus' Dominion over Satan

Lent 4

O.T.:	Gn 41:25-45	Joseph Interprets Pharaoh's Dreams
Ep.:	1 Pe 1:10-16	Redeemed with the Precious Blood of Christ
Gosp.:	Lk 9:10-17	Jesus Feeds the Five Thousand

Passion Sunday (Lent 5)

O.T.:	Lv 16:29-34	The Day of Atonement
Ep.:	He 3:1-6	Jesus Greater Than Moses
Gosp.:	Lk 13:31-35	Jesus Laments over Jerusalem

Palm Sunday

O.T.:	Is 45:22-25	Before the Lord Every Knee Will Bow
Ep.:	2 Cor 4:11-18	We Believe And Therefore Speak
Gosp.:	Mk 11:1-10	Jesus Enters Jerusalem

Maundy Thursday

O.T.:	Lv 16:15-22	The Scapegoat Ritual
Ep.:	Re 19:6-10	The Marriage Supper of the Lamb
Gosp.:	Jn 13:16-20	Jesus Predicts His Betrayal

Good Friday

O.T.:	Zch 13:6-9	The Shepherd Struck, the Sheep Scattered
Ep.:	Re 12:7-12	Satan's Defeat
Gosp.:	Lk 23:26-38	Jesus' Crucifixion

Easter — The Resurrection Of Our Lord

O.T.:	Jon 2:1-10	Jonah's Prayer And Deliverance
Ep.:	1 Cor 15:20-28	The Last Enemy Is Death
Gosp.:	Jn 20:1-10	The Empty Sepulcher

Easter 1

O.T.:	Jos 3:9-17	Israel Crosses the Jordan
Ep.:	2 Cor 2:5-11	Forgiveness for the Sinner
Gosp.:	Lk 11:29-36	The Sign of Jonah

Easter 2

O.T.:	Is 40:6-11	He Shall Feed His Flock
Ep.:	Ro 4:23—5:11	Justified by Faith
Gosp.:	Jn 12:37-45	Belief And Unbelief

Easter 3

O.T.:	2 Kgs 20:1-11	Hezekiah's Illness
Ep.:	Php 3:13-16	Press On toward the Goal
Gosp.:	Mt 9:14-17	Jesus Questioned about Fasting

Easter 4

O.T.:	Jdg 7:15-22	Gideon Defeats the Midianites
Ep.:	1 Cor 14:20-26	Gifts of Prophecy And Tongues
Gosp.:	Jn 21:20-25	Jesus Speaks Concerning John

Easter 5

O.T.:	1 Kgs 3:5-15	Solomon Asks for Wisdom
Ep.:	1 Jn 5:11-15	He That Has the Son Has Life
Gosp.:	Mt 7:7-12	Ask, And It Will Be Given

Ascension

O.T.:	Ps 68:15-20	Christ's Ascension Prophesied
Ep.:	Re 19:11-16	King of Kings And Lord of Lords
Gosp.:	Mt 16:24-28	Jesus Prophesies His Ascension

Sunday after Ascension

O.T.:	Gn 45:1-15	Joseph Reveals Himself
Ep.:	Ac 13:1-12	Paul And Barnabas Commissioned
Gosp.:	Lk 9:51-56	Working with Jesus

Pentecost

O.T.:	Is 32:14-18	The Promise of the Spirit
Ep.:	2 Cor 1:18-24	The Guarantee of the Spirit
Gosp.:	Mt 10:1-15	Jesus Sends Out the Twelve

Trinity Sunday

O.T.:	Jr 10:1-16	The Lord Is the True God
Ep.:	2 Tm 1:7-14	The Saving Work of the Triune God
Gosp.:	Lk 3:21-33	The Baptism of Jesus

Trinity 1

O.T.:	Dt 5:22-33	Moses Receives the Law
Ep.:	2 Tm 2:19-26	A Workman Approved by God
Gosp.:	Jn 6:47-58	Jesus, the Bread of Life

Trinity 2

O.T.:	Dn 1:1-21	Daniel's Training in Babylon
Ep.:	Jas 2:1-13	Don't Show Favoritism
Gosp.:	Jn 7:40-53	Opinions Concerning Christ

Trinity 3

O.T.:	Is 4:2-6	The Branch of the Lord
Ep.:	1 Tm 4:6-11	Godliness Is Profitable
Gosp.:	Lk 18:15-17	Jesus And Little Children

Trinity 4

O.T.:	Is 43:8-13	Apart from Me There Is No Savior
Ep.:	Ac 6:8-15	The Arrest of Stephen
Gosp.:	Mk 11:27-33	Christ's Authority Challenged

Trinity 5

O.T.:	1 Sm 3:1—4:1	The Call of Samuel
Ep.:	1 Pe 5:1-5	Be Shepherds of God's Flock
Gosp.:	Lk 10:1-15	The Seventy-two Commissioned

Trinity 6

O.T.:	Jos 24:14-28	Joshua's Farewell
Ep.:	1 Tm 5:17-25	Paul's Advice to Timothy
Gosp.:	Mk 9:33-37	Who Is the Greatest?

Trinity 7

O.T.:	Gn 41:45-47	Joseph Exalted
Ep.:	He 12:12-17	Strive To Live a Holy Life
Gosp.:	Mk 7:14-23	The Heart the Center of Life

Trinity 8

O.T.:	Ps 119:121-128	Teach Me Your Decrees
Ep.:	2 Cor 6:14—7:1	Do Not Be Yoked with Unbelievers
Gosp.:	Mt 5:33-37	Let Your "Yes" Be "Yes"

Trinity 9

O.T.:	Jos 4:1-18	What Do These Stones Mean?
Ep.:	1 Cor 10:29—11:1	Do All to the Glory of God
Gosp.:	Lk 5:17-26	Christ's Power To Forgive Sin

Trinity 10

O.T.:	Eze 33:30-33	A Prophet Has Been among Them
Ep.:	He 5:11—6:10	Warning against Falling Away
Gosp.:	Lk 20:9-19	The Parable of the Tenants

Trinity 11

O.T.:	Nu 9:15-23	The Cloud above the Tabernacle
Ep.:	Jas 4:7-17	Humble Yourselves
Gosp.:	Mk 11:20-26	The Withered Fig Tree

Trinity 12

O.T.:	Dt 30:11-20	The Offer of Life Or Death
Ep.:	Ro 9:30—10:8	Christ Is the End of the Law
Gosp.:	Mt 19:1-12	Marriage And Divorce

Trinity 13

O.T.:	Pr 2:1-8	In Praise of Wisdom
Ep.:	Ro 2:11-16	The Judgment of the Law
Gosp.:	Lk 20:41-44	Whose Son Is the Christ?

Trinity 14

O.T.:	Nu 12:1-15	Miriam And Aaron Oppose Moses
Ep.:	Jas 3:6-18	The Sins of the Tongue
Gosp.:	Lk 6:6-11	The Lord of the Sabbath

Trinity 15

O.T.:	Ps 37:12-24	The Lord Upholds the Righteous
Ep.:	Ro 3:1-20	All Have Sinned
Gosp.:	Mk 9:14-29	Jesus Heals the Demoniac

Trinity 16

O.T.:	2 Kgs 4:18-37	Is It Well with the Child?
Ep.:	1 Cor 8:1-6	There Is But One God
Gosp.:	Mk 8:22-26	Jesus Heals a Blind Man

Trinity 17

O.T.:	Nu 27:12-23	Joshua Named as Moses' Successor
Ep.:	2 Jn 6-11	Abide in the Doctrine of Christ
Gosp.:	Mk 2:23-28	Jesus Heals on the Sabbath Day

Trinity 18

O.T.:	Ps 138	The Lord Will Fulfill His Purpose for Me
Ep.:	1 Jn 2:24-29	Continue in Pure Teaching
Gosp.:	Lk 11:1-4	Jesus Teaches the Lord's Prayer

Trinity 19

O.T.:	Jr 16:16-21	They Will Know My Name
Ep.:	2 Cor 2:14-17	Our Victory in Christ
Gosp.:	Mk 9:38-50	Various Teachings of Jesus

Trinity 20

O.T.:	Jr 30:12-17	Israel's Restoration
Ep.:	Jas 5:13-20	Effectual Fervent Prayer
Gosp.:	Mk 1:21-28	Jesus Drives Out an Evil Spirit

Trinity 21

O.T.:	Gn 37:12-28	Joseph Sold by His Brothers
Ep.:	2 Cor 10:3-6	Our Spiritual Weapons
Gosp.:	Mt 20:29-34	Two Blind Men Receive Sight

Trinity 22

O.T.:	Ne 1:1-11	Nehemiah's Prayer
Ep.:	He 7:26—8:2	The High Priest of the New Covenant
Gosp.:	Mk 5:1-20	Healing a Demon-Possessed Man

Trinity 23

O.T.:	2 Kgs 18:1-8	Hezekiah's Reform
Ep.:	Ro 16:17-20	Avoid False Doctrine
Gosp.:	Lk 20:20-26	Paying Taxes to Caesar

Trinity 24

O.T.:	Jr 6:10-16	Ask for the Ancient Paths
Ep.:	1 Cor 1:26-31	Our Boasting in the Lord
Gosp.:	Mk 8:10-21	Beware of the Yeast of the Pharisees

Trinity 25

O.T.:	Jl 3:9-21	The Day of the Lord Is Near
Ep.:	Re 7:9-17	The Great Multitude in White Robes
Gosp.:	Mt 24:29-36	Prophecies Concerning the Last Times

Trinity 26

O.T.:	Eze 34:17-24	I Will Save My Flock
Ep.:	Re 22:6-11	Jesus Is Coming Soon
Gosp.:	Mt 24:37-44	Christ's Coming Will Be Unexpected

Trinity 27

O.T.:	Nu 14:10-24	God's Justice And His Love
Ep.:	2 Pe 2:1-11	Punishment And Rescue
Gosp.:	Lk 13:24-30	The Narrow Door

Festival Of Reformation

O.T.:	Hab 2:1-4	The Just Shall Live by Faith
Ep.:	Ga 1:1-12	Only One Gospel
Gosp.:	Lk 11:37-54	Jesus Pronounces Six Woes

Festival Of Harvest

O.T.:	Gn 9:1-15	God's Covenant with Noah
Ep.:	1 Tm 6:17-19	A Charge to the Rich
Gosp.:	Lk 22:35-37	Did You Lack Anything?

Mission Festival

O.T.:	Is 43:1-7	God Will Gather His Church
Ep.:	1 Cor 12:26-31	Desire the Greater Gifts
Gosp.:	Lk 22:31-32	Strengthen Your Brothers

Thanksgiving Day

O.T.:	Dt 28:1-10	Blessings for Obedience
Ep.:	2 Cor 8:8-15	Generosity Encouraged
Gosp.:	Jn 6:22-27	The Food Which Endures

THE ILCW SERIES

The most recent pericope in Lutheran circles came about as the result of work done through an Inter-Lutheran Commission on Worship and published in 1973. Participating bodies were the Lutheran Church in America, the American Lutheran Church, the Evangelical Lutheran Church of Canada and the Lutheran Church-Missouri Synod.

Based upon the traditional pericope systems, the ILCW Series provides for a number of revisions. Actually it is a three-year system offering Old Testament, Epistle and Gospel selections in three cycles. Since the Gospel sets the tone for the Sunday, Series A is built around selections from Matthew, Series B from Mark, and Series C from Luke. The Old Testament selections in each case support more closely the Gospel theme for the Sunday than is the case in the ancient pericopes. Epistle selections were chosen for their relationship to the Gospel, or they present consecutive readings on successive Sundays so that an overview of an entire Epistle is given. The Gospel of John is given prominence in the post-Easter season in each series. On festival occasions the traditional readings have often been maintained.

There are several rather significant changes in the way in which the Sundays of the church year are designated.

The Sundays after Epiphany serve as a direct bridge between the Christmas and the Lenten seasons. Thus the last Sunday after the Epiphany, the Transfiguration of our Lord, is the Sunday before Ash Wednesday. The pre-Lenten season has been dropped.

The Sundays following Easter are designated as the Sundays "of Easter." They lead into the Day of Pentecost as the culmination of the Easter celebration. The long season which follows is called the "Season after Pentecost" rather than "after Trinity." This is done in order to emphasize the significance of the "Easter-Pentecost event" in the life of the church of Jesus Christ throughout the remainder of the church year. Some students of liturgics claim that this "after Pentecost" arrangement has more historical tradition behind it than the "after Trinity" designation.

Another variation of the ILCW Series is the substitution of selected readings from the book of Acts in place of the Old Testament on the six Sundays of Easter. This shift brings in the story of the early church prior to the celebration of Pentecost.

The strengths of the ILCW Series lie in its Old Testament selections, which show a greater correlation with the church year than most other pericopes, its varied use of the Gospels and its consecutive readings of the Epistles.

Because of variations in the designation of the Sundays, as mentioned above, the sequence in the ILCW selections is as follows:

Advent 1 — First Sunday in Advent
Christmas 1 — First Sunday after Christmas
Epiphany 1 — First Sunday after Epiphany
Lent 1 — First Sunday in Lent

Easter 2 — First Sunday of Easter (Sunday after Easter)
Pentecost 1 — First Sunday after Pentecost (Trinity Sunday)
Pentecost 2 — Second Sunday after Pentecost

These designations apply to all three ILCW Series.

6. ILCW — SERIES A

Advent 1

O.T.:	Is 2:1-5	Christ's Advent Establishes Peace
Ep.:	Ro 13:11-14	Christ's Advent Calls Us To Wake Up
Gosp.:	Mt 24:37-44	Be Ready for Christ's Second Advent

Advent 2

O.T.:	Is 11:1-10	Jesse's Branch Brings Righteousness
Ep.:	Ro 15:4-13	Jesse's Branch Is the Hope of the Gentiles
Gosp.:	Mt 3:1-12	John Preaches Repentance

Advent 3

O.T.:	Is 35:1-10	Christ's Advent Brings Joy to the Redeemed
Ep.:	Jas 5:7-10	Wait Patiently for the Lord's Coming
Gosp.:	Mt 11:2-11	In Preparing the Way for Christ, John Was the Greatest Prophet

Advent 4

O.T.:	Is 7:10-14 (15-17)	The Christ Born of a Virgin Will Be Immanuel
Ep.:	Ro 1:1-7	Christ Is True God And True Man
Gosp.:	Mt 1:18-25	The Virgin's Child Is Savior And Immanuel

The Nativity Of Our Lord — The First Service (Christmas Eve)

O.T.:	Is 9:2-7	God's Son Is Born As a Child
Ep.:	Tt 2:11-14	God's Grace Has Appeared to All Men
Gosp.:	Lk 2:1-20	The Birth of Jesus Is Good News

The Nativity Of Our Lord — The Second Service (Christmas Dawn)

O.T.:	Is 52:7-10	All Will See the Salvation of Our God
Ep.:	He 1:1-9	God Has Spoken to Us by His Son
Gosp.:	Jn 1:1-14	The Word Became Flesh

The Nativity Of Our Lord — The Third Service (Christmas Day)

O.T.:	Is 62:10-12	The Savior Comes to the Daughter of Zion
Ep.:	Tt 3:4-7	The Holy Spirit Is Poured Out on Us Generously through Jesus Our Savior
Gosp.:	Lk 2:1-20	The Birth of Jesus Is Good News

First Sunday after Christmas

O.T.:	Is 63:7-9	In His Love And Mercy God Redeemed His People
Ep.:	Ga 4:4-7	God Sent His Son To Make Us His Sons
Gosp.:	Mt 2:13-15, 19-23	God Guides Joseph To Flee to Egypt

New Year's Day

O.T.:	Nu 6:22-27	God's Name Brings Blessings to His People
Ep.:	Ro 1:1-7	Grace And Peace Are Ours in Jesus' Name
Gosp.:	Lk 2:21	He Is Named Jesus

Second Sunday after Christmas

O.T.:	Is 61:10—62:3	Christ's Robe of Righteousness
Ep.:	Eph 1:3-6, 15-18	Know the Hope to Which He has Called You
Gosp.:	Jn 1:1-18	The Eternal Word Made Flesh

The Epiphany Of Our Lord

O.T.:	Is 60:1-6	The Savior Brings Light to the Nations
Ep.:	Eph 3:2-12	The Gentiles Are Heirs with Israel
Gosp.:	Mt 2:1-12	The Magi Follow the Star

Epiphany 1 — The Baptism of Our Lord

O.T.:	Is 42:1-7	God Sends His Spirit on His Chosen Servant
Ep.:	Ac 10:34-38	God Anointed Jesus with the Holy Spirit And Power
Gosp.:	Mt 3:13-17	God's Son Is Baptized

Epiphany 2

O.T.:	Is 49:1-6	God Displays His Splendor through His Servant
Ep.:	1 Cor 1:1-9	We Know Jesus Christ Is Our Lord
Gosp.:	Jn 1:29-41	Jesus Is the Son of God And the Messiah

Epiphany 3

O.T.:	Is 9:1-4	The People Walking in Darkness Have Seen a Great Light
Ep.:	1 Cor 1:10-17	Let Followers of Christ Be Perfectly United
Gosp.:	Mt 4:12-23	Jesus Calls His First Disciples

Epiphany 4

O.T.:	Mic 6:1-8	The Lord Requires Us To Act Justly And Love Mercy
Ep.:	1 Cor 1:26-31	The Gospel Is Both Foolishness And Wisdom
Gosp.:	Mt 5:1-12	The Beatitudes Show True Spiritual Riches

Epiphany 5

O.T.:	Is 58:5-9a	Christianity Is Not Dead Ceremony
Ep.:	1 Cor 2:1-5	Jesus Christ And Him Crucified
Gosp.:	Mt 5:13-20	Doing God's Will to God's Glory

Epiphany 6

O.T.:	Dt 30:15-20	To Obey God Brings Blessings; To Disobey Brings Curses
Ep.:	1 Cor 2:6-13	What No Eye Has Seen Or Ear Heard
Gosp.:	Mt 5:20-37	Jesus Teaches God's Will

Epiphany 7

O.T.:	Dt 19:1-2, 17-18	Do Not Seek Revenge, But Love Your Neighbor
Ep.:	1 Cor 3:10-11, 16-23	To Build on Any Foundation But Christ Is Foolishness
Gosp.:	Mt 5:38-48	Repay Evil with Love

Epiphany 8

O.T.:	Is 49:13-18	The Lord Cannot Forget Those Who Are His
Ep.:	1 Cor 4:1-13	Faithfulness Is Required
Gosp.:	Mt 6:24-34	God Provides All Needs

The Transfiguration Of Our Lord

O.T.:	Ex 24:12, 15-18	The Glory of the Lord Appeared to Israel
Ep.:	2 Pe 1:16-19	Eyewitnesses of Christ's Majesty
Gosp.:	Mt 17:1-9	Christ's Transfiguration

Ash Wednesday

O.T.:	Jl 2:12-19	The Lord Calls His People to True Repentance
Ep.:	2 Cor 5:20b—6:2	Do Not Receive God's Grace in Vain
Gosp.:	Mt 6:1-6, 16-21	Don't Do the Father's Will To Be Rewarded by Men

Lent 1

O.T.:	Gn 2:7-9, 15-17; 3:1-7	Disobedience Brings Sin into the World
Ep.:	Ro 5:12, 17-19	Christ's Obedience Justifies All Men
Gosp.:	Mt 4:1-11	Jesus Overcomes the Devil's Temptation

Lent 2

O.T.:	Gn 12:1-8	Abraham Believes God's Promises
Ep.:	Ro 4:1-5, 13-17	Abraham Was Justified by Faith, Not by Works
Gosp.:	Jn 4:5-26	Jesus Gives Living Water to the Samaritan Women

Lent 3

O.T.:	Is 42:14-21	Nothing Could Keep God from Bringing the Light of Salvation
Ep.:	Eph 5:8-14	Live as Children of the Light
Gosp.:	Jn 9:13-17; 34-39	Jesus Gives Physical And Spiritual Sight to a Blind Man

Lent 4

O.T.:	Ho 5:15—6:2	The Law Tears Us to Pieces, But God's Grace Heals Us
Ep.:	Ro 8:1-10	Our Sinful Nature Brings Death, But the Spirit Gives Us Life
Gosp.:	Mt 20:17-28	Jesus Came To Serve by Giving His Life as a Ransom

Passion Sunday (Lent 5)

O.T.:	Eze 37:1-3, (4-10), 11-14	God Can Make Dry Bones Live Again
Ep.:	Ro 8:11-19	God Gives Us Spiritual And Eternal Life
Gosp.:	Jn 11:47-53	Jesus Is the Resurrection And the Life

Palm Sunday

O.T.:	Is 50:4-9a	The Servant Submits to Shame And Suffering
Ep.:	Php 2:5-11	God's Son Humbled Himself to Death on a Cross
Gosp.:	Mt 27:11-54	Jesus' Trial, Crucifixion And Death

Maundy Thursday

O.T.:	Ex 12:1-14	The Blood of the Lamb Saves the Firstborn of Israel
Ep.:	1 Cor 11:23-26	Christ Gives Us His Body And Blood
Gosp.:	Jn 13:1-17,34	Peter Learns To Let Jesus Serve Him

Good Friday

O.T.:	Is 52:13—53:12	The Servant Suffers the Punishment for Our Sins
Ep.:	He 4:14-16; 5:7-9	Jesus Serves as Our High Priest
Gosp.:	Jn 19:17-30	Jesus' Crucifixion

Easter — The Resurrection Of Our Lord

Acts:	Ac 10:34-43	God Raised Jesus To Assure Us of Our Forgiveness
Ep.:	Col 3:1-4	Christ Is Our Life
Gosp.:	Jn 20:1-9	Mary of Magdala Sees Her Risen Lord

Easter 2

Acts:	Ac 2:14a, 22-32	God's Holy One Did Not See Decay
Ep.:	1 Pe 1:3-9	Christ's Resurrection Gives Us a Living Hope
Gosp.:	Jn 20:19-31	Doubting Thomas Hails Jesus as His Lord And God

Easter 3

Acts:	Ac 2:14a, 36-47	Christians Live in the Joy of Their Risen Savior
Ep.:	1 Pe 1:17-21	God Raised the Lamb Who Shed His Blood for Us
Gosp.:	Lk 24:13-35	The Risen Christ Revives the Hopes of the Emmaus Disciples

Easter 4

Acts:	Ac 6:1-9; 7:2a, 51-60	Stephen Is Chosen, Testifies And Is Stoned
Ep.:	1 Pe 2:19-25	The Shepherd Calls Straying Sheep To Return
Gosp.:	Jn 10:1-10	The Sheep Know And Follow Their Shepherd

Easter 5

Acts:	Ac 17:1-15	Paul Is Persecuted in Thessalonica And Berea
Ep.:	1 Pe 2:4-10	The Church's Living Stones
Gosp.:	Jn 14:1-12	The Way to the Father's House

Easter 6

Acts:	Ac 17:22-31	Paul Preaches about the "Unknown God"
Ep.:	1 Pe 3:15-22	Set Christ Apart as Lord in Your Hearts
Gosp.:	Jn 14:15-21	The Spirit Leads Us To Love And Obey

The Ascension Of Our Lord

Acts:	Ac 1:1-11	The Ascended Savior Sends Out His Disciples
Ep.:	Eph 1:16-23	The Ascended Savior Rules Over Everything for the Church
Gosp.:	Lk 24:44-53	Jesus' Ascension Moves His Disciples to Joyful Service

Easter 7

Acts:	Ac 1:8-14	The Disciples Await Jesus' Gift of the Holy Spirit
Ep.:	1 Pe 4:12-17; 5:6-11	Praise God That You Are a Christian
Gosp.:	Jn 17:1-11	To Know Jesus as God's Son Is Eternal Life

Pentecost

O.T.:	Jl 2:28-29	God Promises To Pour Out His Spirit
Ep.:	Ac 2:1-21	God Pours Out His Spirit
Gosp.:	Jn 16:5-11	The Work of the Holy Spirit

Pentecost 1 — The Holy Trinity

O.T.:	Dt 4:32-34, 39-40	The Lord Is the Only True God
Ep.:	2 Cor 13:11-14	The God of Love And Peace Be with You
Gosp.:	Mt 28:16-20	We Are Baptized into the Name of the Triune God

Pentecost 2

O.T.:	Dt 11:18-21, 26-28	God Wants His People To Remember His Words And Be Blessed
Ep.:	Ro 3:21-25a, 27,28	A Man Is Justified by Faith
Gosp.:	Mt 7:21-29	Only He Who Does the Will of God Will Enter Heaven

Pentecost 3

O.T.:	Ho 5:15—6:6	God Desires Mercy, Not Sacrifice
Ep.:	Ro 4:18-25	God Credits Faith in the Savior to Us as Righteousness
Gosp.:	Mt 9:9-13	The Savior's Love Reaches Out to Lost Sinners

Pentecost 4

O.T.:	Ex 19:2-8a	God Wants His People To Be a Holy Nation
Ep.:	Ro 5:6-11	Christ Died for Us Sinners
Gosp.:	Mt 9:35—10:8	Jesus Sends Out the Twelve

Pentecost 5

O.T.:	Jr 20:7-13	The Lord Rescues Us from the Hands of the Wicked
Ep.:	Ro 5:12-15	As by One Man Sin Came, by One Man Grace Came
Gosp.:	Mt 10:24-33	Confess Christ Fearlessly

Pentecost 6

O.T.:	Jr 28:5-9	False Prophets Mislead the People
Ep.:	Ro 6:1b-11	Live as Those Who Died to Sin But Are Alive in Christ
Gosp.:	Mt 10:34-42	Following Christ Will Bring Choices And Opportunities

Pentecost 7

O.T.:	Zch 9:9-12	Christ Brings the Peace of Salvation to All Nations
Ep.:	Ro 7:15-25a	Christ Rescues Us from the Sin at Work in Our Bodies
Gosp.:	Mt 11:25-30	Jesus Invites Us To Come to Him for Rest

Pentecost 8

O.T.:	Is 55:10-11	God's Word Accomplishes What He Desires
Ep.:	Ro 8:18-25	We Wait for the Glory Which Is To Be Revealed
Gosp.:	Mt 13:1-9 (18-23)	The Parable of the Sower

Pentecost 9

O.T.:	Is 44:6-8	There Is No God Besides the Lord
Ep.:	Ro 8:26-27	The Spirit Intercedes for Us
Gosp.:	Mt 13:24-30 (36-43)	The Parable of the Weeds among the Wheat

Pentecost 10

O.T.:	1 Kgs 3:5-12	Solomon's Request for Wisdom
Ep.:	Ro 8:28-30	God Preserves His Elect in All Things
Gosp.:	Mt 13:44-52	Some Treasure God's Kingdom, Others Only Seem To Do So

Pentecost 11

O.T.:	Is 55:1-5	God Offers Salvation Freely to All
Ep.:	Ro 8:35-39	Nothing Can Separate Us from the Love of Christ
Gosp.:	Mt 14:13-21	Jesus Feeds the Five Thousand

Pentecost 12

O.T.:	1 Kgs 19:9b-18	God Assures Elijah of the Power of His Word
Ep.:	Ro 9:1-8, 30-33	Israel Stumbled Because It Rejected God's Word
Gosp.:	Mt 14:22-33	Jesus Teaches Peter Not To Doubt His Word

Pentecost 13

O.T.:	Is 56:1, 6-8	God Provides Righteousness for All Nations
Ep.:	Ro 11:13-15; 29-32	Mercy for All the Disobedient
Gosp.:	Mt 15:21-28	Christ Shows Mercy to the Believing Canaanite Woman

Pentecost 14

O.T.:	Ex 6:2-8	God Promises To Free His People from Slavery
Ep.:	Ro 11:33-36	God's Unfathomable Wisdom
Gosp.:	Mt 16:13-20	Peter's Confession Is the Rock of Christ's Church

Pentecost 15

O.T.:	Jr 15:15-21	God Promises To Save His Repentant People
Ep.:	Ro 12:1-8	God's Mercy Moves Us to Lives Pleasing to Him
Gosp.:	Mt 16:21-26	Jesus Asks Us To Take Up Our Cross And Follow Him

Pentecost 16

O.T.:	Eze 33:7-9	God Holds His Watchman Responsible
Ep.:	Ro 13:1-10	Submit to the Government; Love One Another
Gosp.:	Mt 18:15-20	Win Back Your Erring Brother

Pentecost 17

O.T.:	Gn 50:15-21	Joseph Assures His Brothers of Forgiveness
Ep.:	Ro 14:5-9	Whether We Live Or Die We Belong to the Lord
Gosp.:	Mt 18:21-35	Forgive Your Brother from the Heart

Pentecost 18

O.T.:	Is 55:6-9	Turn to the Lord, For He Will Freely Pardon
Ep.:	Php 1:3-5, 19-27	The Believer Exalts Christ in Life And in Death
Gosp.:	Mt 20:1-16	The Parable of the Vineyard Workers

Pentecost 19

O.T.:	Eze 18:1-4, 25-32	God Has No Pleasure in the Death of the Unrepentant

Ep.:	Php 2:1-5 (6-11)	Imitate Christ's Self-Sacrificing Humility
Gosp.:	Mt 21:28-32	God Rejoices in the Repentance of a Sinner

Pentecost 20

O.T.:	Is 5:1-7	God Judges Those Who Sin in His Blessings
Ep.:	Php 3:12-21	Press On Because Your Citizenship Is in Heaven
Gosp.:	Mt 21:33-43	The Parable of the Tenant Farmers

Pentecost 21

O.T.:	Is 25:6-9	The Lord Prepares a Joyous Feast for His People
Ep.:	Php 4:4-13	Learn the Secret of Being Content in Every Situation
Gosp.:	Mt 22:1-10	Don't Refuse God's Invitation to His Banquet

Pentecost 22

O.T.:	Is 45:1-7	God Controls the Events of History
Ep.:	1 Th 1:1-5a	The Holy Spirit Works a Living Faith through the Gospel
Gosp.:	Mt 22:15-21	Jesus' Enemies Fail To Trap Him

Pentecost 23

O.T.:	Lv 19:1-2, 15-18	God Demands Holiness
Ep.:	1 Th 1:5b-10	Believers Receive the Word with Joy
Gosp.:	Mt 22:34-40 (41-46)	Jesus Teaches the Heart of the Law (And the Gospel)

Pentecost 24

O.T.:	Am 5:18-24	The Day of the Lord Demands Justice and Righteousness
Ep.:	1 Th 4:13-14 (15-18)	Those Who Sleep in Jesus Will Rise to Life Eternal
Gosp.:	Mt 25:1-13	The Parable of the Ten Virgins

Pentecost 25

O.T.:	Ho 11:1-4, 8,9	God's Love Saves His People from His Wrath
Ep.:	1 Th 5:1-11	Let Us as Sons of Light Be Ready for Our Savior's Coming
Gosp.:	Mt 25:14-30	The Parable of the Talents

Pentecost 26 — Third-Last Sunday in the Church Year

O.T.:	Mal 2:1-2, 4-10	God Wants the Lips of His Messenger To Speak True Instruction
Ep.:	1 Th 2:8-13	Work Hard To Share the Gospel
Gosp.:	Mt 23:1-12	Put Away All Pride

Pentecost 27 — Second-Last Sunday in the Church Year

O.T.:	Jr 26:1-6	God Will Punish All Who Do Not Listen to His Word
Ep.:	1 Th 3:7-13	God Strengthens Our Faith
Gosp.:	Mt 24:1-14	Jesus Reveals the Signs of His Coming

Last Sunday in the Church Year

O.T.:	Eze 34:11-16, 23,24	God Promises To Gather His Sheep
Ep.:	1 Cor 15:20-28	The Last Enemy Christ Will Destroy Is Death
Gosp.:	Mt 25:31-46	The Lord Will Divide the Sheep from the Goats

Reformation Day

O.T.:	Jr 31:31-34	God Will Establish a New Covenant with Israel
Ep.:	Ro 3:19-28	Justified by Grace through Faith
Gosp.:	Jn 8:31-36	Abraham's True Children

Mission Festival

O.T.:	Is 62:1-7	The Nations Will See God's Righteousness
Ep.:	Ro 10:11-17	How Can They Hear without a Preacher?
Gosp.:	Lk 24:44-53	Proclaim Forgiveness to All Nations

Harvest Festival

O.T.:	Dt 26:1-11	Israel's Thankoffering of Firstfruits
Ep.:	2 Cor 9:6-15	Share Generously
Gosp.:	Mt 13:24-30	The Parable of the Final Harvest

Thanksgiving Day

O.T.:	Dt 8:1-10	Do Not Forget the Lord Your God
Ep.:	1 Tm 2:1-4	Offer Prayers And Thanksgiving
Gosp.:	Lk 17:11-19	Return And Give Praise to God

7. ILCW — SERIES B

Advent 1

O.T.:	Is 63:16b-17; 64:1-8	Make Your Name Known, O Lord
Ep.:	1 Cor 1:3-9	Wait for the Lord Jesus Christ
Gosp.:	Mk 13:33-37	Be on Guard; Be Alert

Advent 2

O.T.:	Is 40:1-11	Prepare the Way for the Lord
Ep.:	2 Pe 3:8-14	The Day of the Lord Will Come
Gosp.:	Mk 1:1-8	John the Baptist Prepares the Way

Advent 3

O.T.:	Is 61:1-3, 10-11	The Year of the Lord's Favor
Ep.:	1 Th 5:16-24	Paul's Final Instructions
Gosp.:	Jn 1:6-8, 19-28	John the Baptist's Testimony

Advent 4

O.T.:	2 Sm 7:8-11, 16	God's Promise to David
Ep.:	Ro 16:25-27	To God Be Glory Forever
Gosp.:	Lk 1:26-38	The Angel Appears to Mary

The Nativity Of Our Lord — The First Service (Christmas Eve)

O.T.:	Is 9:2-7	God's Son Is Born as a Child
Ep.:	Tt 2:11-14	God's Grace Has Appeared to All Men
Gosp.:	Lk 2:1-20	The Birth of Jesus Is Good News

The Nativity Of Our Lord — The Second Service (Christmas Dawn)

O.T.:	Is 52:7-10	All Will See the Salvation of Our God
Ep.:	He 1:1-9	God Has Spoken to Us by His Son
Gosp.:	Jn 1:1-14	The Word Became Flesh

The Nativity Of Our Lord — The Third Service (Christmas Day)

O.T.:	Is 62:10-12	The Savior Comes to the Daughter of Zion
Ep.:	Tt 3:4-7	The Holy Spirit Is Poured Out on Us Generously through Jesus Our Savior
Gosp.:	Lk 2:1-20	The Birth of Jesus Is Good News

First Sunday after Christmas

O.T.:	Is 45:22-25	Turn to the Lord And Be Saved
Ep.:	Col 3:12-21	Let the Peace of Christ Rule in Your Hearts
Gosp.:	Lk 2:25-40	Jesus Is Presented in the Temple

New Year's Day

O.T.:	Nu 6:22-27	God's Name Brings Blessings to His People
Ep.:	Ro 1:1-7	Grace And Peace Are Ours in Jesus' Name
Gosp.:	Lk 2:21	He Is Named Jesus

Second Sunday After Christmas

O.T.:	Is 61:10—62:3	Christ's Robe of Righteousness
Ep.:	Eph 1:3-6, 15-18	Know the Hope to Which He has Called You
Gosp.:	Jn 1:1-18	The Eternal Word Made Flesh

The Epiphany Of Our Lord

O.T.:	Is 60:1-6	The Nations Come to Zion's Light
Ep.:	Eph 3:2-12	To the Gentiles Christ's Unsearchable Riches
Gosp.:	Mt 2:1-12	Wise Men Worship the Christchild

Epiphany 1 — The Baptism of Our Lord

O.T.:	Is 42:1-7	God Will Put His Spirit on Christ
Ep.:	Ac 10:34-38	God Anointed Jesus of Nazareth
Gosp.:	Mk 1:4-11	The Baptism of Jesus

Epiphany 2

O.T.:	1 Sm 3:1-10	The Lord Calls Samuel
Ep.:	1 Cor 6:12-20	Honor God with Your Body
Gosp.:	Jn 1:43-51	Jesus Calls Philip And Nathanael

Epiphany 3

O.T.:	Jon 3:1-5, 10	Jonah Goes to Nineveh
Ep.:	1 Cor 7:29-31	This World Is Passing Away
Gosp.:	Mk 1:14-20	The Calling of the First Disciples

Epiphany 4

O.T.:	Dt 18:15-20	A Prophet like Moses Will Come
Ep.:	1 Cor 8:1-13	Food Sacrificed to Idols
Gosp.:	Mk 1:21-28	Jesus Drives Out an Evil Spirit

Epiphany 5

O.T.:	Job 7:1-7	Job Complains about the Shortness of Life
Ep.:	1 Cor 9:16-23	All Things to All Men
Gosp.:	Mk 1:29-39	The Healing Ministry of Jesus

Epiphany 6

O.T.:	2 Kgs 5:1-14	Elisha Heals Naaman's Leprosy
Ep.:	1 Cor 9:24-27	Go into Training To Get the Crown
Gosp.:	Mk 1:40-45	Jesus Heals a Man with Leprosy

Epiphany 7

O.T.:	Is 43:18-25	God's Mercy And Israel's Unfaithfulness
Ep.:	2 Cor 1:18-22	God's Promises Are "Yes" in Christ
Gosp.:	Mk 2:1-12	Jesus Heals a Paralytic

Epiphany 8

O.T.:	Ho 2:14-16; 19-20	The Lord Promises To Be Israel's Husband
Ep.:	2 Cor 3:1b-6	Ministers of the New Covenant
Gosp.:	Mk 2:18-22	New Wineskins for New Wine

The Transfiguration Of Our Lord

O.T.:	2 Kgs 2:1-12c	Elijah Ascends into Heaven
Ep.:	2 Cor 3:12—4:2	The Glory of the New Covenant
Gosp.:	Mk 9:2-9	The Transfiguration of Our Lord

Ash Wednesday

O.T.:	Jl 2:12-29	The Lord Calls His People to True Repentance
Ep.:	2 Cor 5:20b—6:2	Do Not Receive God's Grace in Vain
Gosp.:	Mt 6:1-6, 16-21	Don't Do the Father's Will To Be Rewarded by Men

Lent 1

O.T.:	Gn 22:1-14	Abraham's Test of Faith
Ep.:	Ro 8:31-39	We Are More than Conquerors
Gosp.:	Mk 1:12-15	The Temptation of Jesus

Lent 2

O.T.:	Gn 28:10-17	Jacob's Dream at Bethel
Ep.:	Ro 5:1-11	We Have Peace And Joy through Christ
Gosp.:	Mk 8:31-38	Jesus Predicts His Death

Lent 3

O.T.:	Ex 20:1-17	The Lord Is Serious about His Commandments
Ep.:	1 Cor 1:22-25	The Preaching of the Cross Is God's Wisdom
Gosp.:	Jn 2:13-22	Jesus Clears the Temple

Lent 4

O.T.:	Nu 21:4-9	The Bronze Snake
Ep.:	Eph 2:4-10	By Grace You Have Been Saved
Gosp.:	Jn 3:14-21	So the Son of Man Must Be Lifted Up

Passion Sunday (Lent 5)

O.T.:	Jr 31:31-34	The New Covenant
Ep.:	He 5:7-9	Jesus, Our Perfect High Priest
Gosp.:	Jn 12:20-33	Jesus Predicts His Death

Palm Sunday

O.T.:	Zch 9:9-10	See, Your King Comes to You
Ep.:	Php 2:5-11	The Humiliation And Exaltation of Christ
Gosp.:	Mk 15:1-39	Christ's Trial, Crucifixion And Death

Maundy Thursday

O.T.:	Ex 24:3-11	The Sinaitic Covenant Confirmed
Ep.:	1 Cor 10:16-17	One Body in Christ
Gosp.:	Mk 14:12-26	Jesus Institutes the Lord's Supper

Good Friday

O.T.:	Is 52:13—53:12	The Servant Suffers the Punishment for Our Sins
Ep.:	He 4:14—5:10	Jesus Serves as Our High Priest
Gosp.:	Jn 19:17-30	Jesus' Crucifixion

Easter — The Resurrection of Our Lord

O.T.:	Is 25:6-9	The Lord Will Swallow Up Death
Ep.:	1 Cor 15:19-28	Christ Has Indeed Been Raised
Gosp.:	Mk 16:1-8	The Resurrection of Jesus

Easter 2

Acts:	Ac 3:13-15, 17-26	You Killed the Author of Life
Ep.:	1 Jn 5:1-6	The Victory of Believers
Gosp.:	Jn 20:19-31	The Risen Lord Appears to His Disciples

Easter 3

Acts:	Ac 4:8-12	Salvation Is Found Only in Jesus
Ep.:	1 Jn 1:1—2:2	Walking in the Light of Christ
Gosp.:	Lk 24:36-49	The Risen Lord Commissions His Disciples

Easter 4

Acts:	Ac 4:23-33	The Believers in Jerusalem: One in Heart And Mind
Ep.:	1 Jn 3:1-2	The Blessings of God's Children
Gosp.:	Jn 10:11-18	I Am the Good Shepherd

Easter 5

Acts:	Ac 8:26-40	Philip Converts the Ethiopian Eunuch
Ep.:	1 Jn 3:18-24	Love One Another
Gosp.:	Jn 15:1-8	The Vine And the Branches

Easter 6

Acts:	Ac 11:19-30	Peter at Cornelius' House
Ep.:	1 Jn 4:1-11	Test the Spirits
Gosp.:	Jn 15:9-17	Remain in My Love

The Ascension Of Our Lord

Acts:	Ac 1:1-11	The Ascended Savior Sends Out His Disciples
Ep.:	Eph 1:16-23	The Ascended Savior Rules over Everything for the Church
Gosp.:	Lk 24:44-53	Jesus' Ascension Moves His Disciples to Joyful Service

Easter 7

Acts:	Ac 1:15-26	Matthias Chosen To Replace Judas
Ep.:	1 Jn 4:13-21	God's Love And Ours
Gosp.:	Jn 17:11b-19	Jesus Prays for His Disciples

Pentecost

O.T.:	Eze 37:1-14	I Will Put My Spirit in You
Ep.:	Ac 2:22-36	On Pentecost Peter Preaches Christ Crucified And Risen
Gosp.:	Jn 7:37-39a	Jesus Promises the Spirit

Pentecost 1 — The Holy Trinity

O.T.:	Dt 6:4-9	The Lord Our God Is One
Ep.:	Ro 8:14-17	The Spirit Makes Us God's Children And Coheirs with Christ
Gosp.:	Jn 3:1-17	Jesus Teaches Nicodemus

Pentecost 2

O.T.:	Dt 5:12-15	Observe the Sabbath Day
Ep.:	2 Cor 4:5-12	We Have This Treasure in Jars of Clay
Gosp.:	Mk 2:23-28	Jesus Is Lord of the Sabbath

Pentecost 3

O.T.:	Gn 3:9-15	The Protevangel
Ep.:	2 Cor 4:13-18	We Also Believe And Therefore Speak
Gosp.:	Mk 3:20-35	Jesus And Beelzebub

Pentecost 4

O.T.:	Eze 17:22-24	I Will Take a Shoot And Plant It
Ep.:	2 Cor 5:1-10	We Live by Faith, Not by Sight
Gosp.:	Mk 4:26-34	Jesus Teaches in Parables

Pentecost 5

O.T.:	Job 38:1-11	The Lord Speaks out of the Storm
Ep.:	2 Cor 5:14-21	A New Creation in Christ
Gosp.:	Mk 4:35-41	Jesus Calms the Storm

Pentecost 6

O.T.:	Lm 3:22-33	The Lord's Compassions Never Fail
Ep.:	2 Cor 8:1-9, 13,14, 21-24a	Generous Giving Encouraged
Gosp.:	Mk 5:21-24a, 35-43	Jesus Raises Jairus' Daughter

Pentecost 7

O.T.:	Eze 2:1-5	Ezekiel's Call to a Rebellious Israel
Ep.:	2 Cor 12:7-10	My Grace Is Sufficent for You
Gosp.:	Mk 6:1-6	Jesus, A Prophet without Honor

Pentecost 8

O.T.:	Am 7:10-15	Amos And Amaziah
Ep.:	Eph 1:3-14	God Predestined Us in Christ
Gosp.:	Mk 6:7-13	Jesus Sends Out the Twelve

Pentecost 9

O.T.:	Jr 23:1-6	The Lord Our Righteousness
Ep.:	Eph 2:13-22	Paul Prays for the Ephesians
Gosp.:	Mk 6:30-34	Jesus' Compassion on the Multitudes

Pentecost 10

O.T.:	Ex 24:3-11	The Sinaitic Covenant Confirmed
Ep.:	Eph 4:1-7, 11-16	Unity in the Body of Christ
Gosp.:	Jn 6:1-15	Jesus Feeds the Five Thousand

Pentecost 11

O.T.:	Ex 16:2-15	Manna in the Wilderness
Ep.:	Eph 4:17-24	Put On the New Self
Gosp.:	Jn 6:24-35	The Jews Seek a Sign

Pentecost 12

O.T.:	1 Kgs 19:4-8	An Angel Strengthens Elijah
Ep.:	Eph 4:30—5:2	Be Imitators of God
Gosp.:	Jn 6:41-51	Jesus, the Bread of Life

Pentecost 13

O.T.:	Pr 9:1-6	Wisdom Has Set Her Table
Ep.:	Eph 5:15-20	Be Filled with the Spirit
Gosp.:	Jn 6:51-58	Eating And Drinking Christ by Faith

Pentecost 14

O.T.:	Jos 24:1-2a, 14-18	Choose Whom You Will Serve
Ep.:	Eph 5:21-31	Advice to Wives And Husbands
Gosp.:	Jn 6:60-69	Lord, to Whom Shall We Go?

Pentecost 15

O.T.:	Dt 4:1-2, 6-8	Obey God's Commands
Ep.:	Eph 6:10-20	Put On the Full Armor of God
Gosp.:	Mk 7:1-8, 14,15, 21-23	Jesus Teaches True Obedience

Pentecost 16

O.T.:	Is 35:4-7a	The Joy of the Redeemed
Ep.:	Jas 1:17-22, 26,27	Be Doers of the Word
Gosp.:	Mk 7:31-37	The Healing of a Deaf-mute

Pentecost 17

O.T.:	Is 50:4-10	The Obedience of the Servant of the Lord
Ep.:	Jas 2:1-5, 8-10, 14-18	Faith And Deeds Go Together
Gosp.:	Mk 8:27-35	Peter's Confession — Jesus' Prediction

Pentecost 18

O.T.:	Jr 11:18-20	The Plot against Jeremiah
Ep.:	Jas 3:16—4:6	Heavenly Wisdom Opposes Envy And Quarrels
Gosp.:	Mk 9:30-37	Who Is the Greatest?

Pentecost 19

O.T.:	Nu 11:4-6, 10-16, 24-29	The Elders Who Prophesied
Ep.:	Jas 4:7-12	Submit Yourselves to God
Gosp.:	Mk 9:38-50	Jesus Warns against Giving Offense

Pentecost 20

O.T.:	Gn 2:18-24	God Institutes Marriage
Ep.:	He 2:9-11	Perfect through Suffering
Gosp.:	Mk 10:2-16	Marriage And Divorce

Pentecost 21

O.T.:	Am 5:6-7, 10-15	Hate Evil; Love Good
Ep.:	He 3:1-6	Jesus Is Greater Than Moses
Gosp.:	Mk 10:17-27	The Rich Young Man

Pentecost 22

O.T.:	Is 53:10-12	The Suffering Servant of the Lord
Ep.:	He 4:9-16	We Have a Sympathetic High Priest
Gosp.:	10:35-45	The Request of James And John

Pentecost 23

O.T.:	Jr 31:7-9	The Return of the Remnant
Ep.:	He 5:1-10	Jesus, a Priest in the Order of Melchizedek
Gosp.:	Mk 10:46-52	Blind Bartimaeus Receives His Sight

Pentecost 24

O.T.:	Dt 6:1-9	Love the Lord Your God
Ep.:	He 7:23-28	Jesus, Our Eternal High Priest
Gosp.:	Mk 12:28-34	The Greatest Commandment Is Love

Pentecost 25

O.T.:	1 Kgs 17:8-16	Elijah And the Widow at Zarephath
Ep.:	He 9:24-28	Christ Was Sacrificed Once
Gosp.:	Mk 12:41-44	The Widow's Offering

Pentecost 26 — Third-Last Sunday in the Church Year

O.T.:	Dn 12:1-3	Daniel Prophesies the End Times
Ep.:	He 12:26-29	Our God Is a Consuming Fire
Gosp.:	Mk 13:1-13	Signs of the End of the Age

Pentecost 27 — Second-Last Sunday in the Church Year

O.T.:	Dn 7:9-10	The Ancient of Days
Ep.:	He 12:1-2	Jesus, the Author and Perfecter of Our Faith
Gosp.:	Mk 13:24-31	The Second Coming of the Son of Man

Last Sunday in the Church Year

O.T.:	Is 51:4-6	The Day of God's Righteousness Draws Near
Ep.:	Re 1:4b-8	I Am the Alpha And the Omega
Gosp.:	Mk 13:32-37	The Day And Hour Is Known Only to the Father

Reformation Day

O.T.:	Jr 31:31-34	God Will Establish a New Covenant with Israel
Ep.:	Ro 3:19-28	Justified by Grace through Faith
Gosp.:	Jn 8:31-36	Abraham's True Children

Mission Festival

O.T.:	Is 62:1-7	The Nations Will See God's Righteousness
Ep.:	Ro 10:11-17	How Can They Hear without a Preacher?
Gosp.:	Lk 24:44-53	Proclaim Forgiveness to All Nations

Harvest Festival

O.T.:	Dt 26:1-11	Israel's Thankoffering of Firstfruits
Ep.:	2 Cor 9:6-15	Share Generously
Gosp.:	Mt 13:24-30	The Parable of the Final Harvest

Thanksgiving Day

O.T.:	Dt 8:1-10	Do Not Forget the Lord Your God
Ep.:	Php 4:6-20	Be Content with God's Gifts
Gosp.:	Lk 17:11-19	Return And Give Praise to God

8. ILCW — SERIES C

Advent 1

O.T.:	Jr 33:14-16	A Righteous Branch from David's Line
Ep.:	1 Th 3:9-13	Be Strong until Jesus Comes Again
Gosp.:	Lk 21:25-36	Your Redemption Is Drawing Near

Advent 2

O.T.:	Mal 3:1-4	A Messenger To Prepare the Way
Ep.:	Php 1:3-11	Paul, a Faithful Messenger of Christ
Gosp.:	Lk 3:1-6	The Advent Voice of John the Baptist

Advent 3

O.T.:	Zph 3:14-18a	Sing, O Daughter of Zion
Ep.:	Php 4:4-7	Rejoice in the Lord Always
Gosp.:	Lk 3:7-18	God's Herald Prepares the Way

Advent 4

O.T.:	Mic 5:2-4	A Ruler Will Come Out of Bethlehem
Ep.:	He 10:5-10	Christ Came To Do God's Will
Gosp.:	Lk 1:39-45	Mary's Song of Praise

The Nativity Of Our Lord — The First Service (Christmas Eve)

O.T.:	Is 9:2-7	God's Son Is Born as a Child
Ep.:	Tt 2:11-14	God's Grace Has Appeared to All Men
Gosp.:	Lk 2:1-20	The Birth of Jesus Is Good News

The Nativity Of Our Lord — The Second Service (Christmas Dawn)

O.T.:	Is 52:7-10	All Will See the Salvation of Our God
Ep.:	He 1:1-9	God Has Spoken to Us by His Son
Gosp.:	Jn 1:1-14	The Word Became Flesh

The Nativity Of Our Lord — The Third Service (Christmas Day)

O.T.:	Is 62:10-12	The Savior Comes to the Daughter of Zion
Ep.:	Tt 3:4-7	The Holy Spirit Is Poured Out on Us Generously through Jesus Our Savior
Gosp.:	Lk 2:1-20	The Birth of Jesus Is Good News

First Sunday after Christmas

O.T.:	Jr 31:10-13	The Lord Will Ransom Jacob
Ep.:	He 2:10-18	Christ Came as Our Brother
Gosp.:	Lk 2:41-52	The Boy Jesus In the Temple

New Year's Day

O.T.:	Nu 6:22-27	God's Name, a Blessing to His People
Ep.:	Ro 1:1-7	For His Name's Sake We Received Grace
Gosp.:	Lk 2:21	Jesus Receives His Name

Second Sunday After Christmas

O.T.:	Is 61:10—62:3	Christ's Robe of Righteousness
Ep.:	Eph 1:3-6, 15-18	Know the Hope to Which He Has Called You
Gosp.:	Jn 1:1-18	The Eternal Word Made Flesh

The Epiphany Of Our Lord

O.T.:	Is 60:1-6	The Nations Come to Zion's Light
Ep.:	Eph 3:2-12	To the Gentiles Christ's Unsearchable Riches
Gosp.:	Mt 2:1-12	Wise Men Worship the Christchild

Epiphany 1 — The Baptism of Our Lord

O.T.:	Is 42:1-7	God Will Put His Spirit on Christ
Ep.:	Ac 10:34-38	God Anointed Jesus of Nazareth
Gosp.:	Lk 3:15-17, 21-22	John Baptizes Jesus

Epiphany 2

O.T.:	Is 62:1-5	The Nations Will See Christ's Righteousness
Ep.:	1 Cor 12:1-11	The Gifts of the Spirit
Gosp.:	Jn 2:1-11	Jesus Reveals His Glory at the Wedding in Cana

Epiphany 3

O.T.:	Is 61:1-6	The Year of the Lord's Favor
Ep.:	1 Cor 12:12-21, 26,27	You Are the Body of Christ
Gosp.:	Lk 4:14-21	Today This Scripture Is Fulfilled

Epiphany 4

O.T.:	Jr 1:4-10	The Call of Jeremiah
Ep.:	1 Cor 12:27—13:13	Love, the Greatest Gift
Gosp.:	Lk 4:21-32	Isn't This Joseph's Son?

Epiphany 5

O.T.:	Is 6:1-8	The Call of Isaiah
Ep.:	1 Cor 14:12b-20	Gifts That Build Up the Church
Gosp.:	Lk 5:1-11	Jesus Calls His First Disciples

Epiphany 6

O.T.:	Jr 17:5-8	The Blessedness of the Believers
Ep.:	1 Cor 15:12, 16-20	Christ, the Firstfruits of the Dead
Gosp.:	Lk 6:17-26	Blessings And Woes

Epiphany 7

O.T.:	Gn 45:3-8a, 15	Joseph Makes Himself Known
Ep.:	1 Cor 15:35-38a, 42-50	The Resurrection Body
Gosp.:	Lk 6:27-38	Love Which Springs from Faith

Epiphany 8

O.T.:	Jr 7:1-7	God Demands a Reform in Word And Deed
Ep.:	1 Cor 15:51-58	Where, O Death Is Your Victory?
Gosp.:	Lk 6:39-49	Jesus Speaks about Judging Others

The Transfiguration Of Our Lord

O.T.:	Dt 34:1-12	The Death of Moses
Ep.:	2 Cor 4:3-6	The Light of Christ in Our Hearts
Gosp.:	Lk 9:28-36	The Transfiguration of Our Lord

Ash Wednesday

O.T.:	Jl 2:12-19	Joel's Call to Repentance
Ep.:	2 Cor 5:20b—6:2	Now Is the Day of Salvation
Gosp.:	Mt 6:1-6; 16-21	Fasting And Praying Sincerely

Lent 1

O.T.:	Dt 26:5-10	Remember the Lord's Blessings
Ep.:	Ro 10:8b-13	Salvation Is for Jew And Gentile
Gosp.:	Lk 4:1-13	Jesus Overcomes the Devil's Temptation

Lent 2

O.T.:	Jr 26:8-15	Jeremiah's Call to Repentance
Ep.:	Php 3:17—4:1	Stand Firm in the Lord!
Gosp.:	Lk 13:31-35	Jesus' Sorrow over Jerusalem

Lent 3

O.T.:	Ex 3:1-8a, 10-15	The Lord Reveals Himself to Moses on Horeb
Ep.:	1 Cor 10:1-13	Warnings from Israel's History
Gosp.:	Lk 13:1-9	Christ's Call to Repentance

Lent 4

O.T.:	Is 12:1-6	Water from the Wells of Salvation
Ep.:	1 Cor 1:18-31	We Preach Christ Crucified
Gosp.:	Lk 15:1-3, 11-32	The Parable of the Lost Son

Passion Sunday (Lent 5)

O.T.:	Is 43:16-21	God's Mercies to His People Israel
Ep.:	Php 3:8-14	Pressing On toward the Heavenly Goal
Gosp.:	Lk 20:9-19	The Parable of the Tenant Farmers

Lent 6 — Palm Sunday

O.T.:	Dt 32:36-39	God Wounds And Also Heals
Ep.:	Php 2:5-11	Imitate Christ's Humility
Gosp.:	Lk 23:1-49	Christ's Trial, Crucifixion And Death

Maundy Thursday

O.T.:	Jr 31:31-34	A New Covenant with the House of Israel
Ep.:	He 10:15-39	Christ's Sacrifice Once for All
Gosp.:	Lk 22:7-20	A New Covenant Replaces the Old

Good Friday

O.T.:	Is 52:13—53:12	Isaiah Prophesies the Suffering And Glory of Christ
Ep.:	He 4:14-16, 5:7-9	Jesus, the Great High Priest
Gosp.:	Jn 19:17-30	Christ's Suffering And Death on the Cross

Easter — The Resurrection of Our Lord

O.T.:	Ex 15:1-11	The Lord's Right Hand Is Majestic in Power
Ep.:	1 Cor 15:1-11	The Resurrection Gospel
Gosp.:	Lk 24:1-11	The First Visit to the Grave on Easter

Easter 2

Acts:	Ac 5:12, 17-32	The Apostles Are Imprisoned
Ep.:	Re 1:4-18	John on Patmos Hears the Voice of the Lord God
Gosp.:	Jn 20:19-31	Jesus Appears to Thomas

Easter 3

Acts:	Ac 9:1-20	Saul's Conversion Near Damascus
Ep.:	Re 5:11-14	John's Vision of the Heavenly Chorus
Gosp.:	Jn 21:1-14	The Risen Lord's Appearance in Galilee

Easter 4

Acts:	Ac 13:15,16a, 26-33	Paul's Testimony at Antioch
Ep.:	Re 7:9-17	John's Vision of the Lamb
Gosp.:	Jn 10:22-30	Jesus' Witness Concerning Himself

Easter 5

Acts:	Ac 13:44-52	Paul And Barnabas Turn to the Gentiles
Ep.:	Re 21:1-5	John Sees the New Jerusalem
Gosp.:	Jn 13:31-35	Christ's New Commandment: Love One Another

Easter 6

Acts:	Ac 14:8-18	Paul Heals the Crippled Man at Lystra
Ep.:	Re 21:10-14, 22,23	The New Jerusalem
Gosp.:	Jn 14:23-29	Jesus Promises the Holy Spirit

The Ascension Of Our Lord

Acts:	Ac 1:1-11	Jesus Is Taken Up into Heaven
Ep.:	Eph 1:16-23	God Placed All Things under Christ's Feet
Gosp.:	Lk 24:44-53	Jesus Prepares for His Ascension

Easter 7

Acts:	Ac 16:6-10	Paul's Vision of the Man of Macedonia
Ep.:	Re 22:12-17, 20	Jesus Is Coming Soon
Gosp.:	Jn 17:20-26	Jesus Prays for All Believers

Pentecost

O.T.:	Gn 11:1-9	The Confusion of Languages at Babel
Ep.:	Ac 2:37-47	The Unity of the Jerusalem Congregation
Gosp.:	Jn 15:26,27; 16:4b-11	The Work of the Holy Spirit

Pentecost 1 — The Holy Trinity

O.T.:	Pr 8:22-31	The Triune God Active in Creation
Ep.:	Ro 5:1-5	Peace And Joy in the Triune God
Gosp.:	Jn 16:12-15	Our Salvation — A Work of the Triune God

Pentecost 2

O.T.:	1 Kgs 8:41-43	Solomon's Prayer for the Foreigner
Ep.:	Ga 1:1-10	No Other Gospel
Gosp.:	Lk 7:1-10	The Faith of the Centurion

Pentecost 3

O.T.:	1 Kgs 17:17-24	Elijah Raises the Widow's Son
Ep.:	Ga 1:11-24	Paul Called by God
Gosp.:	Lk 7:11-17	Jesus Raises a Widow's Son

Pentecost 4

O.T.:	2 Sm 11:26—12:10, 13-15	David's Repentance And Absolution
Ep.:	Ga 2:11-21	Paul Opposes Peter
Gosp.:	Lk 7:36-50	Jesus Anointed by a Sinful Woman

Pentecost 5

O.T.:	Zch 12:7-10	Zechariah Foretells the Messiah's Suffering
Ep.:	Ga 3:23-29	All One in Christ Jesus
Gosp.:	Lk 9:18-24	The Necessity of the Cross

Pentecost 6

O.T.:	1 Kgs 19:14-21	Elijah Casts His Cloak around Elisha
Ep.:	Ga 5:1, 13-25	Freedom in Christ
Gosp.:	Lk 9:51-62	The Cost of Discipleship

Pentecost 7

O.T.:	Is 66:10-14	Isaiah Prophesies the Glories of the New Testament Church
Ep.:	Ga 6:1-10, 14-16	Let Us Do Good to All People
Gosp.:	Lk 10:1-12, 16	Jesus Sends Out the Seventy-two

Pentecost 8

O.T.:	Dt 30:9-14	Moses Provides for the Reading of the Law
Ep.:	Col 1:1-14	We Have Not Stopped Praying for You
Gosp.:	Lk 10:25-37	The Parable of the Good Samaritan

Pentecost 9

O.T.:	Gn 18:1-10a	Three Visitors Have a Message for Abraham
Ep.:	Col 1:21-28	Christ in Us, the Hope of Glory
Gosp.:	Lk 10:38-42	At the Home of Martha and Mary

Pentecost 10

O.T.:	Gn 18:20-32	Abraham Intercedes for Sodom And Gomorrah
Ep.:	Col 2:6-15	Continue To Live in Christ
Gosp.:	Lk 11:1-13	Lord, Teach Us To Pray

Pentecost 11

O.T.:	Ec 1:2; 2:18-26	All Earthly Things Are Meaningless
Ep.:	Col 3:1-11	Put On the New Self
Gosp.:	Lk 12:13-21	The Parable of the Rich Fool

Pentecost 12

O.T.:	Gn 15:1-6	The Lord's Promise to Abram
Ep.:	He 11:1-3, 8-16	Old Testament Examples of Faith
Gosp.:	Lk 12:32-40	Be Prepared for the Lord's Second Coming

Pentecost 13

O.T.:	Jr 23:23-29	A Warning against False Prophets
Ep.:	He 12:1-13	God Disciplines His Children
Gosp.:	Lk 12:49-53	Interpret the Times Wisely

Pentecost 14

O.T.:	Is 66:18-23	God Will Gather All Nations And Tongues
Ep.:	He 12:18-24	The City of the Living God
Gosp.:	Lk 13:22-30	The Narrow Door to Heaven

Pentecost 15

O.T.:	Pr 25:6-7	Humility Becomes the Christian
Ep.:	He 13:1-8	Exhortations To Live a Life of Loving Concern
Gosp.:	Lk 14:1, 7-14	Jesus Pictures True Humility

Pentecost 16

O.T.:	Pr 9:8-12	The Fear of the Lord — the Beginning of Wisdom
Ep.:	Phm 10-21	Paul's Plea for Onesimus
Gosp.:	Lk 14:25-33	The Cost of Being a Disciple

Pentecost 17

O.T.:	Ex 32:7-14	Moses Intercedes for the Lord's People
Ep.:	1 Tm 1:12-17	Christ Came To Save Sinners
Gosp.:	Lk 15:1-10	Joy over One Sinner Who Repents

Pentecost 18

O.T.:	Am 8:4-7	A Warning against Dishonest Management
Ep.:	1 Tm 2:1-8	Instructions on Worship
Gosp.:	Lk 16:1-13	The Parable of the Shrewd Manager

Pentecost 19

O.T.:	Am 6:1-7	Woe to the Complacent
Ep.:	1 Tm 6:6-16	Fight the Good Fight of Faith
Gosp.:	Lk 16:19-31	The Rich Man And Lazarus

Pentecost 20

O.T.:	Hab 1:1-3; 2:2-4	The Just Shall Live by Faith
Ep.:	2 Tm 1:3-14	Encouragement To Be Faithful
Gosp.:	Lk 17:1-10	Increase Our Faith

Pentecost 21

O.T.:	Ru 1:1-19a	Naomi And Ruth
Ep.:	2 Tm 2:8-13	Remember Jesus Christ Raised from the Dead
Gosp.:	Lk 17:11-19	Ten Healed of Leprosy

Pentecost 22

O.T.:	Gn 32:22-30	Jacob Wrestles with God
Ep.:	2 Tm 3:14—4:5	Paul's Charge to Timothy
Gosp.:	Lk 18:1-8a	Pray Always And Do Not Give Up

Pentecost 23

O.T.:	Dt 10:12-22	Fear the Lord Your God And Serve Him
Ep.:	2 Tm 4:6-8, 16-18	I Have Fought the Good Fight
Gosp.:	Lk 18:9-14	The Pharisee And the Tax Collector

Pentecost 24

O.T.:	Ex 34:5-9	The Sermon on the Name of the Lord
Ep.:	2 Th 1:1-5, 11,12	May the Name of Christ Be Glorified in You
Gosp.:	Lk 19:1-10	Jesus And Zacchaeus

Pentecost 25

O.T.:	1 Chr 29:10-13	David's Prayer of Thanksgiving
Ep.:	2 Th 2:13—3:5	Pray That the Gospel Spread
Gosp.:	Lk 20:27-38	Jesus Answers the Sadducees

Pentecost 26 — Third-Last Sunday in the Church Year

O.T.:	Ex 32:15-20	The Golden Calf Angers Moses
Ep.:	2 Th 3:6-13	A Warning against Idleness
Gosp.:	Lk 21:5-19	Signs of the Last Days

Pentecost 27 — Second-Last Sunday in The Church Year

O.T.:	Is 52:1-6	The Church Prepares for Its Deliverance
Ep.:	1 Cor 15:54-58	Your Labor in the Lord Is Not in Vain
Gosp.:	Lk 19:11-27	The Parable of the Ten Minas

Last Sunday in the Church Year

O.T.:	Mal 3:14-18	The Lord Distinguishes between the Righteous And Wicked
Ep.:	Col 1:13-20	Christ Is King over All
Gosp.:	Lk 12:42-48	The Wise Servant Is Always Ready for His Master's Coming

Reformation Day

O.T.:	Jr 31:31-34	God Will Establish a New Covenant with Israel
Ep.:	Ro 3:19-28	Justified by Grace through Faith
Gosp.:	Jn 8:31-36	Abraham's True Children

Mission Festival

O.T.:	Is 62:1-7	The Nations Will See God's Righteousness
Ep.:	Ro 10:11-17	How Can They Hear without a Preacher?
Gosp.:	Lk 24:44-53	Proclaim Forgiveness to All Nations

Harvest Festival

O.T.:	Dt 26:1-11	Israel's Thankoffering of Firstfruits
Ep.:	2 Cor 9:6-15	Share Generously
Gosp.:	Mt 13:24-30	The Parable of the Final Harvest

Thanksgiving Day

O.T.:	Dt 8:1-10	Do Not Forget the Lord Your God
Ep.:	Php 4:6-20	Be Thankful for God's Gifts
Gosp.:	Lk 17:11-19	Return And Give Praise to God

PART TWO

FREE TEXTS FOR FESTIVALS AND SEASONS

1. The Christmas Cycle
    - A. The Advent Season
        - Advent Free Texts
        - Advent Series
    - B. Christmas
    - C. New Year's Eve
    - D. New Year's Day
    - E. Epiphany
2. The Easter Cycle
    - A. The Lenten Season
        - Lenten Series
    - B. Holy Week
    - C. Easter
3. The Pentecost Cycle
    - A. Ascension
    - B. Pentecost
    - C. Trinity Sunday
4. The Trinity Cycle (Pentecost)
    - A. Mission Festival
    - B. Harvest And Thanksgiving
    - C. Reformation

1. THE CHRISTMAS CYCLE

The Christmas Cycle extends from the first Sunday in Advent to the last Sunday after the Epiphany.

A. The Advent Season

The purple paraments which are customarily used during this season indicate the emphasis is on repentance. As John the Baptist prepared the people of his day to receive the Messiah by calling upon them to repent, so it is still necessary for Christians to acknowledge their sins so that they may recognize their need for the Savior and so be prepared to welcome the good news that the Savior has been born.

Other emphases are also proper during the Advent season. The suggested Advent series which follow show the variety of thoughts the preacher may treat.

The pericopes for the four Sundays in Advent will in the main reflect the desire of the original compiler to present texts which contain Advent thoughts. The historic pericopes have set the tone for the Advent Sundays:

Advent 1 — Mt 21:1-9	Your King Comes to You (His Coming in Word And Sacrament)
Advent 2 — Lk 21:25-36	The Lord's Second Coming (at the End of the World)
Advent 3 — Mt 11:2-10	John Prepares for the Lord's Coming in the Flesh
Advent 4 — Jn 1:19-28	The Big Question Concerning Christ

Suggested Free Texts for Advent

Gn 3:15	The First Promise of a Savior
Gn 12:3	The Lord's Promise to Abraham
Gn 49:10	A Messiah from the Tribe of Judah
Dt 18:15	A Prophet Like Moses Will Come
2 Sm 7:12,13	An Everlasting House for David
Ps 24:7-10	The King of Glory Will Come
Is 2:2-4	The Mountain of the Lord's House Shall Be Established
Is 21:11	Watchman, What of the Night?
Is 61:1-3	To Proclaim the Year of the Lord's Favor
Jr 23:5-6	A Righteous Branch from David's Seed
Zch 2:10,11	Sing And Rejoice, O Daughter of Zion
Mal 3:1	I Will Send My Messenger
Mt 3:2	The Kingdom of Heaven Is at Hand
Mt 11:28,29	Come unto Me
Mk 13:24-27	The Son of Man Will Come with Power And Glory
Jn 6:14	The Prophet Who Is To Come
2 Cor 6:2	Now Is the Day of Salvation
1 Tm 1:15	Christ Jesus Came To Save Sinners
Re 21:1-4	The New Jerusalem
Re 22:12	Behold, I Am Coming Soon
Re 22:17	And the Spirit And the Bride Say, Come
Re 22:20	Amen. Come, Lord Jesus

Series for the Advent Season (Arranged for Three Midweek Services)

Old Testament Prophecies of the Messiah

a.	Gn 3:15	The Woman's Seed
	Gn 12:3	The Seed of Abraham
	Gn 49:10	The Descendant of Judah

b.	Ps 2:1-12	The Lord's Anointed
	Ps 14:1-7	Salvation for Israel
	Ps 24:1-10	The King of Glory
c.	Nu 24:17	The Star out of Jacob
	Is 49:6	The Light of the Gentiles
	Dn 7:13,14	The Son of Man
d.	Gn 49:10	Until Shiloh Come
	Dt 18:15	A Prophet Like Moses
	Mal 3:1	The Lord Will Suddenly Come
e.	Gn 3:15	Advent Announced
	Ps 14:7	Advent Awaited
	Mal 3:1	Advent at Hand

Nazarites as Types of Christ

Jdg 13:8	Samson
1 Sm 12:22-24	Samuel
Lk 1:13-17	John

Women of the Old Testament And the Coming Savior

Gn 21:67 and He 11:11	Sarah
Jos 6:25 and He 11:31	Rahab
Ru 1:16,17 and Mt 1:5	Ruth

Advent Messages from Isaiah

a.	Is 7:14	The Savior's Birth
	Is 9:6,7	The Savior's Name
	Is 61:1-3	The Savior's Work
b.	Is 40:1,2	Advent Reminds Us of a Promised Blessing
	Is 40:3-8	Advent Brings a Call to Repentance
	Is 40:9-11	Advent Points to a Person
c.	Is 40:1-8	The Promised Messiah Is at Hand
	Is 40:9-11	The Redeemer of All Men Is Come
	Is 40:25-31	The Holy One of Israel Is Revealed

Your King Comes; Go Out To Meet Him

Is 62:10-12	How Shall I Know Him?
Ps 118:25-29	How Shall I Greet Him?
Is 40:1-8	How Shall I Receive Him?

Christ's Offices Foretold

Dt 18:18,19	Foretold as Prophet
Ps 110:4	Foretold as Priest
Ps 2:1-12	Foretold as King

God's Faithful People Await Christmas

Lk 1:5-22	They Prepare
Lk 1:26-38	They Are Humble
Mt 1:18-25	They Are Saved

Advent Hymns

Lk 1:67-79	The Benedictus
Lk 1:46-55	The Magnificat
Lk 2:14	The Gloria in Excelsis

To Whom Does Jesus Come?

Lk 1:18-20	With Proof to Him Who Doubts
Lk 1:26, 31-33	With Comfort to Him Who Waits
Mt 1:20-23	With Enlightenment to Him Who Does Not Understand

Lord Jesus, Come to Me

1 Jn 4:7-12	With Your Love
1 Jn 4:1-6	With Your Truth
1 Jn 4:17-19	With Your Power

John's Message of the Coming Savior

Re 22:12,13	He Is Coming Soon
Re 22:17	The Spirit and the Bride Say, Come
Re 22:20	Amen. Come, Lord Jesus

B. Christmas

The service Christmas Day is the high point in the entire Christmas cycle. It is regrettable if the children's Christmas Eve service or the family customs which cluster around Christmas are allowed to obscure this fact. The man entrusted with the privilege of being the Lord's herald will in his Christmas sermon try his best to show that what he has to tell is indeed good news of great joy. While the sermon on Christmas Day will focus upon the objective truths revealed by the Savior's birth, the Sunday after Christmas may emphasize the believer's response to what he has seen and heard. Only the more obvious free texts appropriate for the occasion are listed here:

Is 60:1	Your Light Has Come
Ez 17:22-24	A Tender Branch

Mt 18:22-25	The Savior-God Is with Us
Lk 2:14	Glory to God in the Highest
Lk 2:15-20	Responding to the Savior's Birth
Jn 1:1-14	The Word Made Flesh
Jn 3:16-21	The Greatest Christmas Gift
Rm 8:31,32	How Will He Not Give Us All Things?
2 Cor 8:9	We Are Rich For He Was Poor
Ga 4:4,5	God Sent His Son
He 2:14-18	Made Like His Brothers
1 Jn 3:15	God Loves Me Dearly

C. New Year's Eve

Since New Year's Eve and New Year's Day are only hours apart, some of the free texts suggested are appropriate for either one. However to avoid becoming repetitious the preacher will do well to observe a distinction in emphasis and let New Year's Eve be an occasion for looking back and New Year's Day an occasion for looking ahead.

We look back upon a year in which the Lord blessed us in our personal, family, congregational, synodical and national life. We will also count the calamities as hidden blessings. In the spirit of Genesis 32:10, we will admit that these blessings are undeserved because we have sinned and deserved only wrath and rejection. This could be an occasion for briefly reviewing the Ten Commandments which should lead to self - examination and the recognition of specific sins. The sermon, however, dare not fail to include a reference to the pardoning grace of our God which enables us to cross over into the new year with a clean slate. Occasionally it would be appropriate to focus upon the fleeting nature of time and how transitory human life is in contrast to the unchanging and eternal nature of our God. The following are suggested free texts for New Year's Eve:

Gn 32:10	I Am Unworthy
Ex 3:13,14	I Am Who I Am
Dt 33:27	Underneath Are the Everlasting Arms
1 Sm 7:12	Thus Far Has the Lord Helped Us
Ezr 9:13	Less Than Our Sins Have Deserved
Ps 39:4-7,12	Show Me, O Lord
Ps 90	Teach Us To Number Our Days
Ps 116:5-7	The Lord Has Been Good to You
Ps 130:1-8	He Will Redeem Israel from All Their Sins
Ps 136:1	His Love Endures Forever
Is 1:18	Let Us Reason Together
Is 12:1-6	Praise the Lord for His Blessings
Is 63:7-17	You Are Our Father
Lm 3:22,23	His Compassions Never Fail
Na 1:2-8	The Lord Knows His Own

Mt 6:16-18	When You Fast
Mt 11:20	Because They Did Not Repent
Lk 12:48	Much Will Be Demanded
Lk 13:6-9	The Lord Looks for Fruit
Lk 24:29	Lord, Abide with Us
2 Tm 4:7,8	I Have Kept the Faith
He 13:5c	Never Will I Leave You
He 13:14	Here There Is No Enduring City
1 Jn 2:17	The World And Its Desires Pass Away

D. New Year's Day

New Year's Day has double significance. As the octave of Christmas it is the festival of the circumcision and the name of Jesus. But it also marks the beginning of the calendar year. In general our people have come to expect that the emphasis will be upon the latter. In treating the historic Gospel for the festival, Luke 2:21, the preacher without doing violence to the text can combine both emphases of the day. In sermons focusing upon the beginning of a new year a number of thoughts may be emphasized. People are apprehensive about what the new year may bring and need to be reassured that their future is in the hands of a loving God. Since the day for many is the occasion for making resolutions to improve in one or more areas, the preacher may want to suggest good resolutions for personal, family and church life. Suggested free texts for New Year's Day:

Ex 14:13-15	Tell the People To Move On
Ex 33:14,15	My Presence Will Go with You
Jos 1:1-9	Be Strong And Courageous
Jos 3:1-6	And the Ark Went Ahead
Ps 90:1-17	From Everlasting to Everlasting
Ps 91:1-16	I Will Protect You
Ps 121:1-8	My Help Comes from the Lord
Is 40:29-31	Hope in the Lord
Jr 3:12,13	The Lord Is Merciful
Mt 7:24-28	A House Built on a Rock
Mt 16:24-26	Come after Me
Mt 16:27,28	The Son of Man Is Going To Come
Mt 28:20b	I Will Be with You Always
Lk 12:32	Do Not Be Afraid, Little Flock
Ro 8:28	God Works for the Good of Those Who Love Him
Ro 8:31-39	More Than Conquerors
Ro 14:7-9	Life's Purpose And Goal
Jas 4:13-17	What Will Happen Tomorrow?
1 Pe 5:7	Cast All Your Anxiety on Him

2 Pe 3:8,9	Time from the Lord's Viewpoint
Re 1:8	I Am the Alpha And the Omega
Re 3:20	I Stand at the Door And Knock

E. Epiphany

In our circles the Epiphany festival itself is not commonly observed unless January 6 happens to fall on a Sunday. But we do have the Sundays after Epiphany. The Epiphany emphasis is vital, for it reminds us that he whom we beheld as a helpless infant at Christmas time and who walked among men in the form of a servant did at times let rays of divine glory shine through. We need to be aware of his divinity if we are to be sure that he was able to accomplish what he set out to accomplish in his suffering and death which are the focus of the Lenten season.

Other important truths may also be emphasized during the Epiphany season. The Historic Gospel for Epiphany, Matthew 2:1-12, tells of the adoration of the Magi. For that reason Epiphany was regarded as the Christmas of the Gentiles. That in turn suggests a mission emphasis during the Epiphany season. The Historic Epistles suggest that as the Savior let his hidden glory shine forth, so his people in their good works are to let their light shine (Mt 5:16). The last Sunday of the Epiphany season is known as Transfiguration Sunday when the Historic Gospel (Mt 17:1-9) and Epistle (2 Pe 1:16-21) tell of the grandest manifestation of the hidden glory of the Son of Man. Suggested free texts for the Epiphany season:

Ps 22:27,28, 31	All the Ends of the Earth Will Turn to the Lord
Ps 72:8-11	The King of Sheba Will Present Him Gifts
Is 9:2	The People in Darkness Have Seen a Great Light
Hg 2:6,7	The Desire of All Nations Shall Come
Zch 9:10	His Dominion Shall Be from Sea to Sea
Lk 1:78,79	The Rising Sun Will Come to Us
Lk 3:6	All Mankind Will See
Jn 1:14	We Have Seen His Glory
Ro 10:14-18	The Gospel Is Universal
2 Cor 4:6	True Epiphany Light

2. THE EASTER CYCLE

A. The Lenten Season

This cycle begins on Ash Wednesday and reaches its climax on Easter Sunday. Texts for the six midweek Lenten services are not included in pericopic systems. As a result pastors will have to develop their own series or adopt and adapt those available in the marketplace. The passion history itself provides the most appropriate texts, enough for five years of midweek Lenten sermons. Then there are prophecies of the passion and Old Testament types of the suffering Savior. Characters, both good and bad, who appear in the passion history can provide enough material for several series. Key passages which treat the doctrines involved in the passion and death of Jesus make an edifying series.

Several cautions need to be sounded. The preacher will have to guard against maudlin sentimentality in speaking of what Jesus suffered. While sympathy is in place, gratitude for what the Savior accomplished for us is much more in place. Although we may direct attention to characters in the passion history whose example we ought either to emulate or avoid, we must take care that the Savior and what he accomplished for us remain predominant. The call to repentance must be earnest, never as an end in itself but always and only preparatory for the good news of the forgiveness which the Savior won for sinners. Good works will be encouraged, but the encouragement must not be allowed to degenerate into moralizing. It should be motivated by gratitude for what the Savior has done. In thc suggestions for midweek Lenten series some contain six texts and do not include Good Friday, while those with seven texts do. Suggested Lenten Series:

The Passion History

a.	Mt 26:1-5	The Decision To Kill Jesus
	Mt 14:3-9	Mary Anoints Jesus
	Mt 26:14-16	Judas' Bloody Bargain
	Lk 22:24-30	Jesus Stills Strife among the Twelve
	Jn 13:1-17	Jesus Washes the Disciples' Feet
	Jn 13:18-30	The Betrayer Revealed
	Mt 26:26-28	The Supper Instituted (Maundy Thursday)
b.	Mt 26:30-35	You Will All Fall Away
	Mt 26:36-46	The Agony of Prayer
	Jn 18:3-12	Jesus Taken Captive
	Jn 18:13,14, 19-24	Jesus before Annas
	Mt 26:57-68	Jesus before Caiaphas
	Lk 22:54-62	Peter Denies Jesus

c.	Mt 27:1-10	The Death of Judas
	Jn 18:28-30	Jesus before Pilate
	Lk 23:5-12	Jesus before Herod
	Mt 27:15-26	Barabbas Preferred
	Jn 19:1-16a	Pilate's Futile Attempt To Free Jesus
	Lk 23:26-31	The Weeping Women
	Lk 23:39-46	Jesus' Death (Good Friday)
d.	Jn 19:19-22	The Superscription
	Mt 27:35,36, 38-44	Jesus Mocked
	Mt 27:45, 51-56	The Signs Accompanying the Crucifixion
	Jn 19:31-37	The Pierced Side
	Jn 19:38-42	The Burial
	Mt 27:62-66	The Tomb Sealed

Lenten Characters

a.	Jn 12:1-8	Mary of Bethany, Model of Faith
	Lk 23:5-12	Herod of Galilee, Example of Unbelief
	Mk 15:42-46	Joseph, a Weak Man Becomes Strong
	Mk 26:24	Pontius Pilate, a Strong Man Becomes Weak
	Mk 15:39	The Centurion, a Stranger Won
	Mt 26:57-68	Caiaphas, a Son Cast Out
b.	Mt 26:14-16	Judas — the Fallen Disciple
	Jn 19:26,27	John — the Faithful Disciple
	Mt 15:10	The Chief Priests — the Worst Element of the Nation
	Lk 23:27-31	The Weeping Women — the Better Element of the Nation
	Lk 22:54-62	Simon Peter — the Cross-Shirker
	Mt 15:21	Simon of Cyrene — the Cross-Bearer
	Mt 15:6-15	Barabbas — the Type of Sinners (Good Friday)

Places of the Passion

Mt 26:17-29	The Upper Room
Mt 26:36-46	Gethsemane
Mt 26:57-66	The High Priest's Palace
Mt 27:2, 11-26	Pilate's Court
Lk 23:26-31	The Way of Sorrows
Mt 27:33,56	Golgotha
Mt 27:57-66	The Place of Burial (Good Friday)

Words from the Cross

Lk 23:34	The Word of Forgiveness
Lk 23:43	The Word of Assurance
Jn 19:26,27	The Word of Concern
Mt 27:45,46	The Word of Desolation
Jn 14:28,29	The Word of Fulfillment
Jn 19:30	The Word of Triumph
Lk 23:46	The Word of Committal (Good Friday)

Lenten Questions

Mt 26:40	Could You Not Keep Watch with Me for One Hour?
Mt 26:50	Friend, Why Have You Come?
Mt 26:54	How Then Would the Scripture Be Fulfilled?
Lk 22:70	Are You the Son of God?
Jn 18:37	You Are a King Then?
Mt 27:22	What Shall I Do with Jesus?
Mt 27:46	Why Have You Forsaken Me?

What They Said When Jesus Went to Calvary

Mt 26:25	Master, Is It I?
Mt 26:66	He Is Guilty of Death
Mt 26:74	I Know Not the Man
Jn 18:38	What Is Truth?
Mt 27:25	His Blood Be on Us
Lk 23:43	Lord, Remember Me
Lk 23:47	Surely, This Was a Righteous Man (Good Friday)

"When I Survey the Wondrous Cross"

Mk 15:21	Those Who Bear the Cross
Lk 23:27-31	Those Who Lament the Cross
Lk 23:32-34	Those Who Nail to the Cross
Jn 19:25-27	Those in the Shadow of the Cross
Lk 23:35	Those Who Revile the Cross
Lk 23:42	Those Who Surrender to the Cross
1 Cor 11:26	Those Who Find Fellowship in the Cross

Lenten Shadow and Light

Judas (Mt 27:5), Peter (Lk 22:62)	Two Disciples
Caiaphas (Mt 26:57), Nicodemus (Jn 19:39)	Two Masters in Israel
Barabbas (Mk 15:6,7), Jesus (Mk 15:12,13)	Two Prisoners
Women of Jerusalem (Lk 23:27-31), Women at the Foot of the Cross (Jn 19:25)	Two Kinds of Sorrows
Pilate (Jn 18:28,29), The Centurion (Mt 27:54)	Two Romans
"Testas" (Lk 23:39); "Dismas" (Lk 23:40-43)	Two Malefactors

Christ Calls to Calvary

Lk 18:31-33	The Faithful
Mt 26:50	The Fallen
Lk 22:61	The Erring
Jn 18:34-37	The Worldly
Lk 23:34	The Ignorant
Lk 23:43	The Penitent
Mk 15:39	The Confessing

Contrasts of the Cross

Ro 6:23	Sin And Grace
1 Jn 3:16	Hatred And Love
He 10:23	Betrayal And Faithfulness
Is 53:3,4	Sorrow And Joy
2 Cor 5:21	Justice And Mercy
Ga 6:14	Shame And Glory
Lk 23:32,33	Life And Death

Triumphs of the Savior's Passion

Mt 26:36-39	Triumph in Gethsemane
Mk 14:53, 55-63	Triumph in the Jewish Court
Lk 22:54-62	Triumph in the Courtyard
Lk 23:13-15	Triumph in the Gentile Court
Lk 23:39-43	Triumph at Calvary
Jn 19:30	Triumph on the Cross
Lk 23:46	Triumph in Dying

What Do You Think of Christ?

Ps 2	Does His Majesty Attract You?
Ps 130	Does His Grace Fill You?
Ps 22:1-6	Does the Intensity of His Agony Amaze You?
Ps 22:7-11	Does His Confidence Instruct You?
Ps 22:12-18	Does His Ordeal Humble You?
Ps 22:19-26	Does His Praying Inspire You?
Ps 22:27-31	Does His Victory Sustain You?

Series on Lenten Hymns

Lk 18:34	Jesus I Will Ponder Now
Is 53:6,7	A Lamb Goes Uncomplaining Forth
1 Pe 3:18	O Dearest Jesus, What Law Hast Thou Broken?
Jn 19:5	O Sacred Head, Now Wounded
1 Pe 2:21-24	Upon the Cross Extended
Jn 19:41,42	O Darkest Woe
Ro 12:1,2	Christ, the Life of All the Living (Good Friday)

The Searching Questions of Lent

Jn 13:36-38	"Will You Really Lay Down Your Life for Me?"
Jn 18:1-6	"Who Is It You Want?"
Jn 18:10,11	"Shall I Not Drink the Cup?"
Jn 18:15-17	"Surely You Are Not Another of This Man's Disciples?"
Jn 18:37,38	"What Is Truth?"
Mt 27:15-22	"What Shall I Do, Then, with Jesus?"
Lk 23:27-31	"What Will Happen When the Tree Is Dry?" (Good Friday)

The Lord's Prayer in the Light of the Lord's Passion

1 Jn 3:1a	"How Great That We Should Be Called Children of God"
Jn 18:36,37	"My Kingdom Is Not of This World"
Lk 22:31,32	"I Have Prayed for You . . . That Your Faith May Not Fail"
Jn 19:28	"I Am Thirsty"
Lk 23:34	"Father, Forgive Them"
Mt 26:41	"Watch And Pray So That You Will Not Fall into Temptation"
Jn 17:15	"My Prayer Is That You Protect Them from the Evil One" (Good Friday)

Triumphs of the Cross

Mt 26:36-46	Dedication to the Father's Will Triumphs over the Horror of the Cross
Lk 22:54ff	A Straying Sheep Reclaimed by the Good Shepherd
Mt 26:53ff	Every Word of the Scripture Is Fulfilled to the Letter
Lk 23:43	A Sinner Snatched from the Jaws of Hell
Lk 23:46	An Important Life Comes to a Victorious Conclusion
Jn 19:38	A Feeble Faith Grows Bold
Mt 26:26-28	A Precious Supper Instituted
Jn 19:30	The Father's Plan Carried Out to the Last Detail

Lenten Sermons Preached by Christ's Enemies

Jn 11:49-53	Caiaphas: "It is Better That One Man Die for the People."
Mt 27:19	Pilate's Wife: "Don't Have Anything To Do with That Innocent Man."
Lk 22:70ff	Sanhedrin: "We Have Heard It from His Own Lips."
Mt 27:4	Judas: "I Have Sinned, For I Have Betrayed Innocent Blood."
Jn 19:2ff	Pilate's Soldiers: "Hail, O King of the Jews!"
Mt 27:42	Chief Priests: "He Saved Others, But He Can't Save Himself."
Mt 27:54	Centurion: "Surely He Was the Son of God."

What Did the Prophets Say about the Son of Man? (Lk 18:31)

Zch 9:8-10	Zechariah Foretold That Jesus Would Come as Israel's King
Ps 41:9	David Foretold the Tragedy of Jesus' Betrayal by a Friend
Is 50:5-7	Isaiah Shows the Savior's Attitude on the Way to the Cross
Is 53:3-6	Isaiah Shows Us the Heart of Jesus' Suffering
Ps 69:20f	David Predicted the Agony of the Savior's Thirst
Ps 22:1ff	David Shows Us What Went On In the Soul of the Dying Savior
Ex 12:21-27, 43-47	The Passover, an Old Testament Picture of the Lord's Supper (Maundy Thursday)
Is 53:9-12	Isaiah Helps Us To Understand Christ's Passion

B. Holy Week: Palm Sunday, Maundy Thursday, Good Friday

It has been traditional to call the week which begins with Palm Sunday and ends with Easter Holy Week. Likc the other Sundays during Lent Palm Sunday does not share in the solemn tone of Lent. All Sundays are considered joyous anniversaries of Easter. The Historic Gospel for Palm Sunday commemorates the triumphant entrance of Jesus into Jerusalem. It gives the assurance in advance that the Savior whose death will be commemorated on Good Friday is God's appointed King whom death cannot defeat. Pericope series contain appropriate texts for Palm Sunday. In congregations which, in keeping with tradition, have confirmation on Palm Sunday the sermon for the day will be a confirmation sermon. Confirmation texts will be suggested among free texts for special occasions.

The Historic Gospel for Maundy Thursday is the account of Jesus washing the disciples' feet (Jn 13:1-15). Since the Lord's Supper was instituted on the first Maundy Thursday, the sermon may well treat of it. This becomes especially appropriate if those who have been confirmed on Palm Sunday at this time receive their first communion. Texts for sermons about the Lord's Supper will be included among free texts for special occasions.

Good Friday centers our attention upon the suffering and dying Savior and what he accomplished for us. As was mentioned previously, the Good Friday sermon may conclude the Lenten series. Texts for Good Friday are included in the pericope series.

Free Texts for Good Friday

Ps 22:1-31	David's Prophecy of the Suffering Savior
Is 52:13—53:12	Isaiah's Prophecy of the Suffering Servant
Jn 1:29	Behold the Lamb of God
Jn 3:14,15	As Moses Lifted Up the Snake in the Desert
Jn 3:23,24	Jesus Glorified in His Death
Ro 3:24,25	God Demonstrates His Justice
Ro 5:8	Christ Died for Us
1 Cor 1:23,24	We Preach Christ Crucified
2 Cor 5:19-21	A World of Sinners Reconciled
Ga 6:14	I Boast in the Cross
Eph 2:14	The Barrier between God And Man

C. Easter

Easter celebrates both the triumph of our Savior in his glorious resurrection and its importance for us. The resurrection of Jesus will be treated as the historical fact it is without devoting an undue amount of time to refuting the error of those who deny his physical resurrection. It is more important to stress the following comforting truths which are established by the resurrection:

1. Jesus is proved to be true God with the Father.
2. The fact that he rose as he said proves that all his words are true and that all of the Bible is true.
3. By raising him the Father showed that he had accepted Christ's atoning sacrifice as sufficient and completed.
4. Because he rose, we too shall rise as he promised.
5. Because he lives never to die again, we may be sure that he will always be with us.

Free Texts for Easter

Job 19:25-27	I Know That My Redeemer Lives
Ps 16:8-11	Therefore My Heart Is Glad
Is 25:8	Death Is Swallowed Up in Victory

Jn 6:40	Everlasting Life Now
Jn 11:25,26	I Am the Resurrection And the Life
Jn 14:19	Because I Live
Jn 20:11-18	Mary And the Risen Christ
Ro 4:25	Raised for Our Justification
Ro 6:3-8,11	The Resurrection, of Daily Significance
1 Cor 15:13-20	Christ Is Risen Indeed
1 Cor 15:55-57	Where, O Death, Is Your Victory?
2 Cor 5:15	The Fruits of Christ's Resurrection
1 Th 4:13-18	Concerning Those Who Sleep in Jesus
2 Tm 1:9,10	Life And Immortality Brought to Light
1 Pe 1:3,4	Living Hope through the Resurrection
1 Jn 3:2	We Shall Be Like Him
Re 5:1-14	Worthy Is the Lamb

3. THE PENTECOST CYCLE

A. Ascension

The first three Sundays after Easter (Quasimodogeniti, Misericordias Domini or Good Shepherd, Jubilate) still belong to the Easter cycle, and the pericopes refer to the resurrection event. Beginning with the fourth Sunday after Easter (Cantate) the pericopes refer to Christ's promise of the Holy Spirit and thus prepare for Pentecost. We have therefore included Ascension Day in the Pentecost cycle, although traditionally this festival was simply considered as part of a fifty-day period from Easter to Pentecost in which the entire work of redemption was commemorated.

The ascension of our Lord is commemorated forty days after Easter, ten days before Pentecost. The ascension, the third phase of our Lord's exaltation, shows that he had successfully finished the work for which he had come down to earth. He could now return to the glory which he had with the Father before he came to earth to assume the role of the suffering servant. Now he rules as head over all things and uses his power for the good of his church in general and of every believer in particular. Now he pleads for us with the Father. One day he will come back to take us to be with him, so that his ascension is the harbinger of our own.

Free Texts for Ascension

Ps 47:5-8	The Psalmist's Prophecy of Our Ascended King
Dn 7:13,14	Daniel's Vision of Christ's Dominion
Lk 24:50-53	Jesus Was Taken Up into Heaven
Jn 14:1-6	The Way to the Father's House
Ro 8:34	Christ's Intercession at God's Right Hand
1 Cor 15:25-28	Everything Is under Christ's Feet
2 Cor 4:17,18	The Temporal Versus the Eternal
Eph 1:20-23	Christ's Rule at God's Right Hand
Eph 4:8-10	Gifts from Our Ascended Lord
Php 2:9-11	Before Whom Every Knee Should Bow
Php 3:20,21	Our Citizenship Is in Heaven
Eph 4:8-10	He Ascended And Gave Gifts to Men
He 4:14-16	Our Heavenly High Priest
He 6:17-20	Jesus, A High Priest Forever
He 13:14	The Enduring City That Is To Come
Re 7:9-17	A Glimpse of Our Heavenly Home

B. Pentecost

The outpouring of the Holy Spirit upon the first disciples is our assurance that he is an abiding gift for every believer. He creates, strengthens and sustains saving faith. He prompts our prayers. He helps us in our struggle against our sinful flesh. The church is his creation.

Free Texts for Pentecost

Ps 51:10-12	Create in Me a Clean Heart, O God
Jr 31:33,34	They Will All Know Me
Jl 2:28	Joel's Pentecost Prophecy
Jn 3:5-8	Born Again of the Spirit
Jn 6:41-46	They Will All Be Taught by God
Jn 15:25-27	Jesus Promises To Send the Holy Spirit
Jn 16:5-16	The Work of the Holy Spirit, the Counselor
Ac 2:42-47	The Fellowship of Believers
Ro 8:14-16	Let God's Spirit Lead You
1 Cor 2:6-16	Wisdom from God's Spirit
1 Cor 3:16,17	You Are God's Temple
1 Cor 12:1-11	The Gifts of the Spirit
Ga 5:16-25	Live by the Spirit
He 8:8-12	They Will All Know Me

C. Trinity Sunday

This festival has been observed regularly since 1334, although it had been inserted into the calendar as early as 1305. It concludes the festival half of the church year. It becomes the occasion for reviewing the truth that the only true God is the triune God. It is he who performed the saving work to which our attention was directed during the festival half of the church year.

Free Texts for Trinity Sunday

Nu 6:22-27	A Threefold Blessing
Mt 3:16,17	The Triune God Revealed at Jesus' Baptism
Mt 28:19	Baptize in the Name of the Triune God
Jn 14:23	God's Home within Us
Ac 2:37-41	The Fruit of Preaching
1 Jn 4:13,14	A Threefold Assurance of Discipleship

4. THE TRINITY CYCLE (PENTECOST)

According to traditional pericope series (such as the Historic, Eisenach, Thomasius etc.) the non-festival portion of the church year is comprised of "Sundays after Trinity." The ILCW series, calling upon a tradition which antedates A.D. 1300, names these "Sundays after Pentecost." Both designations refer to Sundays representing the *Time of the Church*, which points especially to the life of believers as they respond to the wonderful works of God presented in the festival half of the church year. Since the various pericopes offer sufficient text material for this long season, no added free texts are included. Toward the close of the church year a number of special church festivals have become a part of church usage for which the following free texts are suggested.

A. Mission Festival

The observance began in Europe. The state church as such was concerned only with the spiritual affairs of the citizens of the state. However earnest Christians who read their Bibles realized that their Lord had made it their obligation and privilege to reach beyond the confines of their own nation to bring the gospel to the heathen. So they organized mission societies to train and send out missionaries. To stimulate interest in mission work they arranged for mission festivals, which were often held outdoors and drew people from far and near. The sermons sought to inform and inspire. The offerings supported the missionary enterprises of the mission societies.

When these dedicated souls emigrated to the United States, they felt constrained to continue having mission festivals. But things began to change. Information about mission work was provided to congregations throughout the year. Instead of depending upon one large mission festival offering to support the church's mission program, congregations introduced weekly envelope offerings. But there was one need which mission festivals continued to meet — the need for inspiration.

Generally it is a guest pastor who is expected to supply this inspiration from God's Word. If it is possible, missionaries on furlough are accorded the privilege. The spiritual need of the unchurched millions in the world, evidences of the converting power of the Word, opportunities, problems and difficulties are brought to the attention of Christ's people. Since the Lord has laid this work upon their hearts, the appeal goes out to support it with their interest, their prayers and their contributions.

Suggested Free Texts for Mission Festival

Gn 12:1-3	A Blessing for All People
Ex 19:6	You Will Be a Kingdom of Priests
Nu 10:35	The Church's Marching Orders
Jdg 18:9	God's Command To Possess the Earth
1 Kgs 8:41-43	Solomon's Prayer for the Foreigner
2 Kgs 5:2,3	The Witness of a Little Girl
2 Kgs 6:15-17	Surrounded by Hosts of Angels
Ps 2:8	The Nations Are Our Inheritance
Ps 87	This One Was Born in Zion
Ps 96:10	Say among the Nations, the Lord Reigns
Ps 107:2	Let the Redeemed of the Lord Say So
Ps 133:1-3	Our Mission Calling
Pr 30:24-28	The Wisdom of a Little Strength
Is 2:1-4	Many Peoples Will Come
Is 12:1-6	Make Known What God Has Done
Is 40:9	Here Is Your God
Is 42:1-4	He Will Bring Justice to the Nations
Is 45:22	Turn to Me And Be Saved
Is 49:22,23	See, I Will Beckon to the Gentiles
Is 52:7	How Beautiful on the Mountains
Is 57:19	Peace to Those Far And Near
Is 54:1-3	Enlarge the Place of Your Tent
Is 61:1-6	Beauty Instead of Ashes
Jr 16:19-21	Then the Nations Will Know

Jr 31:10-14	Hear the Word of the Lord, O Nations
Ez 37:1-14	Dry Bones Made Alive
Jon 3:1-10	Go to the Great City of Nineveh
Jon 4:1-11	Have You Any Right To Be Angry?
Hab 2:14	The Earth Will Be Filled
Mic 4:1-5	Let Us Go Up to the Mountain of the Lord
Zch 9:9,10	His Rule Will Extend from Sea to Sea
Mal 1:11	My Name Will Be Great among the Nations
Mt 5:13-16	The Salt, the Light, the Candle
Mt 6:9,10	The First Three Petitions
Mt 6:10	Your Kingdom Come
Mt 9:35-38	The Harvest And the Workers
Mt 13:31-33	Like Mustard Seed — Like Leaven
Mt 24:14	The Gospel in All the World
Mt 28:18-20	The Great Commission
Mk 16:16	Good News to All Creation
Lk 6:31	Do to Others . . .
Lk 15:1-10	A Cause for Rejoicing
Lk 15:7,10,32	Lost And Found
Lk 16:9	Use Worldly Wealth To Gain Friends
Lk 19:1-10	The Seeking Savior
Lk 19:11-27	Put This Money to Work
Lk 24:45-48	Beginning at Jerusalem
Jn 1:42	He Brought Him to Jesus
Jn 3:16	God So Loved the World
Jn 7:37-39	Streams of Living Water
Jn 9:4	While It Is Day
Jn 10:16	Other Sheep
Jn 12:32	I Will Draw All Men to Myself
Jn 14:12	The Greater Work of Jesus' Followers
Jn 17:3	The Only True God
Jn 20:19-23	I Am Sending You
Ac 1:8	You Will Be My Witnesses
Ac 2:1-23	World Communications
Ac 2:39	The Promise Is for All
Ac 4:12	Salvation in No One Else
Ac 4:18-21	We Cannot Help Speaking
Ac 5:38-42	A Story of Success
Ac 13:6-12	The Power Struggle in Mission Work
Ac 14:26,27	A Mission Report
Ac 15:6-12	Wonders Done among the Gentiles
Ac 16:6-10	Come And Help Us

Ac 26:25-32	It Was Not Done in a Corner
Ac 28:23,24	Some Were Convinced by What Was Said
Ro 1:14-16	Not Ashamed of the Gospel
Ro 10:15	Unless They Are Sent
1 Cor 16:9	A Great Door Is Opened to Me
2 Cor 4:6	The Light of the Glory of the Lord
2 Cor 4:13,14	We Believe And Therefore Speak
2 Cor 2:14,15	We Try To Persuade Men
Eph 2:16-18	He Came And Preached Peace
Eph 3:8	The Heart of a Missionary
Php 4:15-18	An Acceptable Sacrifice
Col 4:3	Pray That God May Open a Door
2 Th 3:1	Pray That the Message May Spread
1 Tm 2:1-7	Mission Goals And Guidelines
2 Tm 2:1,2	A Worker-Training Program for Missions
He 11:1	Mission Work — a Work of Faith
1 Pe 2:9,10	A Royal Priesthood
3 Jn 5-8	The Mission Work of Layman Gaius
Re 3:8	A Little Strength — An Open Door
Re 7:13-17	Preparing for Heaven
Re 14:6,7	The Reformation's Mission Heritage
Re 22:17	The Spirit And the Bride Say Come

B. Harvest And Thanksgiving

With the increasing urbanization of our country separate harvest festivals are becoming increasingly rare. They were set for the time when the year's harvest had been pretty well completed. People were urged to recognize that there could be a harvest only because the Lord had granted it. If the harvest was good, it was easy to urge people to thank God for it. The warning was issued not to abuse the Lord's bounty by setting the heart upon riches or by using it to cater to the flesh, but rather to use it to the glory of God and the benefit of one's fellow men. If the harvest was scant, people were urged to submit to the Lord's chastening and to depend upon him to see them through.

If there is no harvest festival, one of the blessings for which people can be urged to give thanks on Thanksgiving Day is the year's harvest. City dwellers need to be reminded that the supermarket is not the genesis for the many foods so attractively displayed. Needless to say, there are many other blessings for which Christian people should be encouraged to give thanks on the day of national thanksgiving. In personal and family life, in congregational and synodical life, and in national life we receive countless blessings, some of which may be singled out to provide concreteness in the sermon. Our response to the blessings should also be pointed out — thanking in thought, word and deed, sharing with the needy, avoiding the complaining mind-set, praying for our government.

Suggested Texts for Harvest And Thanksgiving

Gn 8:20-22	God's Promise to Noah
Gn 32:10	A Time for Humble Reflection
Lv 19:9,10	When You Reap the Harvest, Remember
Dt 8:10,11	Praise the Lord for the Good Land
1 Sm 12:24	Consider What Great Things He Has Done
Job 1:21	The Lord Gave, the Lord Has Taken Away
Ps 24:1	The Earth Is the Lord's
Ps 34:1-8	Glorifying the Lord with Me
Ps 65:1-4	Praise Awaits You, O God, in Zion
Ps 67:1-7	May the People Praise You
Ps 92:1-15	Too Much of a Good Thing?
Ps 100:1-5	Shout for Joy, All the Earth
Ps 103:1-22	Praise the Lord, O My Soul
Ps 105:105	Give Thanks to the Lord
Ps 106:1ff	Give Thanks to the Lord
Ps 107:1ff	Give Thanks to the Lord
Ps 116:12-14	How Can I Repay the Lord?
Ps 117:1,2	Praise the Lord
Ps 145:15-21	The Eyes of All Look to You
Ps 148:1ff	Praise the Lord
Pr 3:9,10	Honor the Lord with Your Wealth
Mt 6:11	Give Us Today Our Daily Bread
Mt 15:29-39	Jesus Feeds Four Thousand
Mt 16:5-12	Do You Still Not Understand?
Lk 12:16-21	The Rich Fool
Lk 17:17	Where Are the Other Nine?
Ro 2:4	God's Kindness Leads toward Repentance
1 Cor 6:20	Therefore Honor Your God
1 Cor 10:10	Do Not Grumble
Eph 5:20	Always Giving Thanks
Php 4:6	In Everything with Thanksgiving
Php 4:12	Content in Every Situation
1 Th 5:18	Give Thanks in All Circumstances
Jas 1:17	Every Good And Perfect Gift Is from Above

C. Reformation

According to Nesper, October 31 began to be observed as the festival of the Reformation as early as 1617. This was not the case, however, in all Lutheran churches until two centuries later. By 1917 other Protestant churches also began to make the day an occasion for recalling the debt which they too owed the Reformation.

Recently the more liberal Lutherans have joined with Roman Catholics in observing the day as a festival of reconciliation, emphasizing areas of agreement and downgrading the serious doctrinal differences still separating the two groups. We do well to retain the original emphasis of the festival of the Reformation and to stress the work of the great Reformer and its continuing significance — the discovery of the cardinal truth that a man is justified by faith without works, of the truth of the individual's accountability to his God, of the privilege and duty of using the Bible, of the dignity of marriage, of the separate functions of church and state, of the need for Christian education, of the universal priesthood of all believers. Gifts such as the translation of the Bible into the language of the people, the Small and Large Catechisms, hymns and congregational singing could also be gratefully acknowledged.

References to Reformation history will of necessity introduce a measure of polemics, but the positive note of gratitude for our heritage will predominate. This will lead in turn to the admonition to appreciate and preserve our heritage and to be eager to share it with others who do not have it.

Suggested Free Texts for Reformation

1 Kgs 8:57,58	As He Was with Our Fathers
2 Kgs 23:1-3	A True Reformation
Ps 31:1-3	Deliver Me in Your Righteousness
Ps 46:1-11	Our Refuge And Strength
Ps 119:92	If Your Law Had Not Been My Delight
Ps 119:105	God's Word, A Lamp
Jr 23:29	God's Word, Like a Fire
Hab 2:1-4	The Just Shall Live by Faith
Mt 16:18	The Rock of Our Lutheran Confession
Lk 12:48	Much Will Be Demanded
Jn 2:15-17	Zeal for God's House
Jn 5:39	Search the Scriptures
Jn 8:31,32	Continue in Christ's Word
Jn 17:6-11	Keep the Word of God
Ro 1:16,17	Not Ashamed of the Gospel of Christ
Ro 3:28	Justified by Faith
Ro 4:1-8	Not by Works, But by Faith
Ro 5:1,2	Therefore, Since We Have Been Justified through Faith

Ro 7:24,25	I Thank God through Jesus Christ
Ro 8:31-34	God Is for Us
2 Cor 4:1-6	We Preach Christ
2 Cor 4:13	We Believe And Therefore Speak
2 Cor 5:14,15	Christ's Love Compels Us
Ga 1:8,9	No Other Gospel
Ga 2:16	Not by Works, But by Faith
Ga 3:11-13	The Just Shall Live by Faith
Ga 5:1	Stand Firm in Your Christian Liberty
Eph 2:8-10	By Grace, Through Faith
Eph 6:10-17	Put On the Full Armor of God
Col 3:16,17	Let Christ's Word Dwell in You
1 Th 5:20-22	Test All Things by the Word
2 Tm 1:12	I Know Whom I Have Believed
2 Tm 1:13,14	Guard the Good Deposit
He 10:23-25	Hold Unswervingly to the Hope You Profess
He 13:7	Remember Your Leaders
1 Pe 2:2	Crave Pure Spiritual Milk
1 Pe 2:8,9	The Priesthood of Believers
2 Pe 1:19-21	We Have a Certain Word
1 Jn 4:1,2	Test the Spirits
Jd 3	Contend for the Faith
Re 3:8	The Church of the Open Door
Re 3:11	Hold On to What You Have
Re 14:6,7	The Angel with the Everlasting Gospel

PART THREE

FREE TEXTS FOR SPECIAL OCCASIONS

1. Confirmation
2. Holy Communion
3. Marriage
4. Funerals
   - A. General
   - B. Children
   - C. Sudden or Tragic Death
   - D. After Prolonged Illness
   - E. Aged Christian
   - F. Doubtful Cases
5. Ordination — Installation
6. Introductory — Farewell
7. Christian Education — Graduation
8. The Christian Family
9. Stewardship
10. Dedication
    - A. Cornerstone
    - B. Church
    - C. School
    - D. Parsonage
    - E. Organ

FREE TEXTS FOR SPECIAL OCCASIONS

Not only is a pastor expected to preach regularly in the Sunday, festival and midweek services, but also on a vast variety of special occasions, some of which, like marriages and funerals, come more or less frequently depending upon the size of his congregation. Others may come only rarely or not at all in his career, as, e.g., the dedication of a church or parsonage. The purpose of this brief survey is to provide somewhat of a perspective and also to present some suggestions and occasionally words of caution.

1. CONFIRMATION

Experience and observation show that the pastor who has prepared a class of young people or adults for confirmation holds a unique place in their affection. He will want to capitalize upon this reverence by trying to bring a message in his confirmation sermon which will stay with the members of his class through life. He will do so not without a tinge of sadness as he recalls others of previous classes who have since proved to be like the seed which fell upon the rock. He will remind the class of the blessings which they have received from the Lord in their baptism, their Christian training, and the new blesssing which they are soon to receive in the Lord's Supper. He will encourage them to remain faithful to their Lord, to his Word, to their church and warn them against the temptations and dangers which face them in the lust of the flesh, the pride of reason, indifference and apostasy. He will direct them to their source of strength in Word and sacrament, and encourage active participation in the life of their congregation and good works in general. He will also remind especially the parents, families, friends and then also the entire congregation of their continuing obligation to pray for the confirmands and to encourage them by word and example. Keep the sermon brief!

Suggested Texts

Dt 4:39,40	A Solemn Covenant with the Lord
Dt 39:19,20a	Now Choose Life
Dt 31:6	Be Strong And Courageous
Dt 32:46,47	Take These Words to Heart
Jos 1:5-8	The Lord's Promise And Advice
Jos 24:15-18	Choose Whom You Will Serve
1 Sm 17:45,46	Do Battle in the Name of the Lord
1 Kgs 8:57,58	Keep What the Lord Commanded Our Fathers
2 Chr 29:11	Do Not Be Negligent Now
Neh 8:10	The Joy of the Lord Is Your Strength
Ps 1:1-6	The Way of the Righteous
Ps 20:7	We Trust in the Name of the Lord Our God
Ps 25:4-6	Show Me Your Way, O Lord
Ps 40:8	I Delight To Do Your Will, O My God
Ps 43:3	Let Your Light And Truth Lead Me
Ps 71:5	You Are My Trust from My Youth, O Lord
Ps 86:11	I Will Walk in Your Truth, O Lord
Ps 119:105	Your Word — a Lamp And a Light
Pr 3:5,6	Trust in the Lord
Pr 14:27	The Fear of the Lord — a Fountain of Life
Pr 23:26	Give Me Your Heart This Day
Is 40:26-31	They Shall Run And Not Be Weary
Is 41:10	Let God Be with You

Is 43:1	You Belong to God
Hab 3:18,19	The Lord God Is My Strength
Mt 6:33	Seek First the Kingdom of God
Mt 7:13,14	Enter through the Narrow Gate
Mt 10:32,33	Confess Christ before Men
Mt 11:28-30	Take Christ's Yoke upon You
Mt 24:13	Stand Firm to the End
Lk 10:23,24	Blessed Are the Eyes That See What You See
Jn 6:27	Food That Endures to Eternal Life
Jn 6:60-69	Lord, to Whom Shall We Go?
Jn 8:31,32	Hold to My Teaching
Jn 10:27,28	My Sheep Hear My Voice
Jn 12:28	The Vine And the Branches
Jn 17:3	This Is Life Eternal
Ac 4:23-31	Help Us To Speak Your Word
Ro 1:16	I Am Not Ashamed of the Gospel
Ro 8:14	Let the Spirit of God Lead You
Ro 12:2	Not Conformed, But Transformed
1 Cor 1:8,9	God Shall Confirm You
1 Cor 6:19,20	You Are Not Your Own
1 Cor 15:58	Stand Firm
Ga 2:20	Life in Christ
Ga 5:16	Walk in the Spirit
Eph 2:10	We Are God's Workmanship
Eph 4:14,15	Grow Up into Him
Php 3:14	Pressing toward the Mark
Col 2:6,7	Continue To Live in Christ
1 Th 5:23,24	May the God of Peace Sanctify You Through And Through
1 Tm 2:2-4	Fight the Good Fight of Faith
2 Tm 2:2-4	Endure Hardship as a Good Soldier of Christ
2 Tm 3:14-16	Continue in What You Have Learned
He 10:23-25	Hold Unswervingly to the Hope We Profess
He 11:24-26	By Faith Moses
He 12:2	Fix Your Eyes on Jesus
1 Pe 3:15	Be Prepared To Give an Answer
1 Pe 5:10,11	May the God of Grace Make You Strong
1 Jn 2:12-14	I Write to You, Dear Children
Re 2:10	Be Faithful, Even to the Point of Death

2. HOLY COMMUNION

With the welcome development that Communion services are increasing in frequency in our circles, it can hardly be expected that a special sermon be preached whenever Communion is celebrated. The experienced pastor will try to make some reference to the comfort in the Sacrament in his regular sermon when Holy Communion is to be celebrated. From time to time it would wholesome to devote a special sermon to a fuller exposition of the Lord's Supper on the basis of a fitting text. As indicated previously, this may be done on Maundy Thursday, or when the confirmation class receives the Sacrament for the first time. The nature, the benefits and the right use of the Sacrament should be presented. The sermon can also take on the nature of a confessional address, pointing to the seriousness of sin and the blessings of forgiveness, assured through the sacrifice of Christ's body and blood.

Suggested Texts

Gn 32:26	Unless You Bless Me
Ex 33:18,19	The Glory of the Lord
2 Sm 12:13	Confession And Absolution
2 Sm 24:14	Let Us Fall into the Hands of the Lord
Job 9:2,3, 14,15	A Plea for Mercy
Ps 6:1,2	Have Mercy on Me, O Lord
Ps 13:1-6	Look on Me And Answer, O Lord
Ps 22:26a	The Poor Will Eat And Be Satisfied
Ps 23:5	You Prepare a Table before Me
Ps 25:11	Forgive My Iniquity, For It Is Great
Ps 32:1	The Blessedness of Forgiveness
Ps 34:8	Taste And See That the Lord Is Good
Ps 34:18	The Lord Is Close to the Brokenhearted
Ps 40:12,13	Be Pleased, O Lord, To Save Me
Ps 51:10-12	Create in Me a Clean Heart, O God
Ps 51:16-19	The Sacrifices of God Are a Broken Spirit
Ps 65:3	You Atoned for Our Transgressions
Ps 103:8-12	So Great Is His Mercy
Ps 103:1-8	With You, O Lord, There Is Forgiveness
Ps 139:23,24	Search Me, O God, And Know My Heart
Pr 28:13	The Blessings of Forthright Confession
Is 1:18	A Conference with God
Is 6:5-7	Your Guilt Is Taken Away
Is 38:17	All My Sins behind God's Back
Is 40:29-31	He Gives Strength to the Weary
Is 42:3	A Bruised Reed — a Smoldering Wick

Is 44:22	I Have Swept Away Your Offenses
Is 55:1	Come, All You Who Are Thirsty
Is 61:10	Clothed with Garments of Salvation
Mt 11:28-30	Come to Me, I Will Give You Rest
Lk 5:8	Depart from Me, For I Am a Sinful Man
Lk 6:20,21	You Will Be Satisfied
Lk 15:21,22	Celebrating the Return of the Sinner
Lk 18:13	God, Be Merciful to Me, a Sinner
Lk 22:19	Do This in Remembrance of Me
Lk 24:28-31	Lord, Stay with Us
Jn 1:29	Behold the Lamb of God
Jn 13:1-17	Do You Understand What Jesus Has Done for You?
Jn 15:5	The Vine And the Branches
Jn 15:13-16	Friendship with Christ
Rm 7:18-25a	The Way to True Repentance
1 Cor 10:3,4	That Rock Was Christ
1 Cor 10:14-21	We Who Are Many Are One Body
1 Cor 11:26	The Sermon Preached in the Sacrament
1 Cor 11:27-29	A Man Ought To Examine Himself
1 Cor 12:12,13	Union with Christ
2 Cor 5:17	A New Creation in Christ
Ga 6:4	Test Your Own Actions
Ga 2:20	I Have Been Crucified with Christ
Col 1:27,28	Christ In Us, the Hope of Glory
1 Tm 1:15	Christ Came To Save Sinners
He 4:16	Approach the Throne of Grace with Confidence
1 Pe 1:18,19	Redeemed with the Precious Blood of Christ
1 Pe 2:24	By His Wounds You Have Been Healed
1 Jn 1:7	Purified by the Blood of Christ
1 Jn 3:20	God Is Greater Than Our Hearts
Re 19:9	Called to the Marriage Supper of the Lamb
Re 22:17	Whoever Is Thirsty, Let Him Come

3. MARRIAGE

This is not the place to discuss whether it is wise for a congregation to make the wedding sermon obligatory or, on the other hand, to rule it out. For devout Christians their wedding text will have a cherished place in their memory. At times the pastor may ask whether the couple has any text which they would prefer. There are cases when they have anticipated the question by asking whether the pastor would use a certain text. In our day the sacredness of marriage as a divine institution and a lifelong union needs to be emphasized. Other general thoughts which are appropriate are — the assurance of the Lord's providence, the reminder that also the trials which come in wedded life work together for good to those who love God, a review of the duties which are incumbent upon each spouse, the comfort for Christians that when death does part them there will be a reunion in bliss. Since the audience at many marriages is mixed, the pastor will not neglect to preach sin and grace. The sermon will have to be kept brief. It will be addressed primarily to the bridal pair, but dare not be kept so confidential in tone that others will have difficulty in hearing what is said.

The nature of the observance of silver and golden wedding anniversaries varies greatly. If the pastor is requested to deliver an address for the occasion, he will gladly consent. If there is a formal church service, the sermon is self-evident. Thanksgiving for the preservation of life and health, material and spiritual blessings received in the past, assurance of the Lord's continuing nearness and the hope of everlasting life will be the dominant themes.

Suggested Texts

Gn 2:18	It Is Not Good for the Man To Be Alone
Nu 6:24-26	The Aaronic Blessing
Dt 33:25b	Your Strength Will Equal Your Days
Dt 33:27a	The Eternal God Is Your Refuge, And Underneath Are the Everlasting Arms
Jos 1:8	Meditate on It Day And Night
Jos 24:15b	As for Me And My Household, We Will Serve the Lord
Ru 1:16,17	Where You Go, I Will Go
1 Chr 17:27	Bless the House of Your Servant
Ps 23:1-6	I Will Dwell in the House of the Lord Forever
Ps 23:1	The Lord Is My Shepherd
Ps 23:1-3	My Shepherd Guides Me in Paths of Righteousness
Ps 23:3b	He Guides Me for His Name's Sake
Ps 23:6	All the Days of My Life And Forever
Ps 27:4	One Thing I Ask of the Lord
Ps 31:3b	For the Sake of Your Name Lead And Guide Me
Ps 37:5	Commit Your Way to the Lord
Ps 51:17-19	The Sacrifices of God

Ps 103:1,2	Praise And Forget Not
Ps 118:14	The Lord Is My Strength
Ps 119:97	Oh, How I Love Your Law
Ps 121:8	The Lord Will Watch over Your Coming And Going
Ps 127:1	Unless the Lord Builds the House
Pr 3:5,6	Trust in the Lord
Pr 3:33	The Lord Blesses the Home of the Righteous
Pr 18:22	He Who Finds a Wife Finds What Is Good
Pr 19:14	A Prudent Wife Is from the Lord
Is 41:10	Do Not Fear; I Will Uphold You
Is 54:10	My Unfailing Love for You Will Not Be Shaken
Is 62:5b	As a Bridegroom Will Your God Rejoice over You
Jr 17:7	Blessed Is the Man Who Trusts in the Lord
Jr 31:3	I Have Loved You with an Everlasting Love
Ez 16:60	I Will Establish an Everlasting Covenant with You
Mt 6:33	Seek First His Kingdom And His Righteousness
Mt 7:24,25	A House Founded on a Rock
Mt 19:6b	What God Has Joined Together, Let Man Not Separate
Mt 28:20	Surely I Will Be with You Always
Lk 10:41,42	One Thing Is Needed
Lk 12:15b	A Man's Life Does Not Consist in the Abundance of His Possessions
Lk 14:20	I Just Got Married, So I Can't Come
Lk 24:20	Stay with Us
Jn 2:2	Jesus And His Disciples Invited to the Wedding
Jn 3:29	The Bride Belongs to the Bridegroom
Jn 10:11	I Am the Good Shepherd
Jn 10:27,28	My Sheep Listen to My Voice
Ro 8:16	The Spirit Himself Testifies That We Are God's Children
Ro 8:28	In All Things God Works for the Good of Those Who Love Him
Ro 8:31,32	If God Is For Us, Who Can Be Against Us?
Ro 12:12	Be Joyful in Hope, Patient in Affliction, Faithful in Prayer
1 Cor 11:11	Interdependency in Marriage
1 Cor 13:1-13	The Greatest of These Is Love
2 Cor 11:2	I Promised You to One Husband, to Christ
Eph 4:32	Be Kind And Compassionate, Forgiving Each Other
Eph 5:20	Always Giving Thanks
Eph 5:22-33	Wives, Submit — Husbands, Love
Eph 5:29	Just As Christ Feeds And Cares for the Church
Php 4:7	The Peace of God Will Guard Your Hearts And Your Minds in Christ Jesus

Php 4:19	My God Will Meet All Your Needs
He 13:5	Never Will I Leave You; Never Will I Forsake You
1 Pe 5:7	Cast All Your Anxiety on Him Because He Cares for You
Re 19:7,8	The Wedding of the Lamb Has Come
Re 19:9	Blessed Are Those Who Are Invited to the Wedding Supper of the Lamb

4. FUNERALS

The test of a good funeral sermon is not how successful the preacher has been in causing tears, but how successful he has been in drying them. As with occasional sermons and other addresses, strict homiletical procedure may be relaxed, but a clear progression of thought is still called for. The funeral sermon should remind the listeners that the cause of all death is sin. It will proclaim the Savior's pardoning grace. It will herald the comfort which lies in the resurrection of the body and life everlasting. The preacher will not take for granted that the bereaved know what happens when a Christian dies — that his soul goes to be with the Lord. They know, but when this truth has an immediate and personal meaning for them because their dear one has died, they want to be reminded. So too with the truths concerning the resurrection of the body in a glorified state, security in the last judgment by virtue of the justification which is ours by faith, and the glories of life everlasting. Christians will appreciate hearing about these glories in some detail. If a pastor has a considerable number of funerals during the course of a year, he may fear that he is becoming repetitious. But as indicated, for the bereaved the comforting truths of our faith take on a new meaning when the blow of bereavement has struck them. While it is not amiss to take note of the good example set by the deceased if he was rich in good works, the main thrust of the funeral sermon is not to be a eulogy, but to eulogize the Savior. Never say more to the credit of the deceased than is incontrovertible knowledge, lest those who knew him better than you have reason to doubt what you say and thereby becloud not only what you have said about the deceased, but your whole message.

At times the pastor may ask whether the family has a particular text in mind, although in so doing he is taking a calculated risk. The season of the church year may influence the choice of text, e.g., during the Christmas season, Simeon's song; during Lent, the promise to the dying malefactor or Jesus' own dying prayer; at Easter the connection is obvious; near Ascension Day we may turn to Jesus' promise to come again to receive us to himself. The fact that funeral sermons may be heard by unchurched and non-Christians must also be borne in mind so that the essentials of saving truth are put into the foreground. In funeral sermons beware of polemics.

A. General Funeral Texts

Gn 5:24	Enoch Walked with God . . . God Took Him Away
Gn 28:17b	This Is the Gate of Heaven
Ex 15:22-27	The Waters of Marah And Elim
Nu 23:10b	Let Me Die the Death of the Righteous
Jos 1:9	The Lord Will Be with You
Job 7:16	I Would Not Live Forever
Job 19:25-27	In My Flesh I Will See God
Ps 4:8	I Will Lie Down And Sleep in Peace
Ps 13:5,6	My Heart Rejoices in Your Salvation
Ps 16:9b	My Body Will Rest Secure
Ps 17:15	I Will Be Satisfied with Seeing Your Likeness
Ps 23:1	The Lord Is My Shepherd
Ps 23:4	The Valley of the Shadow of Death
Ps 23:6	In the House of the Lord Forever
Ps 31:3	For the Sake of Your Name Lead And Guide Me
Ps 31:15	My Times Are in Your Hands
Ps 34:19	The Lord's Deliverance from Many Troubles
Ps 48:14	Our Guide Even to the End
Ps 51:12a	The Joy of Your Salvation
Ps 71:5-9	God, Our Refuge from Birth to Death
Ps 73:23,24	Afterward You Will Take Me into Glory
Ps 73:25,26	God Is My Portion Forever
Ps 84:1-4	Forever with the Lord
Ps 90:1-17	Teach Us To Number Our Days Aright
Ps 92:12-15	The Righteous Will Flourish
Ps 103:1,2	Forget Not All His Benefits
Ps 103:15-18	The Lord's Everlasting Love
Ps 116:15	Precious Is the Death of His Saints
Ps 121:1-8	Both Now And Forevermore
Ps 126:1-6	Reap with Songs of Joy
Pr 4:18	The Path of the Righteous
Pr 10:7a	The Memory of the Righteous Will Be a Blessing
Pr 10:28a	The Prospect of the Righteous Is Joy
Pr 14:32b	In Death the Righteous Have a Refuge
Ec 7:2	It Is Better to Go to a House of Mourning
Is 43:1	You Are Mine
Jr 17:7,8	Blessed Is the Man Who Trusts in the Lord
Jr 29:11	I Know the Plans I Have for You
Jr 31:3	I Have Loved You with an Everlasting Love
Dn 12:13	You Will Rise To Receive Your Inheritance
Mt 6:9b	Hallowed Be Your Name

Mt 11:28-30	Come to Me And I Will Give You Rest
Mt 16:21-26	Whoever Loses His Life for Me Will Find It
Mt 16:26	What Can a Man Give in Exchange for His Soul?
Mt 20:6-15	The Man Who Was Hired Last
Mt 26:39	Not As I Will, But As You Will
Lk 1:38	May It Be to Me As You Have Said
Lk 1:78,79	The Tender Mercy of Our God
Lk 2:25,26	He Would Not Die before He Had Seen the Lord's Christ
Lk 2:29	Now Dismiss Your Servant in Peace
Lk 12:37	Whose Master Finds Them Watching When He Comes
Lk 23:39-43	The Penitent Criminal
LK 23:43	Today You Will Be with Me in Paradise
Lk 23:56	Into Your Hands I Commit My Spirit
Lk 24:29	Stay with Us
Jn 3:16	God So Loved the World
Jn 3:17,18	Whoever Believes in Him Is Not Condemned
Jn 5:24	Whoever Believes Has Crossed Over from Death to Life
Jn 5:28,29	Those Who Have Done Good Will Rise To Live
Jn 6:20	Don't Be Afraid; It Is I
Jn 6:53-54	I Will Raise Him Up at the Last Day
Jn 10:27-30	I Give Them Eternal Life
Jn 11:11	Our Friend Lazarus Has Fallen Asleep
Jn 11:25,26	I Am the Resurrection And the Life
Jn 11:33	Jesus Was Deeply Moved in Spirit And Troubled
Jn 11:35-37	Jesus Wept
Jn 12:26	Where I Am, My Servant Also Will Be
Jn 14:1-6	I Will Come Back And Take You To Be with Me
Jn 14:19	Because I Live, You Also Will Live
Ac 4:12	Salvation Is Found in No One Else
Ac 7:59	Lord Jesus, Receive My Spirit
Ro 3:22-24	Justified Freely by His Grace
Ro 4:25	Raised to Life for Our Justification
Ro 5:8	God Demonstrates His Love
Ro 6:23	The Gift of God Is Eternal Life
Ro 8:1	No Condemnation
Ro 8:38,39	Death Will Not Be Able to Separate Us from the Love of God
Ro 10:10	You Believe And Are Justified
Ro 14:9	Christ Is the Lord of the Dead
1 Cor 15:17-20	Christ, the Firstfruits of Those Who Have Fallen Asleep
1 Cor 15:42-44	Sown in Weakness, It Is Raised in Power
1 Cor 15:55-57	Where, O Death, Is Your Victory?

2 Cor 4:17,18	What Is Unseen Is Eternal
2 Cor 5:1-8	At Home with the Lord
2 Cor 8:9	Rich through His Poverty
Ga 4:4,5	The Full Rights of Sons
Ga 6:14	Boast in the Cross
Eph 2:8,9	Saved by Grace through Faith
Php 1:20	Christ Exalted by Death
Php 3:7-9	That I Might Be Found in Christ
Php 3:20,21	Our Lowly Bodies Will Be Like His Glorious Body
Col 1:12-14	The Inheritance of the Saints in the Kingdom of Light
1 Th 4:13-18	We Will Be with the Lord Forever
1 Th 5:9,10	God Did Not Appoint Us To Suffer Wrath
1 Tm 1:15	Christ Jesus Came into the World To Save Sinners
1 Tm 6:12	Take Hold of the Eternal Life
2 Tm 1:10	Christ Jesus Brought Life And Immortality to Light
2 Tm 4:18	The Lord Will Bring Me Safely to His Heavenly Kingdom
He 2:14,15	Free Those Held in Slavery by Their Fear of Death
He 4:9	A Sabbath-Rest for the People of God
He 13:14	The City That Is To Come
1 Pe 1:3,4	An Inheritance That Can Never Perish
1 Pe 1:24,25	The Word of the Lord Stands Forever
1 Jn 3:2	We Shall Be Like Him
1 Jn 4:10	God Sent His Son as an Atoning Sacrifice
Re 2:10c	I Will Give You the Crown of Life
Re 7:13-17	God Will Wipe Away Every Tear
Re 19:9	The Wedding Supper of the Lamb
Re 21:3-5	I Am Making Everything New

B. Death of Children

Since death is no respecter of age or persons, there will be a wide variety of situations and cases which will influence to a degree the nature of the funeral sermon. An address at the burial of a stillborn child is rare; usually the form in the agenda read at the grave will suffice. The case of a child who died without baptism is difficult. The main purpose of the sermon will be to encourage the parents to submit to the unsearchable ways of God, although some reference will be made to the evidence in Scripture that the Lord can save without baptism even though he has bound us to use it. In the case of children who have been baptized, the comforting promises concerning the saving power of baptism will come to the fore.

Suggested Texts

1 Sm 1:27,28	Lent to the Lord
2 Kgs 4:26	Is It Well with the Child?
Job 1:21	The Lord Gave — The Lord Has Taken Away
Is 40:11	He Gathers the Lambs in His Arms
Mt 9:24	The Girl Is Not Dead But Asleep
Mt 18:2	Jesus Called a Little Child
Mt 18:5	Whoever Welcomes a Child, Welcomes Me
Mt 18:14	The Father's Will for Little Ones
Mk 10:14-16	Let the Little Children Come to Me
Lk 7:13	Weep Not

C. Sudden Or Tragic Death

Ps 46:10	Be Still And Know That I Am God
Ps 73:23-26	God Is the Strength of My Heart
Ps 90:12	Teach Us To Number Our Days Aright
Is 38:1	Put Your House in Order
Is 45:15	Truly A God Who Hides Himself
Is 55:6-11	My Thoughts Are Not Your Thoughts
Mt 24:44	At an Hour When You Do Not Expect Him
Mt 14:12	They Went And Told Jesus
Mt 26:39	Not As I Will, But As You Will
Mt 28:20	I Am with You Always
Jn 13:7	Later You Will Understand
Ro 11:33-36	How Unsearchable Are His Judgments
Eph 1:22	God Placed All Things under His Feet
Jas 4:13-15	You Are a Mist

D. After Prolonged Illness

Job 23:10	He Knows the Way I Take
Ps 34:17-19	Final Deliverance from All Troubles
Mt 6:10	May Your Will Be Done
Jn 11:4	This Sickness Is for God's Glory
Ac 21:12-14	I Am Ready
Ro 5:3-5	Suffering Produces Perseverance
Ro 8:18	Sufferings Not Worth Comparing with Glory
1 Cor 10:13	Not Beyond What You Can Bear
2 Cor 4:17	Fix Your Eyes on What Is Unseen
2 Cor 12:8,9	My Grace Is Sufficient for You
Jas 1:12	Blessed Is the Man Who Perseveres under Trial
Re 7:8-10,13-17	Out of the Great Tribulation
Re 14:13	Blessed Are the Dead
Re 21:1-5	He Will Wipe Away Every Tear

E. Death of an Aged Christian

Gn 15:15	Buried at a Good Old Age
Gn 25:8	Abraham Died at a Good Old Age
Gn 49:18	I Look for Your Deliverance, O Lord
Jos 23:14	Not One Promise Has Failed
1 Kgs 2:10	Then David Rested with His Fathers
Job 42:17	So Job Died, Old And Full of Years
Ps 27:4	All the Days of My Life
Ps 71:18	Even When I Am Old And Gray
Ps 73:23-26	I Am Always with You
Ps 90:10	The Length of Our Days
Ps 91:16	With Long Life Will I Satisfy Him
Pr 16:31	Gray Hair Is a Crown of Splendor
Pr 17:6	Children's Children Are a Crown of the Aged
Lm 3:26	It Is Good To Wait Quietly
Lk 2:29,30	You Now Dismiss Your Servant in Peace
Php 1:23	I Desire To Depart And Be with Christ
2 Tm 4:6-8	In Store for Me a Crown of Righteousness
He 4:9	There Remains a Rest for the People of God
He 11:13	Aliens And Strangers on Earth
1 Pe 5:1-4	To the Elders a Crown of Glory
Re 22:20	Amen. Come, Lord Jesus

F. Doubtful Cases

Suicide and sudden death while intoxicated or involved in crime confront a pastor with hard decisions if his services are requested. If there are circumstances which justify his consenting to officiate, the preparation of a fitting sermon will be difficult. It may be necessary for him to explain why he is officiating. The less said about the eternal state of the deceased, the better. Judgment is the Lord's. The pastor's chief purpose will be to present what comfort he can to those who have been shaken to the very depths of their being by what has transpired. To use the opportunity to inveigh against current sins would be adding salt to already painful wounds.

Suggested Texts

Ps 55:22	Cast Your Cares on the Lord
Ps 130:3,4	If You, O Lord, Kept a Record of Sins
Is 55:8-11	My Thoughts Are Not Your Thoughts
Lk 11:28	Blessed Are Those Who Hear the Word of God
Lk 15:3-7	The Lost Sheep Found
Ro 5:20b	Where Sin Increased, Grace Increased All the More
Ro 10:17	Faith Comes by Hearing
2 Pe 3:9	The Lord Is Patient with You

5. ORDINATION — INSTALLATION

Since it is our policy in general to combine the ordination of a pastor with his installation in his first charge, there is no basic difference between the ordination and installation sermon. Only in case of the former, reference will be made to the nature of a man's entire ministry before application is made to his ministry in a specific field.

The sermon will be addressed first to the pastor, then to the congregation. The content should impress upon the pastor the privilege of being entrusted with the ministry, the duties which are incumbent upon him, his grave responsibility and the results which are promised. The purpose is to use the Word to fill the heart of the one being installed with joy and thankfulness, with dedication and earnestness, with hope and courage.

In addressing the congregation the preacher will remind God's people of the privilege involved in having a pastor, of what it may and what it may not expect of him, and of what it owes him (honor, cooperation, intercession, support). The divinity of the call may well be emphasized.

Mutatis mutandis what has been said above will also apply in the case of the installation of men teachers.

Since the installation of members of the church council occurs annually, the advisability of preaching a special installation sermon for them each year is debatable. As a general rule it might be more effective to insert a reference to the event in the sermon for the day. At intervals it would not be amiss to devote an entire sermon to the need, the importance, the duties and the benefits of congregational offices.

Suggested Texts

Ex 3:1-8	Moses And the Burning Bush
Ex 17:1-7	Water from the Rock
Jos 1:1-9	The Lord Commands Joshua
2 Kgs 2:1-15	The Spirit of Elijah Resting on Elisha
1 Chr 28:8-10	The Lord Has Chosen You
1 Chr 28:20	Be Strong And Courageous
Is 6:1-8	Here Am I, Send Me
Ez 2:1-7a	Ezekiel's Call
Jr 1:4-10	The Call of Jeremiah
Am 7:10-16a	Amos And Amaziah
Mt 3:1-12	John Prepares the Way
Mt 4:19	Come, Follow Me
Lk 4:16-21	Jesus at Nazareth
Jn 21:15-19	Feed My Lambs
Ac 1:21-26	Matthias Chosen
Ac 20:28	The Holy Spirit Has Made You Overseers
1 Cor 2:2	Jesus Christ And Him Crucified

1 Cor 3:6	God Made It Grow
1 Cor 3:10-15	I Laid a Foundation
1 Cor 13:3	If I Have Not Love, I Gain Nothing
2 Cor 3:4-6	Our Sufficiency Is of God
2 Cor 4:7	Earthly Vessels — Heavenly Treasures
2 Cor 5:7	We Live by Faith Not by Sight
2 Cor 5:18	A Ministry of Reconciliation
2 Cor 5:20—6:1	We Urge You Not To Receive God's Grace in Vain
Eph 1:8-10	All Things Together under One Head, Even Christ
Eph 3:8	This Grace Was Given to Me
Eph 4:11,12	To Prepare God's People for Works of Service
1 Th 2:1-13	Men Approved by God To Be Entrusted with the Gospel
1 Tm 3:1	A Noble Task
1 Tm 3:8-13	The Qualities Required of Deacons
1 Tm 4:16	You Will Save Both Yourself And Your Hearers
2 Tm 2:16	Be Strong in the Grace That Is in Christ Jesus
2 Tm 3:14-17	Continue in What You Have Learned
2 Tm 4:2-5	Preach the Word
2 Tm 4:5	Discharge All the Duties of Your Ministry
1 Pe 4:10	A Faithful Administering of God's Grace

6. INTRODUCTORY — FAREWELL

This initial sermon which follows installation has unique significance. The congregation is curious, let's admit it, to see and hear its new pastor, but also prayerfully hopeful that the new pastor's first sermon will bring the promise of future edification through his preaching. The pastor will be eager, in a good sense, to make a good impression. Guiding thoughts in his sermon will be: the privilege of being entrusted with the ministry of the Word; assurance to the congregation that he is dedicated to preaching Christ crucified first and with him the whole counsel of God as revealed in his inspired Word, the Bible; his desire to please God not men; his loyalty to the Lutheran symbols; reference to the blessings which the Lord will bring through his ministry because of the power inherent in the means of grace; a plea for wholehearted cooperation in all phases of his ministry.

The tone of the sermon will be humble and evangelical. If ever legalism or any evidence of haughtiness and pride are out of place, it is in the introductory sermon. It is well not to stress the duties which the congregation has toward its pastor. It is far better for the installing pastor to have mentioned them in his sermon. An outline of them is also incorporated in the order for installation.

The farewell sermon when leaving a charge should avoid sentimentality. It should rather point objectively to the privileges enjoyed in having been entrusted with the duties of the pastoral office as outlined above, with an expression of thanks to God for the grace received in having been able to discharge these duties.

A. Introductory Texts

Ps 22:22	I Will Declare Your Name in the Congregation
Ps 27:11	Teach Me Your Ways, O Lord
Ps 40:9-11	The Content of Preaching
Ps 51:15	O Lord, Open My Lips
Ps 51:18	Make Zion Prosper
Lk 5:5	Because You Say So, I Will Let Down the Net
Ro 1:16	The Gospel, the Power of God unto Salvation
Ro 15:29-32	Working Together for Christ
1 Cor 1:23	We Preach Christ Crucified
1 Cor 2:1-5	Following Paul's Example
2 Cor 4:5-7	We Preach Not Ourselves But Christ Jesus
2 Cor 5:14,15	The All-Compelling Love of Christ
2 Cor 5:20	We Are Ambassadors for Christ
2 Cor 6:1	As God's Fellow Workers We Urge You
Eph 6:19,20	Pray Always for Me
Php 1:9-11	And This I Pray
Php 2:17	The Sacrifice And Service of Your Faith
2 Tm 2:2	Qualified To Teach Others

B. Farewell Texts

Nm 6:24-26	The Lord Bless You And Keep You
Dt 30:19,20	Life And Death
1 Kgs 8:57	May He Never Leave Or Forsake Us
Is 40:6-8	The Word of Our God Stands Forever
Ac 20:27	I Have Proclaimed the Whole Will of God
Ac 20:32	I Commit You to God
1 Cor 1:4-9	I Always Thank God for You
Php 1:3-6	I Thank My God Every Time I Remember You
Col 2:6,7	Continue To Live in Him
2 Th 2:15-17	Stand Firm
He 13:20,21	To Christ Be All Glory
1 Jn 2:24,25	Remain in Christ And He in You
Jd 20,21	Keep Yourselves in God's Love

7. CHRISTIAN EDUCATION — GRADUATION

In some congregations it is customary to observe an annual Christian Education Sunday, usually at the beginning of the school year. The direction which the sermon will take is obvious — the duty of giving a Christian training to children, the assistance which the congregation offers to parents, the advantages of a Christian day school training (dedicated Christian teachers, thorough religious instruction, all subjects taught in the light of God's Word, discipline from the Christian viewpoint), the blessings to be expected for this life and the life to come, the need for cooperation and prayers, the disappointments.

Whether there is a special Christian Education Sunday or not, it is well to bear in mind that by the time school begins parents have pretty well made up their minds to which school their children are going. Therefore it is well to refer to the importance of Christian education at intervals during the year when the text warrants the introduction of such an application. Be positive. Don't damn the public school.

The graduation service for the Christian elementary school, while containing some of the foregoing elements, will exhort the graduates to appreciation and faithfulness also.

To provide a substitute for the unionistic and un-American baccalaureate services, some congregations have a special service for the high school graduates in their membership. The fear of the Lord as the beginning of wisdom, the use of secular knowledge in his service, faithfulness in employment, continued education, and citizenship — all may be emphasized.

Special children's services are arranged by some congregations. These may be an abbreviated service on Sunday morning before or after Sunday school, a special service at intervals in which the sermon is scaled down to the level of the child, or a weekday service for Christian elementary school pupils. The latter especially provides the pastor with an opportunity to school himself in keeping his sermons simple, and to establish rapport with the children of the congregation. Brevity and simplicity will be aimed at.

Suggested Texts

Gn 18:19	He Will Direct His Children
Gn 25:29-34	The Birthright
Ex 2:1,2	The Birth of Moses
Dt 6:4-9	Impress These Things on Your Children
1 Sm 1:28	So Now I Give This Child to the Lord
1 Kgs 2:1-4	David's Charge to Solomon
Neh 12:43	The Women And Children Also Rejoiced
Ps 23	The Shepherd Feeds And Leads His Own
Ps 34:11	Come, My Children, Listen to Me
Ps 78:5-7	From Generation to Generation
Ps 111:10	The Beginning of Wisdom

Ps 119:9-11	How Can a Young Man Keep His Way Pure?
Ps 147:12,13	He Strengthens the Bars of Your Gates
Pr 2:1-5	Turn Your Ear to Wisdom
Pr 4:13	Hold On to Instruction
Pr 4:23	Above All Else Guard Your Heart
Pr 8:10,11	Choose My Instruction
Pr 13:22a	An Inheritance for His Children's Children
Pr 22:6	Train a Child in the Way He Should Go
Pr 23:22	Buy the Truth; Do Not Sell It
Pr 23:26	My Son, Give Me Your Heart
Pr 30:24-28	Four Things on Earth Are Small
Ec 12:1	Remember Your Creator in the Days of Your Youth
Is 40:9-11	He Gathers the Lambs in his Arms
Is 54:13	All Your Sons Will Be Taught by the Lord
Jr 9:23,24	The Boast of a Wise Man
Mt 6:9	Our Father in Heaven
Mt 6:24	No One Can Serve Two Masters
Mt 18:1-14	Whoever Welcomes a Little Child Welcomes Me
Mt 28:20	Teach Them To Obey Everything I Have Commanded
Mk 10:14	Let the Little Children Come to Me
Lk 1:57-66	What Then Is This Child Going To Be?
Jn 21:15-17	Feed My Lambs
1 Cor 1:20-25	Where Is the Wise Man?
1 Cor 2:6-10	Wisdom from the Spirit
1 Cor 3:10-17	God's Temple Is Sacred
1 Cor 12:31	Eagerly Desire the Greater Gifts
2 Cor 1:19-22	God's Promises Are "Yes" in Christ
Eph 6:4	Bring Them Up in the Training of the Lord
Php 2:15,16	You Shine Like Stars
2 Tm 2:1	Be Strong in the Grace That Is in Christ Jesus
2 Tm 2:3	Endure Hardship Like a Good Soldier of Jesus Christ
2 Tm 3:14-17	From Infancy You Have Known the Holy Scriptures
He 11:10	Look Forward to the City with Foundations
Jas 3:13	Who Is Wise And Understanding among You?
1 Pe 2:16,17	Live As Servants of God

8. THE CHRISTIAN FAMILY

Suggested Texts

Gn 2:18-25	The Institution of Marriage
Gn 6:1-4	The Sons of God Married the Daughters of Men
Gn 47:7-12	Joseph Settled His Father in the Best Part of the Land
Jn 19:26,27	Jesus Provides for His Mother
1 Tm 2:9-15	Good Deeds, Appropriate for Women Who Profess To Worship God
1 Tm 5:14	I Counsel Younger Widows To Marry
2 Tm 1:5	Lois And Eunice

Two Series on the Christian Family

A. Marriage And Its Blessings

Gn 2:22-24	God's Institution, Not a Human Custom
Mt 5:31,32	The Sin of Divorce (Mk 10:2-12; Mt 19:2-9)
Gn 2:18	God Blesses Us with Living Companionship in Marriage (1 Cor 7:2-5), with Sexual Happiness (Ps 127:3), And with Children
Eph 5:22-33	The Relationship of Husband And Wife in Christ (1 Cor 11:3,8,9,11,12; Col 3:18,19; 1 Pe 3:1-7)
Sol 5:10-16: 7:1-13	The Physical Attraction of Husband And Wife Is God's Gift, Not a Sin
1 Th 4:3-8	Acquiring a Spouse (cf NIV footnote)
Eph 5:3-7	Do Not Be Partners with the World's Sexual Filth (He 13:4; 2 Pe 2:18-22; Jd 4; Gn 39:6-12; Mt 5:27,28)
1 Cor 6:9,10	Homosexuality Is a Sin (Ro 1:26,27; Jd 7)

B. Children And Their Training:

Ps 127:3	God's Gift, Not a Biological Accident (Gn 1:28; Ps 113:9)
Ex 21:22-24	The Child in the Womb Is a Human Life in God's Eyes (Lk 1:41-44)
Eph 6:4	God Wants Parents To Train Their Children (Dt 6:6,7; Pr 22:6; 2 Tm 3:15-17)
1 Sm 3:13; 2:29	God Condemns Permissive Parents (Pr 13:24; Pr 19:18; Pr 22:15; 23:13,14)
He 12:7b,8,11	The Salutary Purpose of Christian Training (Pr 29:15,17; Col 3:21)
Eph 4:22-24	Christian Training Has a Double Thrust, To Build Up the New Man as Well as To Curb the Old Adam (Col 3:5-14)

9. STEWARDSHIP

Suggested Texts

Ex 35:20-29	Bringing Gifts for the Tabernacle
1 Kgs 17:8-16	The Jar of Flour — The Jug of Oil
2 Kgs 4:42-44	Feeding of a Hundred
1 Chr 29:14	Giving Generously
Ps 96:7-10	Bring an Offering
Pr 3:9,10	Honor the Lord with Your Wealth
Hg 1:2-8	A Call To Build
Mt 10:42	A Cup of Cold Water
Mt 16:18	I Will Build My Church
Mt 20:26-28	Not To Be Served, But To Serve
Mt 25:14-28	Parable of the Talents
Mk 14:3-9	She Did What She Could
Lk 19:11-27	Parable of the Ten Minas
Jn 15:5	Apart from Me You Can Do Nothing
1 Cor 4:2	Faithfulness Required of Stewards
2 Cor 5:14,15	Christ's Love Compels us
Ga 6:10	Let Us Do Good to All People
Php 3:17-21	Live According to the Pattern We Gave You
1 Pe 4:10	Using Gifts To Serve Others

10. DEDICATION

A. Cornerstone

Gn 28:22	This Stone That I Have Set Up
Jos 24:27	This Stone Will Be a Witness
1 Sm 7:12	The Stone Named Ebenezer
Ps 118:22-24	The Stone Has Become the Capstone
Is 28:16	A Precious Cornerstone in Zion
Jn 6:68	To Whom Shall We Go?
Ac 4:11	Christ, the Capstone
Ac 11:23	Remain True to the Lord
Eph 2:20-22	Christ Jesus, the Chief Cornerstone
1 Pe 2:4,5	Come to Him, the Living Stone

B. Church

Gn 28:10-22	Jacob at Bethel
Ex 20:24	Wherever I Cause My Name To Be Honored
Lv 9:23—10:2	The Glory of the Lord Appeared
Lv 26:11	I Will Put My Dwelling Place among You
Jos 3:19-24	What Do These Stones Mean?
2 Sm 6:12-18	David's Love for His Church
1 Kgs 8:22ff	Solomon's Prayer of Dedication
1 Kgs 9:3	I Have Consecrated This Temple
1 Chr 16:5ff	David's Psalm of Thanks (Ps 105)
2 Chr 6:18	Will God Really Dwell on Earth with Men?
2 Chr 6:40-42	Arise, O God, And Come
Ezr 6:16	A Dedication with Joy
Neh 2:18	So They Began This Good Work
Ps 26:8	I Love the House Where You Live, O Lord
Ps 84:1-12	How Lovely Is Your Dwelling Place, O Lord
Ps 90:17	Establish the Work of Our Hands
Ps 118:24	This Is the Day the Lord Has Made
Ps 122:1-9	Let Us Go to the House of the Lord
Ps 127:1	Unless the Lord Builds the House
Ec 5:1-7	When You Go to the House of God
Is 56:7	A House of Prayer for All Nations
Is 61:1-3	A Crown of Beauty Instead of Ashes
Mt 16:13-19	Peter's Confession of Christ
Mt 17:4	Lord, It Is Good for Us To Be Here
Mt 18:20	Where Two or Three Come Together
Lk 6:48	A Building According to God's Blueprint
Lk 10:20	Rejoice That Your Names Are Written in Heaven
Lk 19:1-9	Salvation Has Come to This House
Eph 2:19-22	No Longer Foreigners And Aliens
He 11:8-10	Whose Architect And Builder Is God
Re 21:3	The Dwelling of God Is with Men

C. School

Gn 18:17-19	He Will Direct His Children
Dt 32:44-47	So That You May Command Your Children
Ps 34:11	Come, My Children, Listen to Me
Ps 147	He Strengthened the Bars of Your Gates
Neh 12:43	The Children Also Rejoiced
Lk 2:14	Glory to God in the Highest
Jn 21:15	Feed My Lambs

D. Parsonage

Jos 24:15	As for Me And My Household
Pr 3:33b	The Lord Blesses the Home of the Righteous
Pr 12:7	The House of the Righteous Stands Firm
Lk 10:7	Peace Be to This House
Lk 10:38	Martha Received Jesus into Her House
2 Cor 4:5	Your Servants for Jesus' Sake
1 Th 5:12,13	Hold Them in Highest Regard in Love

E. Organ

Jdg 5:3	I Will Sing to the Lord
Ps 57:7-11	I Will Sing And Make Music
Ps 96:1-3	Sing to the Lord a New Song
Ps 98:1-6	Burst into Jubilant Song with Music
Ps 150:1-6	Praise the Lord with Instruments of Music
Eph 5:19	Sing And Make Music in Your Heart to the Lord
Col 3:16	Sing Psalms, Hymns, Spiritual Songs

BIBLE INDEX

Genesis

2:7-9,15-17, 3:1-7	Lent 1	6
2:18-24	Trinity 19/Pentecost 20	7
3:1-15	Lent 1	4
3:9-15	Trinity 2/Pentecost 3	7
4:3-16	Trinity 6/Pentecost 7	4
5:21-24	Ascension	1
8:15-22	Harvest	4
9:1-15	Harvest	5
11:1-9	Epiphany 5	4
	Pentecost	8
12:1-4	Trinity 1/Pentecost 2	3
12:1-8	Lent 2	6
14:8-20	Passion Sunday/Lent 5	4
15:1-6	Trinity 2/Pentecost 3	3
	Trinity 11/Pentecost 12	8
17:1-9	Trinity 3/Pentecost 4	3
18:1-10a	Trinity 8/Pentecost 9	8
18:16-33	Easter 5/Easter 6	4
18:20-32	Trinity 9/Pentecost 10	8
18:20-33	Trinity 4/Pentecost 5	3
19:15-26	Trinity 5/Pentecost 6	3
19:15-29	Trinity 26/Pentecost 27	4
22:1-19	Lent 2	4
	Lent 3	3
22:1-14	Lent 1	1,2,7
25:7-10	Trinity 6/Pentecost 7	3
27:22-46	Sunday after New Year	5
28:10-17	Lent 2	7
	Trinity 19/Pentecost 20	1
28:10-22	Transfiguration	4
	Trinity 7/Pentecost 8	3
32:22-30	Trinity 21/Pentecost 22	8
32:22-31	Easter 1/Easter 2	1,2,3
37:12-28	Trinity 21/Pentecost 22	5
37:25-45	Lent 4	5
41:45-47	Trinity 7/Pentecost 8	5
45:1-15	Sunday after Ascension/Easter 7	5

1 Historic　　3 Thomasius　　5 Soll　　7 ILCW-B
2 Eisenach　　4 Synodical Conf.　　6 ILCW - A　　8 ILCW-C

45:3-8a,15	Epiphany 7	8
46:28-34	Epiphany 2	5
50:15-21	Trinity 16/Pentecost 17	6
50:15-23	Trinity 22/Pentecost 23	.4

Exodus

3:1-6	Transfiguration	1,2,3
3:1-8a,10-15	Lent 3	8
3:1-14	Trinity 8/Pentecost 9	3
3:1-15	Trinity 5/Pentecost 6	4
6:2-8	Trinity 13/Pentecost 14	6
12:1-14	Maundy Thursday	1,3,4,6
14:13-21	Lent 2	3
14:21-31	Epiphany 4	1
15:1-11	Easter Sunday	8
16:2-15	Trinity 10/Pentecost 11	7
17:1-7	Trinity 9/Pentecost 10	3
19:2-8	Trinity 3/Pentecost 4	6
20:1-17	Lent 3	7
20:18-24	Trinity 13/Pentecost 14	4
24:3-11	Maundy Thursday	7
	Trinity 9/Pentecost 10	7
24:12,15-18	Transfiguration	6
32:1-14	Trinity 9/Pentecost 10	4
32:7-14	Trinity 16/Pentecost 17	8
32:15-20	Trinity 25/Pentecost 26	8
32:15-35	Sexagesima	5
33:11-17	Trinity 25/Pentecost 26	4
33:17-23	Lent 2	2
33:17-25	Lent 2	1
34:5-9	Trinity 23/Pentecost 24	8
34:29-35	Trinity 12/Pentecost 13	4
40:34-38	Transfiguration	5

Leviticus

16:15-22	Maundy Thursday	5
16:29-34	Passion Sunday/Lent 5	5
19:1-2,15-18	Trinity 22/Pentecost 23	6
20:6-8	Lent 2	5

Numbers

6:22-27	New Year's Day	6,7,8
	Trinity Sunday/Pentecost 1	2,3,4
9:15-23	Trinity 11/Pentecost 12	5
11:4-6,10-16,24-29	Trinity 18/Pentecost 19	7
12:1-15	Trinity 14/Pentecost 15	5
14:10-24	Trinity 27/Last Pentecost	5
20:1-13	Lent 1	5
21:4-9	Lent 4	7
	Passion Sunday/Lent 5	1,2,3
	Trinity 14/Pentecost 15	4
24:10-17	Epiphany 3	3
27:12-23	Trinity 17/Pentecost 18	5

Deuteronomy

4:1-2,6-8	Trinity 14/Pentecost 15	7
4:23-31	Trinity 10/Pentecost 11	4
4:32-34,39-40	Trinity Sunday/Pentecost 1	6
5:12-15	Trinity 1/Pentecost 2	7
5:22-33	Trinity 1/Pentecost 2	5
6:1-9	Epiphany 1	3
	Trinity 23/Pentecost 24	7
6:4-9	Trinity Sunday/Pentecost 1	7
6:4-13	Trinity 1/Pentecost 2	1,2
7:6-11	Lent 4	4
8:1-10	Thanksgiving	6,7,8
8:1-20	Thanksgiving	1
8:6-18	Thanksgiving	4
10:12-22	Trinity 22/Pentecost 23	8
11:8-17	Harvest	1
11:18-21,26-28	Trinity 1/Pentecost 2	6
18:15-19	Advent 4	1,2
18:15-20	Epiphany 4	7
18:15-22	Advent 2	4
19:1,2,17,18	Epiphany 7	6
26:1-11	Harvest	3,6,7,8
26:5-10	Lent 1	8
28:1-10	Thanksgiving	5
30:9-14	Trinity 7/Pentecost 8	8
30:11-20	Trinity 12/Pentecost 13	5

1 Historic
2 Eisenach
3 Thomasius
4 Synodical Conf.
5 Soll
6 ILCW - A
7 ILCW - B
8 ILCW - C

30:15-20	Epiphany 6	6
32:1-9	Trinity 10/Pentecost 11	3
32:36-39	Palm Sunday	8
34:1-12	Transfiguration	8
	Septuagesima	5

Joshua

3:9-17	Easter 1/Easter 2	5
4:1-18	Trinity 9/Pentecost 10	5
24:1,2a,14-18	Trinity 13/Pentecost 14	7
24:14-18	New Year's Day	1
24:14-28	Trinity 6/Pentecost 7	5

Judges

2:1-12	Trinity 2/Pentecost 3	4
7:15-22	Easter 4/Easter 5	5

Ruth

1:1-17	Trinity 6/Pentecost 7	1
1:1-19a	Trinity 20/Pentecost 21	8

1 Samuel

2:1-10	Sunday after New Year	1
3:1-10	Epiphany 2	7
3:1—4:1a	Trinity 5/Pentecost 6	5
3:19—4:1a	Reformation	1
7:5-12	Trinity 11/Pentecost 12	3
15:13-26	Trinity 17/Pentecost 18	4
16:1-13	Trinity 12/Pentecost 13	3
17:42-51	Sexagesima	4
20:27-42	Trinity 23/Pentecost 24	4

2 Samuel

7:8-11,16	Advent 4	7
7:17-29	Trinity 21/Pentecost 22	1,2
11:26—12:10,13-15	Trinity 3/Pentecost 4	8
12:1-10	Easter 1/Easter 2	4
	Trinity 13/Pentecost 14	3

1 Kings

3:5-12	Trinity 9/Pentecost 10	6

3:5-15	Easter 5/Pentecost 6	5
8:41-43	Trinity 1/Pentecost 2	8
17:1-16	Trinity 7/Pentecost 8	4
	Trinity 15/Pentecost 16	3
17:8-16	Trinity 15/Pentecost 16	1,2
	Trinity 24/Pentecost 25	7
17:17-24	Trinity 2/Pentecost 3	8
	Trinity 16/Pentecost 17	3
	Trinity 24/Pentecost 25	1
18:21-40	Trinity 15/Pentecost 16	4
19:1-18	Trinity 19/Pentecost 20	3
19:4-8	Trinity 11/Pentecost 12	7
19:9-18	Epiphany 4	4
19:9b-18	Trinity 11/Pentecost 12	6
19:14-21	Trinity 5/Pentecost 6	8
21:17-25	Trinity 20/Pentecost 21	

2 Kings

2:1-12c	Transfiguration	7
2:6-18	Trinity 20/Pentecost 21	4
4:18-37	Trinity 16/Pentecost 17	5
5:1-14	Epiphany 6	7
5:1-19	Epiphany 3	1,2
5:8-19	Trinity 16/Pentecost 17	4
18:1-8	Trinity 23/Pentecost 24	5
20:1-11	Easter 3/Easter 4	5
23:1-3	Trinity 23/Pentecost 24	1
23:21-27	Reformation	

1 Chronicles

29:10-13	Trinity 24/Pentecost 25	8

2 Chronicles

1:7-12	Trinity 18/Pentecost 19	1,2
29:12-19	Reformation	3
33:9-16	Trinity 3/Pentecost 4	4

Nehemiah

1:1-11	Trinity 22/Pentecost 23	5

Job

1:1-22	Epiphany 3	5

1 Historic — 3 Thomasius — 5 Soll — 7 ILCW - B
2 Eisenach — 4 Synodical Conf. — 6 ILCW - A — 8 ILCW - C

2:1-13	Epiphany 4	5
5:17-26	Trinity 16/Pentecost 17	1,2
7:1-7	Epiphany 5	7
14:1-5	Trinity 25/Pentecost 26	1,2
19:22-27	Easter Sunday/Easter 1	3
19:23-27	Easter Sunday/Easter 1	4
38:1-11	Trinity 4//Pentecost 5	7

Psalms

1	Trinity 6/Pentecost 7	2
8	Palm Sunday	4
22:1-11	Good Friday	2
23	Easter 2/Easter 3	2,4
24	Advent 1	4
25	Lent 3	4
32:1-7	Trinity 19/Pentecost 20	2
34:1-9	Harvest	2
37:12-24	Trinity 15/Pentecost 16	5
37:25-40	Trinity 19/Pentecost 20	4
39	Trinity 24/Pentecost 25	2
42	Sunday after Ascension/Easter 7	2
46	Reformation	2,4
47	Ascension	4
50:14-23	Trinity 14/Pentecost 15	2
68:15-20	Ascension	5
73:23-28	Sunday after New Year	2,3
75:4-7	Trinity 17/Pentecost 18	2
78:1-7	Epiphany 1	4
85:6-13	Trinity 23/Pentecost 24	2
87:1-3	Reformation	3
90	New Year's Day	2
93	Epiphany 4	2
98	Easter 4/Easter 5	2
100	Easter 3/Easter 4	4
104:24-35	Epiphany 2	4
110	Ascension	2,3
111	Maundy Thursday	2
118:14-24	Easter Sunday/Easter 1	2
119:121-128	Trinity 8/Pentecost 9	5
121	New Year's Day	4
122	Epiphany 1	2

1 Historic
2 Eisenach
3 Thomasius
4 Synodical Conf.
5 Soll
6 ILCW - A
7 ILCW - B
8 ILCW - C

126	Trinity 26/Pentecost 27	2
	Trinity 27/Last Pentecost	4
138	Trinity 18/Pentecost 19	5
145:15-21	Harvest	3

Proverbs

2:1-8	Trinity 13/Pentecost 14	5
	Trinity 20/Pentecost 21	1
2:1-8	Trinity 20/Pentecost 21	2
3:13-20	Trinity 20/Pentecost 21	7
4:14-23	Trinity 14/Pentecost 15	1,3
8:22-31	Trinity Sunday/Pentecost 1	8
9:1-6	Trinity 12/Pentecost 13	7
9:1-10	Trinity 2/Pentecost 3	1,2
9:8-12	Trinity 15/Pentecost 16	8
11:23-31	Trinity 1/Pentecost 2	4
16:1-9	Trinity 9/Pentecost 10	1,2
	Trinity 17/Pentecost 18	3
24:14-20	Trinity 22/Pentecost 23	1,2
25:6-7	Trinity 14/Pentecost 15	8
25:6-13	Trinity 17/Pentecost 18	1

Ecclesiastes

1:2; 2:18-26	Trinity 10/Pentecost 11	8
12:1-7	Epiphany 1	1

Isaiah

2:1-5	Advent 1	6
2:2-5	Advent 4	3
	Epiphany	1,2
4:2-6	Trinity 3/Pentecost 4	5
5:1-7	Easter 4/Easter 5	3
	Trinity 19/Pentecost 20	6
6:1-6	Trinity Sunday/Pentecost 1	1
6:1-8	Epiphany 5	8
	Trinity Sunday/Pentecost 1	2
6:3-7	Trinity Sunday/Pentecost 1	3
7:10-14(15-17)	Advent 4	6
8:20-22	Epiphany 2	3
9:1-4	Epiphany 3	6
9:2-7	Christmas Day/Christmas Eve	1,4,6,7,8
9:6,7	Christmas Day	2,3

1 Historic — 2 Eisenach — 3 Thomasius — 4 Synodical Conf. — 5 Soll — 6 ILCW - A — 7 ILCW - B — 8 ILCW - C

11:1-10	Advent 2	6
12:1-6	Lent 4	8
	Trinity 3/Pentecost 4	1,2
	Trinity 4/Pentecost 5	4
25:1-8	Easter Sunday/Easter 1	1
25:1-9	Sexagesima	3
25:6-9	Easter Sunday/Easter 1	7
	Trinity 20/Pentecost 21	6
28:14-19	Sunday after Christmas	4
29:18-21	Trinity 12/Pentecost 13	1,2
30:15-19	Trinity 21/Pentecost 22	3
32:14-18	Pentecost	5
32:14-20	Sunday after Ascension/Easter 7	1
35:1-10	Advent 3	6
35:3-10	Trinity 27/Last Pentecost	1,2
35:4-7a	Trinity 15/Pentecost 16	7
35:4-10	Trinity 25/Pentecost 26	3
40:1-8	Advent 3	1,2
40:1-10	Advent 3	3
40:1-11	Advent 2	7
40:6-11	Easter 2/Easter 3	5
40:26-31	Easter 3/Easter 4	1,2
42:1-7	Epiphany 1	6,7,8
42:1-8	Lent 4	3
42:14-21	Lent 3	6
43:1-7	Mission Festival	5
43:8-13	Trinity 4/Pentecost 5	5
43:16-20	Sunday after Christmas	5
43:16-21	Passion Sunday/Lent 5	8
43:18-25	Epiphany 7	7
44:1-6	Pentecost	3
44:6-8	Trinity 8/Pentecost 9	6
45:1-7	Trinity 21/Pentecost 22	6
45:22-25	Sunday after Christmas	7
	Palm Sunday	5
49:1-6	Epiphany 2	6
49:1-9	Epiphany	3
49:1-15	Easter 4/Easter 5	1
49:13-18	Epiphany 8	6
49:22-26	Lent 3	5

50:4-9a	Palm Sunday	6
50:4-6	Trinity 16/Pentecost 17	7
51:1-12	Epiphany 4	3
51:4-6	Trinity 27/Pentecost Last	7
52:1-6	Trinity 26/Pentecost 27	8
52:7-10	Christmas Dawn	6,7,8
	Lent 4	1,2
52:7-17	Lent 2	3
52:13—53:12	Good Friday	1,6,7,8
53	Good Friday	4
53:1-7	Good Friday	1,3
53:8-12	Easter Sunday/Easter 1	3
53:10-12	Trinity 21/Pentecost 22	7
54:7-13	Easter 5/Easter 6	3
	Trinity 24/Pentecost 25	4
55	Sunday after Ascension/Easter 7	4
55:1-5	Trinity 10/Pentecost 11	6
55:6-9	Trinity 17/Pentecost 18	6
55:6-11	Easter 5/Easter 6	1,2
55:10-11	Trinity 7/Pentecost 8	6
55:10-13	Epiphany 8	8
56:1-7	Advent 3	5
56:1,6-8	Trinity 12/Pentecost 13	6
58:5-9a	Epiphany 5	6
60:1-6	Epiphany	1,6,7,8
60:1-11	Epiphany	4
60:17-22	New Year's Day	5
61	Advent 3	4
61:1-3	Advent 1	3
61:1-3,10-11	Advent 3	7
61:1-6	Epiphany 2	1,2
	Epiphany 3	8
61:10—11	Easter 3/Easter 4	3
61:10—62:3	Second Sunday after Christmas	6,7,8
62:1-5	Epiphany 2	8
62:1-7	Mission Festival	6,7,8
62:6-12	Trinity 7/Pentecost 8	1,2
62:10-12	Advent 1	5
	Christmas Day	6,7,8
63:1-9	Trinity 24/Pentecost 25	3

1 Historic 3 Thomasius 5 Soll 7 ILCW - B
2 Eisenach 4 Synodical Conf. 6 ILCW - A 8 ILCW - C

63:7-9	Sunday after Christmas	6
63:7-16	Sunday after Christmas	1,2
63:7-17	Sunday after Christmas	3
63:16b,17; 64:1-8	Advent 1	7
64:1,2	Sunday after Ascension/Easter 7	3
65:17-19,24,25	Trinity 4/Pentecost 5	1,2
66:10-14	Trinity 6/Pentecost 7	8
66:18-23	Trinity 13/Pentecost 14	8

Jeremiah

1:4-10	Epiphany 4	8
2:17-19	Lent 1	3
3:22-23	Lent 1	3
6:10-16	Trinity 24/Pentecost 25	5
7:1-7	Epiphany 8	8
7:1-11	Trinity 10/Pentecost 11	1,2
8:4-9	Quinquagesima	1,2
8:19-22	Quinquagesima	3
9:23-24	Septuagesima	1,2
10:1-16	Trinity Sunday/Pentecost 1	5
11:18-20	Trinity 17/Pentecost 18	7
15:15-21	Easter 4/Easter 5	4
	Trinity 14/Pentecost 15	6
16:16-21	Trinity 19/Pentecost 20	5
17:5-8	Epiphany 6	8
17:5-10	Trinity 18/Pentecost 19	3
18:1-10	Epiphany 5	3
20:7-13	Trinity 4/Pentecost 5	6
23:1-6	Trinity 8/Pentecost 9	7
23:2-6	Trinity 27/Last Pentecost	8
23:16-29	Trinity 8/Pentecost 9	1,2
23:21-32	Trinity 8/Pentecost 9	4
23:23-29	Trinity 12/Pentecost 13	8
26:1-6	Trinity 26/Pentecost 27	6
26:1-15	Lent 3	1,2
26:8-15	Lent 2	8
28:5-9	Trinity 5/Pentecost 6	6
30:12-17	Trinity 20/Pentecost 21	5
31:7-9	Trinity 22/Pentecost 23	7
31:10-13	Sunday after Christmas	8

31:31-34	Advent 1	1,2
	Septuagesima	4
	Passion Sunday/Lent 5	7
	Maundy Thursday	8
	Reformation	6,7,8
33:14-16	Advent 1	8

Lamentations

3:22-32	New Year's Day	3
	Sunday after New Year	4
3:22-32	Trinity 5/Pentecost 6	1,2
3:22-33	Trinity 5/Pentecost 6	7

Ezekiel

2:1-5	Trinity 6/Pentecost 7	7
3:17-21	Trinity 18/Pentecost 19	4
17:22-24	Christmas Day	5
	Trinity 3/Pentecost 4	7
18:1-4,25-32	Trinity 18/Pentecost 19	6
33:7-9	Trinity 15/Pentecost 16	6
33:10-16	Epiphany 5	1,2
33:30-33	Trinity 10/Pentecost 11	5
34:11-16	Easter 2/Easter 3	1,3
34:11-16,23-24	Trinity 27/Last Pentecost	6
34:17-24	Trinity 26/Pentecost 27	5
34:23-31	Easter 2/Easter 3	3
36:22-28	Pentecost	1,2,4
37:1-3(4-10),11-14	Passion Sunday/Lent 5	6
37:1-14	Pentecost	7

Daniel

1:1-21	Trinity 2/Pentecost 3	5
3:19-30	Trinity 21/Pentecost 22	4
4:31-34	Septuagesima	3
5:17-30	Septuagesima	3
6:10-23	Epiphany 3	4
7:9,10	Trinity 26/Pentecost 27	7
7:9-14	Trinity 26/Pentecost 27	1
9:15-18	Trinity 11/Pentecost 12	1
9:15-19	Trinity 11/Pentecost 12	2
12:1-3	Trinity 25/Pentecost 26	7

Hosea

2:14-16,19-20	Epiphany 8	7
5:15—6:2	Lent 4	6
5:15—6:6	Trinity 2/Pentecost 3	6
11:1-4,8,9	Trinity 24/Pentecost 25	6

Joel

2:12-19	Ash Wednesday	1,6,7,8
2:28,29	Pentecost	6
3:9-21	Trinity 25/Pentecost 26	5

Amos

5:6,7,10-15	Trinity 20/Pentecost 21	7
5:18-24	Trinity 23/Pentecost 24	6
6:1-7	Trinity 18/Pentecost 19	8
7:10-15	Trinity 7/Pentecost 8	7
8:4-7	Trinity 17/Pentecost 18	8
8:11,12	Sexagesima	1,2

Jonah

2:1-10	Easter Sunday/Easter 1	5
3:1-5,10	Epiphany 3	7
3:1-9	Quinquagesima	5
3:10—4:11	Quinquagesima	4

Micah

2:7-13	Trinity 11/Pentecost 12	4
5:1-3	Christmas Day	3
5:2-4	Advent 4	8
6:1-8	Epiphany 4	6

Habakkuk

1:1-3; 2:2-4	Trinity 19/Pentecost 20	8
2:1-4	Reformation	5

Zephaniah

1:7-18	Advent 2	5
1:14-16(17,18)	Trinity 23/Pentecost 24	6
3:8-17	Mission Festival	4
3:14-18a	Advent 3	8
	Trinity 22/Pentecost 23	3

1 Historic
2 Eisenach
3 Thomasius
4 Synodical Conf.
5 Soll
6 ILCW - A
7 ILCW - B
8 ILCW - C

Haggai

1:2-14	Epiphany 5	5
2:1-10	Trinity 23/Pentecost 24	3
2:7-10	Advent 4	4

Zechariah

2:10-13	Christmas Day	4
6:12-15	Advent 4	5
7:4-10	Trinity 13/Pentecost 14	1,2
9:8-12	Palm Sunday	1,2,3
9:9-12	Trinity 6/Pentecost 7	6
9:9,10	Palm Sunday	7
12:7-10	Trinity 4/Pentecost 5	8
13:6-9	Good Friday	5
14:8-11	Epiphany	5

Malachi

1:6-11	Epiphany 1	5
2:1,2,4-10	Trinity 25/Pentecost 26	6
3:1-4	Advent 2	8
3:14-18	Trinity 27/Last Pentecost	8
4:1-6	Advent 2	1,2,3

Matthew

1:18-23	Christmas Day	2
1:18-25	Advent 4	6
	Christmas Day	4
2:1-12	Epiphany	1,6,7,8
2:13-15,19-23	Sunday after Christmas	6
2:13-23	Sunday after New Year	1
3:1-11	Advent 3	2
3:1-12	Advent 2	6
	Advent 3	3,4
3:13-17	Epiphany	2,3
	Epiphany 1	6
	Trinity Sunday/Pentecost 1	4
4:1-11	Lent 1	1,6
4:12-17	Epiphany	4
4:12-23	Epiphany 3	6
5:1-6	Trinity 3/Pentecost 4	3

5:1-12	Epiphany 4	6
	Trinity 18/Pentecost 19	4
5:7-12	Trinity 4/Pentecost 5	3
5:13-16	Trinity 4/Pentecost 5	2
	Mission Festival	4
5:13-19	Trinity 13/Pentecost 14	3
5:13-20	Epiphany 5	6
5:17-29	Septuagesima	4
5:20-26	Trinity 6/Pentecost 7	1
5:20-37	Epiphany 6	6
5:33-37	Trinity 8/Pentecost 9	5
5:38-48	Epiphany 7	6
5:42-48	Thanksgiving	4
6:1-4	Harvest	4
6:1-6,16-21	Ash Wednesday	6,7,8
6:5-15	Trinity 18/Pentecost 19	4
6:16-21	Ash Wednesday	1
6:19-23	Trinity 19/Pentecost 20	4
6:24-34	Epiphany 8	6
	Trinity 15/Pentecost 16	1
6:25-34	Thanksgiving	1
7:1-6	Trinity 4/Pentecost 5	4
7:7-12	Easter 5/Easter 6	5
7:15-23	Trinity 8/Pentecost 9	1
7:21-29	Trinity 1/Pentecost 2	6
7:24-29	Epiphany 5	2
	Trinity 5/Pentecost 6	3
	Trinity 20/Pentecost 21	4
8:1-13	Epiphany 3	1
8:19-22	Epiphany 2	5
8:23-27	Epiphany 4	1
9:1-8	Trinity 19/Pentecost 20	1
9:9-13	Sunday after New Year	4
	Trinity 2/Pentecost 3	2,3,6
9:14-17	Easter 3/Easter 4	5
9:18-26	Trinity 24/Pentecost 25	1
9:27-34	Trinity 12/Pentecost 13	4
9:35-38	Mission Festival	4
9:35—10:8	Trinity 3/Pentecost 4	6
10:1-15	Pentecost	5
10:16-22	Trinity 14/Pentecost 15	3
10:24-33	Trinity 23/Pentecost 24	2

1 Historic　3 Thomasius　5 Soll　7 ILCW-B
2 Eisenach　4 Synodical Conf.　6 ILCW - A　8 ILCW-C

10:24-33	Trinity 4/Pentecost 5	6
10:32-39	Epiphany 1	4
10:34-42	Trinity 5/Pentecost 6	6
10:40-42	Trinity 19/Pentecost 20	4
11:2-10	Advent 3	1
11:2-11	Advent 3	6
11:16-24	Trinity 2/Pentecost 3	4
11:20-24	Lent 1	3
11:25-30	Advent 1	4
	Epiphany 3	3
	Trinity 6/Pentecost 7	6
	Trinity 16/Pentecost 17	2
12:1-8	Trinity 17/Pentecost 18	2,4
12:1-13	Trinity 19/Pentecost 20	3
12:9-21	Trinity 14/Pentecost 15	4
12:22-29	Lent 3	5
12:38-42	Easter 1/Easter 2	4
12:46-50	Epiphany 2	4
	Trinity 8/Pentecost 9	2
13:1-9	Trinity 7/Pentecost 8	6
13:1-9,18-23	Sexagesima	5
13:10-17	Epiphany	5
13:24-30	Epiphany 5	1
	Trinity 8/Pentecost 9	6
	Harvest	6,7,8
13:31-35	Epiphany 5	4
	Trinity 1/Pentecost 2	2
	Trinity 12/Pentecost 13	3
13:44-46	Trinity 7/Pentecost 8	3
	Trinity 9/Pentecost 10	2
13:44-52	Trinity 9/Pentecost 10	6
	Trinity 25/Pentecost 26	4
14:13-21	Trinity 10/Pentecost 11	6
14:22-33	Epiphany 4	4
	Trinity 11/Pentecost 12	6
14:22-34	Trinity 9/Pentecost 10	3
15:1-9	Trinity 6/Pentecost 7	4
15:10-20	Trinity 7/Pentecost 8	4
15:21-28	Lent 2	1
	Trinity 12/Pentecost 13	6
15:29-39	Harvest	3
16:1-4	Sunday after New Year	2

1 Historic 3 Thomasius 5 Soll 7 ILCW-B
2 Eisenach 4 Synodical Conf. 6 ILCW - A 8 ILCW-C

16:1-12	Trinity 25/Pentecost 26	4
16:13-20	Sexagesima	4
	Trinity 11/Pentecost 12	3
	Trinity 13/Pentecost 14	6
16:21-23	Quinquagesima	4
16:21-26	Lent 1	2
	Trinity 14/Pentecost 15	6
16:24-28	Ascension	5
17:1-9	Transfiguration	1,6
	Sexagesima	3
17:24-27	Trinity 23/Pentecost 24	4
18:1-14	Trinity 6/Pentecost 7	4
18:15-20	Trinity 15/Pentecost 16	6
18:15-22	Trinity 7/Pentecost 8	4
18:21-35	Trinity 16/Pentecost 17	6
18:23-35	Trinity 22/Pentecost 23	1
19:1-12	Trinity 12/Pentecost 13	5
19:16-26	Trinity 1/Pentecost 2	4
	Trinity 6/Pentecost 7	3
20:1-16	Septuagesima	1
	Trinity 17/Pentecost 18	6
20:17-28	Quinquagesima	4
	Lent 4	6
20:29-34	Trinity 21/Pentecost 22	5
21:1-9	Advent 1	1
	Palm Sunday	1
21:1-11	Palm Sunday	6
21:12-22	Trinity 10/Pentecost 11	4
21:28-32	Trinity 6/Pentecost 7	2
	Trinity 18/Pentecost 19	6
21:33-43	Trinity 19/Pentecost 20	6
21:33-46	Trinity 10/Pentecost 11	4
22:1-10	Trinity 20/Pentecost 21	6
22:1-14	Trinity 20/Pentecost 21	1
22:15-21	Trinity 21/Pentecost 22	6
22:15-22	Trinity 23/Pentecost 24	1
22:23-33	Trinity 16/Pentecost 17	4
22:34-40	Trinity 22/Pentecost 23	6
21:34-46	Trinity 18/Pentecost 19	1
22:1-12	Trinity 25/Pentecost 26	6
	Reformation	4

1 Historic · 2 Eisenach · 3 Thomasius · 4 Synodical Conf. · 5 Soll · 6 ILCW - A · 7 ILCW - B · 8 ILCW - C

23:34-39	Passion Sunday/Lent 5	4
	Trinity 10/Pentecost 11	2,3
24:1-14	Trinity 24/Pentecost 25	3
	Trinity 26/Pentecost 27	6
24:15-28	Trinity 25/Pentecost 26	1
24:29-36	Trinity 25/Pentecost 26	5
24:37-44	Advent 1	6
	Trinity 26/Pentecost 27	5
25:1-13	Trinity 23/Pentecost 24	6
	Trinity 27/Last Pentecost	1
25:13-30	Trinity 27/Last Pentecost	4
25:14-30	Trinity 16/Pentecost 17	3
	Trinity 24/Pentecost 25	6
25:31-46	Trinity 26/Pentecost 27	1
	Trinity 27/Last Pentecost	6
26:17-30	Maundy Thursday	4
26:36-46	Lent 1	5
27:11-54	Palm Sunday	6
27:29-56	Good Friday	3
28:1-8	Easter Sunday/Easter 1	3
28:1-10	Easter Sunday/Easter 1	2,4
28:16-20	Trinity Sunday/Pentecost 1	2,4,6
28:18-20	Trinity Sunday/Pentecost 1	3

Mark

1:1-8	Advent 2	7
1:4-11	Epiphany 1	7
1:12-15	Lent 1	7
1:14-20	Epiphany 3	7
1:21-28	Epiphany 4	7
	Trinity 20/Pentecost 21	5
1:29-39	Epiphany 5	7
1:40-45	Epiphany 3	5
	Epiphany 6	7
2:1-12	Epiphany 7	7
2:13-17	Trinity 11/Pentecost 12	4
2:18-22	Epiphany 8	7
	Easter 3/Easter 4	4
2:23-28	Trinity 1/Pentecost 2	7
	Trinity 17/Pentecost 18	5

1 Historic　3 Thomasius　5 Soll　7 ILCW - B
2 Eisenach　4 Synodical Conf.　6 ILCW - A　8 ILCW - C

3:20-35	Trinity 2/Pentecost 3	7
4:26-29	Trinity 1/Pentecost 2	3
	Trinity 7/Pentecost 8	2
4:26-32	Epiphany 5	4
4:26-34	Trinity 3/Pentecost 4	7
4:35-41	Trinity 4/Pentecost 5	7
5:1-20	Trinity 22/Pentecost 23	5
5:21-24a,35-43	Trinity 5/Pentecost 6	7
6:1-6	Epiphany 5	5
	Trinity 6/Pentecost 7	7
6:7-13	Trinity 7/Pentecost 8	7
6:17-29	Advent 4	4
6:20-29	Sunday after New Year	3
6:30-34	Trinity 8/Pentecost 9	7
6:45-56	Epiphany 4	5
7:1-8,14-15,21-23	Trinity 14/Pentecost 15	7
7:14-23	Trinity 7/Pentecost 8	5
7:24-30	Lent 2	5
7:31-37	Trinity 12/Pentecost 13	1
	Trinity 15/Pentecost 16	7
8:1-9	Trinity 7/Pentecost 8	1
8:10-21	Trinity 24/Pentecost 25	5
8:22-26	Trinity 16/Pentecost 17	5
8:27-35	Trinity 16/Pentecost 17	7
8:27-38	Quniquagesima	3
8:31-38	Lent 2	7
8:34-38	Trinity 8/Pentecost 9	3
	Trinity 24/Pentecost 25	4
9:2-9	Transfiguration	7
9:2-13	Transfiguration	4
9:14-29	Trinity 15/Pentecost 16	5
9:30-32	Quniquagesima	5
9:30-37	Trinity 17/Pentecost 18	7
9:33-37	Trinity 6/Pentecost 7	5
9:38-50	Trinity 18/Pentecost 19	7
	Trinity 19/Pentecost 20	5
10:2-16	Trinity 19/Pentecost 20	7
10:13-16	Trinity 3/Pentecost 4	4
	Trinity 21/Pentecost 22	2

1 Historic
2 Eisenach
3 Thomasius
4 Synodical Conf.
5 Soll
6 ILCW - A
7 ILCW-B
8 ILCW-C

10:17-27	Trinity 18/Pentecost 19	2
	Trinity 20/Pentecost 21	7
10:32-45	Quinquagesima	3
10:35-45	Lent 3	4
	Trinity 21/Pentecost 22	7
10:46-52	Trinity 21/Pentecost 22	4
	Trinity 22/Pentecost 23	7
11:1-10	Palm Sunday	5
11:20-26	Trinity 11/Pentecost 12	5
11:27-33	Trinity 4/Pentecost 5	5
12:28-34	Trinity 23/Pentecost 24	7
12:28-37	Trinity 13/Pentecost 14	4
12:38-44	Trinity 9/Pentecost 10	4
12:41-44	Trinity 13/Pentecost 14	2
	Trinity 24/Pentecost 25	7
13:1-8	Advent 2	5
13:1-13	Trinity 25/Pentecost 26	7
13:24-31	Trinity 26/Pentecost 27	7
13:32-37	Trinity 27/Last Pentecost	7
13:33-37	Advent 1	7
14:12-26	Maundy Thursday	7
15:1-39	Palm Sunday	7
16:1-8	Easter Sunday/Easter 1	1,7
16:14-20	Ascension	1

Luke

1:26-38	Advent 4	7
	Christmas Day	5
1:39-45	Advent 4	8
1:46-55	Advent 4	3
	Christmas Day	4
1:56-66	Advent 4	5
1:67-80	Advent 2	4
1:68-79	Advent 1	2,3
2:1-14	Christmas Day	1
2:1-20	Christmas Day/Christmas Eve	3,6,7,8
2:21	New Year's Day	1,6,7,8
2:22-32	Sunday after Christmas	3,4
2:25-32	Sunday after Christmas	2
2:25-40	Sunday after Christmas	7
2:33-40	Sunday after Christmas	1

2:41-52	Epiphany 1	1
2:41-52	First Sunday after Christmas	8
3:1-6	Advent 2	8
3:3-14	Advent 3	4
3:7-18	Advent 3	8
3:15-17,21,22	Epiphany 1	8
3:21-33	Trinity Sunday/Pentecost 1	5
4:1-13	Lent 1	8
4:1-15	Lent 1	4
4:14-21	Epiphany 3	8
4:14-22	Epiphany 2	3
4:16-21	New Year's Day	2
	Epiphany	4
4:21-32	Epiphany 4	8
4:38-44	Epiphany 3	4
5:1-11	Epiphany 5	8
	Trinity 5/Pentecost 6	1
5:17-26	Trinity 9/Pentecost 10	5
5:27-32	Sunday after New Year	5
6:6-11	Trinity 14/Pentecost 15	5
6:17-26	Epiphany 6	8
6:20-35	Septuagesima	5
6:27-38	Epiphany 7	8
6:36-42	Trinity 4/Pentecost 5	1
6:39-49	Epiphany 8	8
6:43-49	Trinity 20/Pentecost 21	4
7:1-10	Transfiguration	3
	Trinity 1/Pentecost 2	8
7:11-17	Trinity 2/Pentecost 3	8
	Trinity 16/Pentecost 17	1
7:18-26	Advent 3	5
7:27-35	Reformation	4
7:36-50	Trinity 3/Pentecost 4	8
	Trinity 11/Pentecost 12	2
	Trinity 14/Pentecost 15	4
	Trinity 18/Pentecost 19	3
8:4-15	Sexagesima	1
8:27-39	Trinity 22/Pentecost 23	4
9:10-17	Lent 4	5
9:18-24	Trinity 4/Pentecost 5	8
9:18-26	Trinity 5/Pentecost 6	2

9:28-36	Transfiguration	5,8
9:51-56	Lent 3	2
	Sunday after Ascension/Easter 7	5
9:51-62	Trinity 5/Pentecost 6	8
9:57-62	Sunday after Christmas	4
	Trinity 22/Pentecost 23	2
10:1-12,16	Trinity 6/Pentecost 7	8
10:1-15	Trinity 5/Pentecost 6	5
10:17-20	Lent 2	2
10:17-22	Trinity 22/Pentecost 23	3
10:23-37	Trinity 13/Pentecost 14	1
10:25-37	Trinity 7/Pentecost 8	8
10:38-42	Septuagesima	2,4
	Trinity 8/Pentecost 9	8
	Trinity 17/Pentecost 18	3
11:1-4	Trinity 18/Pentecost 19	5
11:1-13	Trinity 9/Pentecost 10	8
11:5-13	Easter 5/Easter 6	2
	Sunday after Ascension/Easter 7	4
	Trinity 15/Pentecost 16	3
11:14-28	Lent 3	1
11:29-36	Easter 1/Easter 2	5
11:37-54	Reformation	5
12:1-3	New Year's Day	5
12:4-9	New Year's Day	4
12:13-21	Trinity 10/Pentecost 11	8
12:15-21	Trinity 21/Pentecost 22	3
	Harvest	1,3
	Thanksgiving	4
12:24-34	Harvest	4
12:32-40	Trinity 11/Pentecost 12	8
12:35-43	Trinity 27/Last Pentecost	2
12:35-46	Trinity 27/Last Pentecost	3
12:42-48	Trinity 27/Last Pentecost	8
12:49-53	Trinity 12/Pentecost 13	8
12:51-59	Epiphany 1	5
13:1-9	New Year's Day	4
	Lent 3	8
13:6-9	New Year's Day	3
13:10-17	Trinity 17/Pentecost 18	4

13:18-24	Sunday after New Year	4
13:22-30	Trinity 13/Pentecost 14	8
13:23-30	Trinity 23/Pentecost 24	3
13:24-30	Trinity 27/Last Pentecost	5
13:31-35	Lent 2	8
	Passion Sunday/Lent 5	5
14:1-11	Trinity 17/Pentecost 18	1
14:1,7-14	Trinity 14/Pentecost 15	8
14:12-15	Trinity 15/Pentecost 16	4
14:16-24	Trinity 2/Pentecost 3	1
14:25-33	Trinity 15/Pentecost 16	8
14:25-35	Trinity 22/Pentecost 23	4
15:1-3,11-32	Lent 4	8
15:1-10	Trinity 3/Pentecost 4	1
	Trinity 16/Pentecost 17	8
15:11-32	Trinity 3/Pentecost 4	2,4
16:1-9	Trinity 9/Pentecost 10	1
16:1-13	Trinity 17/Pentecost 18	8
16:10-17	Trinity 26/Pentecost 27	4
16:19-31	Trinity 1/Pentecost 2	1
	Trinity 18/Pentecost 19	8
17:1-10	Trinity 4/Pentecost 5	4
	Trinity 19/Pentecost 20	8
17:11-19	Trinity 14/Pentecost 15	1
	Trinity 20/Pentecost 21	8
	Thanksgiving	6,7,8
17:20-25	Advent 1	4
17:20-30	Advent 2	2,3
17:26-37	Advent 2	4
18:1-8a	Trinity 21/Pentecost 22	8
18:1-8	Easter 5/Easter 6	4
	Trinity 15/Pentecost 16	3
18:9-14	Trinity 11/Pentecost 12	1
	Trinity 22/Pentecost 23	8
18:15-17	Trinity 3/Pentecost 4	5
18:31-43	Quinquagesima	1
19:1-5	Trinity 20/Pentecost 21	3
19:1-10	Trinity 23/Pentecost 24	8
19:11-27	Trinity 26/Pentecost 27	2,4,8
19:29-40	Advent 1	5
19:41-48	Trinity 10/Pentecost 11	1

20:9-19	Passion Sunday/Lent 5	8
	Trinity 10/Pentecost 11	5
20:20-26	Trinity 23/Pentecost 24	5
20:27-38	Trinity 24/Pentecost 25	8
20:27-40	Trinity 16/Pentecost 17	4
20:41-44	Trinity 13/Pentecost 14	5
21:5-19	Trinity 25/Pentecost 26	8
21:25-36	Advent 1	8
	Advent 2	1
22:7-20	Maundy Thursday	4,8
22:14-20	Maundy Thursday	2
22:14-23	Maundy Thursday	3
22:24-30	Trinity 27/Last Pentecost	4
22:31,32	Mission Festival	5
22:35-37	Harvest	5
23:1-49	Palm Sunday	8
23:26-38	Good Friday	5
23:35-43	Trinity 27/Last Pentecost	8
23:39-46	Good Friday	2
23:39-53	Good Friday	4
24:1-11	Easter Sunday/Easter 1	8
24:1-12	Easter Sunday/Easter 1	4
24:13-35	Easter 2/Easter 3	6
24:36-49	Easter 2/Easter 3	7
24:44-53	Ascension	6,7,8
	Mission Festival	6,7,8
24:50-53	Ascension	2,3,4

John

1:1-14	Christmas Day/Christmas Dawn	3,4, 6,7,8
1:1-8	Second Sunday after Christmas	6,7,8
1:15-18	Advent 4	2
	Christmas Day	4
1:6-8,19-28	Advent 3	7
	Advent 4	1
1:29-34	Advent 4	4
1:29-41	Epiphany 2	6
1:35-42	Epiphany 1	2
	Epiphany 2	4
1:36-51	Epiphany 1	3
1:43-51	Epiphany 2	2,7
	Trinity 5/Pentecost 6	4

1 Historic 3 Thomasius 5 Soll 7 ILCW-B
2 Eisenach 4 Synodical Conf. 6 ILCW - A 8 ILCW-C

7:14-24	Trinity 8/Pentecost 9	4
7:25-31	Trinity 13/Pentecost 14	4
7:33-39	Sunday after Ascension/Easter 7	2
7:37-39a	Pentecost	7
7:37-39	Pentecost	3
7:40-53	Trinity 2/Pentecost 3	5
8:1-11	Trinity 2/Pentecost 3	4
8:12-16	Epiphany 4	3
8:12-20	Sunday after Ascension/Easter 7	4
8:21-30	Lent 2	3
8:25-36	Sexagesima	4
8:30-36	Reformation	3
8:31-36	Trinity 12/Pentecost 13	2
	Reformation	1,6,7,8
8:46-59	Passion Sunday/Lent 5	1
9:1-7	Trinity 11/Pentecost 12	4
9:13-17,34-39	Lent 3	6
9:24-41	Trinity 12/Pentecost 13	4
	Trinity 19/Pentecost 20	2
10:1-10	Easter 3/Easter 4	6
10:1-11	Easter 2/Easter 3	4
	Easter 3/Easter 4	3
10:11-16	Easter 2/Easter 3	1
10:11-18	Easter 3/Easter 4	7
10:17-21	Easter 2/Easter 3	4
10:22-30	Easter 3/Easter 4	8
	Trinity 24/Pentecost 25	4
10:23-30	Trinity 24/Pentecost 25	2
10:24-33	Lent 3	3
10:31-42	Sunday after Christmas	5
11:1-11	Trinity 15/Pentecost 16	2
11:1-16	Easter 3/Easter 4	4
11:17-27	Easter 4/Easter 5	4
11:20-27	Sexagesima	2
11:21-27	Trinity 25/Pentecost 26	3
11:28-45	Easter 5/Easter 6	4
11:46-57	Lent 4	4
11:47-53	Passion Sunday/Lent 5	6
11:47-57	Quinquagesima	2
	Lent 4	3

1 Historic 3 Thomasius 5 Soll 7 ILCW-B
2 Eisenach 4 Synodical Conf. 6 ILCW - A 8 ILCW-C

12:1-8	Palm Sunday	2
12:1-11	Palm Sunday	4
12:1-19	Palm Sunday	3
12:12-19	Palm Sunday	4
12:20-26	Lent 2	4
	Easter 3/Easter 4	2
12:20-33	Passion Sunday/Lent 5	7
12:23-33	Passion Sunday/Lent 5	3
12:27-36	Passion Sunday/Lent 5	4
12:37-45	Easter 2/Easter 3	5
13:1-15	Maundy Thursday	1
13:1-17	Maundy Thursday	3,6
13:16-20	Maundy Thursday	5
13:31-35	Passion Sunday/Lent 5	2
	Easter 4/Easter 5	8
14:1-6	Easter 2/Easter 3	2
14:1-12	Easter 4/Easter 5	6
	Sunday after Ascension/Easter 7	3
14:7-14	Trinity 15/Pentecost 16	4
14:13-21	Easter 5/Easter 6	3
14:15-21	Easter 5/Easter 6	6
	Pentecost	2,4
14:23-29	Easter 5/Easter 6	8
14:23-31	Pentecost	1
15:1-8	Easter 4/Easter 5	7
	Trinity 1/Pentecost 2	4
	Trinity 20/Pentecost 21	2
15:1-11	Easter 4/Easter 5	3
15:9-17	Lent 1	4
	Easter 5/Easter 6	7
15:18-25	Lent 2	4
15:26—16:4	Sunday after Ascension/Easter 7	1
15:26,27; 16:4b-11	Pentecost	8
16:5-11	Pentecost	6
16:5-15	Easter 4/Easter 5	1
16:12-15	Trinity Sunday/Pentecost 1	8
16:16-23	Easter 3/Easter 4	1
16:23-30	Easter 5/Easter 6	1
17:1-11	Sunday after Ascension/Easter 7	6
17:1-16	Lent 4	4
17:11b-19	Sunday after Ascension/Easter 7	7
17:17-26	Ascension	4

17:20-26	Sunday after Ascension/Easter 7	8
18:1—19:42	Good Friday	1
18:33-37	Trinity 27/Last Pentecost	7
19:17-30	Good Friday	4,6,7,8
20:1-9	Easter Sunday/Easter 1	6
20:1-10	Easter Sunday/Easter 1	5
20:19-31	Easter 1/Easter 2	1,6,7,8
21:1-14	Easter 1/Easter 2	4
	Easter 2/Easter 3	3,8
21:15-19	Easter 1/Easter 2	2
	Trinity 5/Pentecost 6	4
21:15-24	Easter 1/Easter 2	3
21:20-25	Easter 4/Easter 5	5

Acts

1:1-11	Ascension	1,6,7,8
1:8-14	Sunday after Ascension/Easter 7	6
1:15-26	Sunday after Ascension/Easter 7	7
2:1-13	Pentecost	1
2:37-47	Pentecost	8
2:14a,36-47	Easter 2/Easter 3	6
2:22-36	Pentecost	7
2:42-47	Easter 1/Easter 2	6
	Trinity 1/Pentecost 2	3
3:1-10	Trinity 2/Pentecost 3	3
3:1-16	Trinity 3/Pentecost 4	2
3:13-15,17-26	Easter 1/Easter 2	7
4:1-12	Trinity 3/Pentecost 4	3
	Trinity 4/Pentecost 5	2
4:23-33	Easter 3/Easter 4	7
4:8-20	Trinity 10/Pentecost 11	4
4:32-35	Trinity 1/Pentecost 2	2
5:12,17-32	Easter 1/Easter 2	8
5:34-42	Trinity 5/Pentecost 6	2
6:1-9; 7:2a,51-60	Easter 3/Easter 4	6
6:1-7	Trinity 17/Pentecost 18	4
6:8-15	Trinity 4/Pentecost 5	5
7:54-59	Trinity 10/Pentecost 11	3
7:54—8:3	Trinity 4/Pentecost 5	4

8:26-38	Trinity 4/Pentecost 5	3
8:26-39	Epiphany	4
8:26-40	Easter 4/Easter 5	7
	Trinity 6/Pentecost 7	2
9:1-19	Trinity 5/Pentecost 6	3
9:1-20	Easter 2/Easter 3	8
9:1-22	Trinity 5/Pentecost 6	4
10:34-38	Epiphany 1	6,7,8
10:34-43	Easter Sunday/Easter 1	6
11:19-30	Easter 5/Easter 6	7
13:1-12	Sunday after Ascension/Easter 7	5
13:15,16a,26-33	Easter 3/Easter 4	8
13:26-39	Easter Sunday/Easter 1	4
13:44-52	Easter 4/Easter 5	8
14:8-18	Trinity 6/Pentecost 7	3
	Easter 5/Easter 6	8
14:11-17	Harvest	4
16:6-10	Sunday after Ascension/Easter 7	8
16:9-15	Trinity 12/Pentecost 13	2
	Mission Festival	4
16:12-15	Trinity 8/Pentecost 9	3
16:16-32	Trinity 8/Pentecost 9	2
16:22-33	Trinity 7/Pentecost 8	3
16:24-35	Sexagesima	4
17:1-15	Easter 4/Easter 5	6
17:15-34	Trinity 11/Pentecost 12	3
17:16-34	Trinity 9/Pentecost 10	2
17:22-31	Thanksgiving	4
	Easter 5/Easter 6	6
18:24-28	Sunday after Christmas	5
19:1-7	Sunday after New Year	3
19:23-40	Trinity 12/Pentecost 13	3
20:17-38	Trinity 10/Pentecost 11	2
	Trinity 13/Pentecost 14	3
20:26-32	Trinity 23/Pentecost 24	4
24:22-26	Trinity 9/Pentecost 10	3

Romans

1:1-7	Advent 4	6
	New Year's Day	6,7,8

1:13-20	Epiphany 3	2
1:16-20	Advent 1	4
2:11-16	Trinity 13/Pentecost 14	5
2:12-16	Advent 3	3
3:1-20	Trinity 15/Pentecost 16	5
3:19-28	Reformation	6,7,8
3:21-26	Sunday after New Year	4
3:21-25a,27,28	Trinity 1/Pentecost 2	6
3:27-31	Lent 1	4
4:1-8	Trinity 22/Pentecost 23	4
4:1-5,13-17	Lent 2	6
4:18-25	Trinity 2/Pentecost 3	6
4:23—5:11	Easter 2/Easter 3	5
5:1-5	Epiphany 3	3
	Trinity Sunday/Pentecost 1	8
5:1-11	Lent 2	7
5:6-11	Trinity 3/Pentecost 4	6
5:12-15	Trinity 4/Pentecost 5	6
5:12(13-16),17-19	Lent 1	6
5:17—6:2	Lent 3	5
6:1-11	Trinity 5/Pentecost 6	6
6:3-11	Trinity 6/Pentecost 7	1
6:12-18	Trinity 6/Pentecost 7	4
6:19-23	Trinity 7/Pentecost 8	1
7:7-16	Epiphany 4	2
7:14-25	Trinity 14/Pentecost 15	4
7:15-25a	Trinity 6/Pentecost 7	6
8:1-9	Epiphany 5	2
8:1-10	Lent 4	6
8:1-11	Trinity 1/Pentecost 2	4
8:11-19	Passion Sunday/Lent 5	6
8:12-17	Trinity 8/Pentecost 9	1
8:14-17	Trinity Sunday/Pentecost 1	7
8:18-23	Trinity 4/Pentecost 5	1
8:18-25	Trinity 7/Pentecost 8	6
8:24-30	Epiphany 3	4
8:24-32	New Year's Day	2
8:26,27	Trinity 8/Pentecost 9	6
8:28-30	Trinity 9/Pentecost 10	6
8:31-39	Lent 1	7
	Trinity 25/Pentecost 26	4

8:33-39	Trinity 11/Pentecost 12	2
8:35-39	Trinity 10/Pentecost 11	6
9:1-8	Sunday after New Year	5
9:1-8,30-33	Trinity 11/Pentecost 12	6
9:30—10:8	Trinity 12/Pentecost 13	5
10:1-12	Epiphany 2	3
10:1-15	Trinity 2/Pentecost 3	2
10:8b-13	Lent 1	8
10:8-18	Epiphany 1	4
10:11-17	Mission Festival	6,7,8
10:12-21	Epiphany 1	3
11:13-15,29-32	Trinity 12/Pentecost 13	6
11:33-36	Trinity Sunday/Pentecost 1	1
	Trinity 13/Pentecost 14	6
12:1-5	Epiphany 1	1
12:1-8	Trinity 14/Pentecost 15	6
12:6-16	Epiphany 2	1
12:17-21	Epiphany 3	1
13:1-10	Trinity 15/Pentecost 16	6
13:8-10	Epiphany 4	1
13:11-14	Advent 1	1,6
14:1-9	Trinity 20/Pentecost 21	2
14:4-12	Trinity 21/Pentecost 22	4
14:5-9	Trinity 16/Pentecost 17	6
14:13-23	Epiphany 1	5
15:4-13	Advent 2	1,6
16:17-20	Trinity 23/Pentecost 24	5
16:25-27	Advent 4	7

1 Corinthians

1:1-9	Epiphany 2	6
1:3-9	Advent 1	7
1:4-9	Trinity 18/Pentecost 19	1
1:10-17	Epiphany 3	6
	Epiphany 4	5
1:18-31	Lent 4	8
1:18-24	Quinquagesima	3
1:18-25	Lent 2	4
1:21-31	Quinquagesima	2
1:22-25	Lent 3	7

1 Historic
2 Eisenach
3 Thomasius
4 Synodical Conf.
5 Soll
6 ILCW - A
7 ILCW - B
8 ILCW - C

1:26-29	Advent 4	3
1:26-31	Epiphany 4	6
	Trinity 24/Pentecost 25	5
2:1-5	Epiphany 5	6
2:6-13	Epiphany 6	6
2:6-16	Epiphany 2	2
	Pentecost	4
3:1-11	Epiphany 4	4
3:10-11,16-23	Epiphany 7	6
3:11-23	Reformation	2
4:1-5	Advent 3	1
4:1-13	Epiphany 8	6
5:6-8	Easter Sunday/Easter 1	1
6:12-20	Epiphany 2	7
7:29-31	Epiphany 3	7
8:1-6	Trinity 16/Pentecost 17	5
8:1-3	Epiphany 4	7
9:16-23	Advent 3	4
	Epiphany 5	7
9:24-27	Epiphany 6	7
9:24—10:5	Septuagesima	1
10:1-13	Lent 3	8
10:6-13	Trinity 9/Pentecost 10	1
10:14-21	Maundy Thursday	4
10:16-21	Maundy Thursday	2,3,7
10:29—11:1	Trinity 9/Pentecost 10	5
11:23-26	Maundy Thursday	6
11:23-32	Maundy Thursday	1
11:28-32	Maundy Thursday	3
12:1-11	Trinity 10/Pentecost 11	1
	Epiphany 2	8
12:4-13	Trinity Sunday/Pentecost 1	3
12:12-21,26,27	Epiphany 3	8
12:26-31	Mission Festival	5
12:27—13:13	Epiphany 4	8
13	Quinquagesima	1
14:12b-20	Epiphany 5	8
15:20-26	Easter 4/Easter 5	5
15:1-10	Trinity 11/Pentecost 12	1
15:1-11	Easter Sunday/Easter 1	8

1 Historic 3 Thomasius 5 Soll 7 ILCW-B
2 Eisenach 4 Synodical Conf. 6 ILCW - A 8 ILCW-C

15:12,16-20	Epiphany 6	8
15:12-20	Easter Sunday/Easter 1	2
15:19-28	Easter Sunday/Easter 1	7
15:20-28	Easter Sunday/Easter 1	5
	Trinity 27/Last Pentecost	6
15:35-38a,42-50	Epiphany 7	8
15:51-58	Epiphany 8	8
15:54-58	Trinity 26/Pentecost 27	8

2 Corinthians

1:3-7	Sexagesima	5
1:18-22	Epiphany 7	7
1:18-24	Pentecost	5
2:5-11	Easter 1/Easter 2	5
2:14-17	Trinity 17/Pentecost 20	5
3:1b-6	Epiphany 8	7
3:4-11	Trinity 12/Pentecost 13	1
3:12-18	Transfiguration	2
	Sexagesima	3
	Trinity 12/Pentecost 13	4
3:12—4:2	Transfiguration	7
4:1-10	Transfiguration	5
4:3-6	Epiphany	2
	Transfiguration	8
4:5-12	Trinity 1/Pentecost 2	7
4:11-18	Palm Sunday	5
4:13-18	Trinity 2/Pentecost 3	7
5:1-9	Sunday after Christmas	2
5:1-10	Sunday after Ascension/Easter 7	4
	Trinity 3/Pentecost 4	7
5:14-21	Trinity 4/Pentecost 5	7
	Good Friday	2,3,4
5:20b—6:2	Ash Wednesday	6,7,8
6:1-10	Lent 1	1
6:14—7:1	Epiphany 1	2
	Trinity 8/Pentecost 9	5
7:4-10	Lent 4	2
7:6-10	Trinity 18/Pentecost 19	3
8:1-9,13,14	Trinity 5/Pentecost 6	7
8:1-12	Trinity 21/Pentecost 22	3

1 Historic · 2 Eisenach · 3 Thomasius · 4 Synodical Conf. · 5 Soll · 6 ILCW - A · 7 ILCW - B · 8 ILCW - C

8:8-15	Harvest	5
	Thanksgiving	5
9:6-11	Trinity 15/Pentecost 16	4
	Harvest	1,2
9:6-15	Harvest	3,6,7,8
10:3-6	Trinity 21/Pentecost 22	5
10:7-18	Advent 2	5
11:19—12:9	Sexagesima	1
12:7-10	Trinity 6/Pentecost 7	7
13:5-14	Septuagesima	5
13:11-14	Trinity Sunday/Pentecost 1	2,6

Galatians

1:1-10	Trinity 1/Pentecost 2	8
1:1-12	Reformation	5
1:11-24	Trinity 2/Pentecost 3	8
2:11-21	Trinity 3/Pentecost 4	8
2:17-21	Lent 3	4
3:5-14	Epiphany 5	5
3:15-22	Trinity 13/Pentecost 14	1
3:23-29	New Year's Day	1
	Trinity 4/Pentecost 5	8
4:1-7	Sunday after Christmas	1
4:4-7	Sunday after Christmas	6
4:21-31	Lent 4	1
5:1,13-25	Trinity 5/Pentecost 6	8
5:16-24	Trinity 14/Pentecost 15	1
5:25—6:10	Trinity 15/Pentecost 16	1
6:1-10,14-16	Trinity 6/Pentecost 7	8

Ephesians

1:3-14	Septuagesima	4
	Trinity Sunday/Pentecost 1	2
	Trinity 7/Pentecost 8	7
1:3-6,15-18	Second Sunday after Christmas	6,7,8
1:15-23	Ascension	3
	Sunday after Ascension/Easter 7	2
1:16-23	Ascension	6,7,8
2:1-10	Passion Sunday/Lent 5	4
2:4-10	Lent 4	7
	Easter 2/Easter 3	2

2:10-22	Pentecost	2
2:11-18	Easter 1/Easter 2	4
2:13-22	Trinity 8/Pentecost 9	7
2:19-22	Easter 4/Easter 5	4
	Trinity 14/Pentecost 15	3
3:2-12	Epiphany	6,7,8
3:13-21	Trinity 16/Pentecost 17	1
4:1-6	Trinity 17/Pentecost 18	1
4:1-7,11-16	Trinity 9/Pentecost 10	7
4:7-16	Ascension	4
4:8-16	Trinity 15/Pentecost 16	3
4:17-24	Trinity 10/Pentecost 11	7
4:22-28	Trinity 19/Pentecost 20	1
4:29-32	Trinity 7/Pentecost 8	4
4:30—5:2	Trinity 11/Pentecost 12	7
5:1-9	Lent 3	1
5:6-14	Advent 1	5
5:8-14	Lent 3	6
5:15-20	Trinity 12/Pentecost 13	7
5:15-21	Trinity 20/Pentecost 21	1
5:21-31	Trinity 13/Pentecost 14	7
5:22-33	Epiphany 2	4
6:1-9	Trinity 20/Pentecost 21	3
	Trinity 21/Pentecost 22	2
6:20-17	Trinity 21/Pentecost 22	1
6:10-20	Trinity 14/Pentecost 15	7

Philippians

1:3-11	Advent 2	8
	Trinity 22/Pentecost 23	1
1:3-5,19-27	Trinity 17/Pentecost 18	6
1:12-21	Sexagesima	2
1:27—2:4	Septuagesima	2
2:1-5	Trinity 18/Pentecost 19	6
2:5-11	Palm Sunday	1,6,7,8
2:12-18	Palm Sunday	4
3:8-14	Passion Sunday/Lent 5	8
3:13-16	Easter 3/Easter 4	5
3:17-21	Trinity 23/Pentecost 24	1
3:17—4:1	Lent 2	8

4:4-7	Advent 3	8
	Advent 4	1
4:4-8	Trinity 19/Pentecost 20	6
4:6-20	Thanksgiving	7,8
4:8-17	New Year's Day	5
4:4-13	Trinity 20/Pentecost 21	6

Colossians

1:1-14	Trinity 7/Pentecost 8	8
1:9-14	Trinity 24/Pentecost 25	1
1:13-20	Trinity 27/Last Pentecost	8
1:21-28	Trinity 8/Pentecost 9	8
2:1-5	Lent 2	5
2:6-15	New Year's Day	4
	Trinity 9/Pentecost 10	8
2:16-23	Epiphany 5	4
3:1-4	Easter Sunday/Easter 1	6
	Ascension	2
	Trinity 23/Pentecost 24	3
3:1-10	Trinity 19/Pentecost 20	4
3:1-11	Trinity 10/Pentecost 11	8
3:12-17	Epiphany 5	1
3:12-21	Sunday after Christmas	7

1 Thessalonians

1:1-5a	Trinity 21/Pentecost 22	6
1:5b-10	Trinity 22/Pentecost 23	6
2:8-13	Trinity 25/Pentecost 26	6
3:7-13	Trinity 26/Pentecost 27	6
3:9-13	Advent 1	8
4:1-7	Lent 2	1
4:13,14	Trinity 23/Pentecost 24	6
4:13-18	Trinity 25/Pentecost 26	1
5:1-11	Trinity 24/Pentecost 25	3,6
	Trinity 27/Last Pentecost	1
5:14-24	Trinity 16/Pentecost 17	3
	Trinity 24/Pentecost 25	2
5:16-24	Advent 3	7

2 Thessalonians

1:1-5,11,12	Trinity 23/Pentecost 24	8

2:1-12	Trinity 25/Pentecost 26	3
2:7-17	Reformation	4
2:13—3:5	Trinity 24/Pentecost 25	8
3:1-5	Trinity 18/Pentecost 19	4
3:5-12	Trinity 19/Pentecost 20	3
3:6-13	Trinity 15/Pentecost 16	2
	Trinity 25/Pentecost 26	8

1 Timothy

1:8-17	Trinity 3/Pentecost 4	4
1:12-17	Trinity 14/Pentecost 15	2
	Trinity 16/Pentecost 17	8
2:1-4	Thanksgiving	6,7,8
2:1-6	Advent 4	4
	Easter 5/Easter 6	2
2:1-8	Trinity 17/Pentecost 18	8
	Thanksgiving	1
3:16	Christmas Day	5
4:4-11	Trinity 23/Pentecost 24	2
4:6-11	Trinity 3/Pentecost 4	5
5:17-25	Trinity 6/Pentecost 7	5
6:3-12	Trinity 21/Pentecost 22	3
6:6-10	Trinity 9/Pentecost 10	4
6:6-12	Trinity 7/Pentecost 8	2
6:6-16	Trinity 18/Pentecost 19	8
6:11-16	Advent 2	3
6:17-19	Harvest	5

2 Timothy

1:3-14	Trinity 19/Pentecost 20	8
1:7-14	Trinity Sunday/Pentecost 1	5
2:3-15	Advent 3	5
2:8-13	Easter 4/Easter 5	2
	Trinity 20/Pentecost 21	8
2:19-26	Trinity 1/Pentecost 2	5
3:10-17	Advent 2	4
3:14—4:5	Trinity 21/Pentecost 22	8
4:1-8	Trinity 11/Pentecost 12	4
4:3-8	Sunday after Christmas	3
4:5-8	Advent 3	2
4:6-8,16-18	Trinity 22/Pentecost 23	8

1 Historic — 2 Eisenach — 3 Thomasius — 4 Synodical Conf. — 5 Soll — 6 ILCW - A — 7 ILCW-B — 8 ILCW-C

Titus

2:1-10	Epiphany 2	5
2:11-14	Christmas Day/Christmas Eve	1,6,7,8
3:4-7	Christmas Day	6,7,8

Philemon

:10-21	Trinity 15/Pentecost 16	8

Hebrews

1:1-6	Christmas Day	3
1:1-9	Christmas Dawn	6,7,8
1:1-12	Christmas Day	4
1:13—2:10	Lent 1	5
2:9-11	Trinity 19/Pentecost 20	7
2:10-15	Lent 2	3
2:10-18	Sunday after Christmas	8
3:1-6	Passion Sunday/Lent 5	5
	Trinity 20/Pentecost 21	7
4:1-13	Easter 2/Easter 3	4
4:9-13	Trinity 17/Pentecost 18	2
	Trinity 23/Pentecost 24	3
4:9-16	Trinity 21/Pentecost 22	7
4:14-16	Passion Sunday/Lent 5	3
	Trinity 26/Pentecost 27	4
4:14-16; 5:7-9	Good Friday	6,7,8
4:15,16	Lent 1	2
5:1-10	Lent 3	3
	Trinity 22/Pentecost 23	7
5:7-9	Passion Sunday/Lent 5	7
5:11—6:10	Trinity 10/Pentecost 11	5
7:23-28	Trinity 23/Pentecost 24	7
7:24-27	Passion Sunday/Lent 5	3
7:26—8:2	Trinity 22/Pentecost 23	5
8:8-11	Pentecost	3
9:11-15	Passion Sunday/Lent 5	1
9:24-28	Trinity 24/Pentecost 25	7
10:1-14	Lent 4	3
10:5-10	Advent 4	8
10:15-39	Maundy Thursday	8
10:19-23	Good Friday	3

10:19-25	Advent 1	2
10:32-39	Trinity 25/Pentecost 26	2
11:1-3,8-16	Trinity 11/Pentecost 12	8
12:1,2	Trinity 26/Pentecost 27	7
12:1-6	Palm Sunday	2,3
12:1-13	Trinity 12/Pentecost 13	8
12:12-17	Trinity 7/Pentecost 8	5
12:14-17	Lent 1	3
12:18-24	Trinity 13/Pentecost 14	8
	Trinity 16/Pentecost 17	2
	Trinity 26/Pentecost 27	3
12:18-29	Quinquagesima	5
12:26-29	Trinity 25/Pentecost 26	7
13:1-8	Trinity 14/Pentecost 15	8
13:1-9	Trinity 2/Pentecost 3	4
	Trinity 22/Pentecost 23	2
13:7-9	Reformation	3
13:8	New Year's Day	3
13:12-21	Quinquagesima	4

James

1:2-12	Trinity 13/Pentecost 14	4
1:16-21	Easter 4/Easter 5	1
1:17-22,26,27	Trinity 15/Pentecost 16	7
1:22-27	Easter 5/Easter 6	1
2:1-5,8-10,14-18	Trinity 16/Pentecost 17	7
2:1-13	Trinity 2/Pentecost 3	5
2:10-17	Trinity 18/Pentecost 19	2
3:6-18	Trinity 14/Pentecost 15	5
3:16—4:6	Trinity 17/Pentecost 18	3,7
4:7-12	Trinity 18/Pentecost 19	7
4:7-17	Trinity 11/Pentecost 12	5
4:13-17	Sunday after New Year	2
5:7-10	Advent 3	6
5:7-11	Trinity 22/Pentecost 23	3
5:13-20	Trinity 19/Pentecost 20	2
	Trinity 20/Pentecost 21	5

1 Peter

1:1-9	Trinity Sunday/Pentecost 1	4

1 Historic · 2 Eisenach · 3 Thomasius · 4 Synodical Conf. · 5 Soll · 6 ILCW - A · 7 ILCW - B · 8 ILCW - C

1:3-9	Easter Sunday/Easter 1	3
	Easter 1/Easter 2	2,6
1:3-21	Transfiguration	3
1:10-16	Lent 4	5
1:13-16	Lent 3	2
1:17-21	Easter 2/Easter 3	6
1:17-25	Passion Sunday/Lent 5	2
1:22-25	Easter 1/Easter 2	3
2:1-10	Sunday after Christmas	4
	Trinity 13/Pentecost 14	2
2:4-10	Easter 4/Easter 5	6
2:11-20	Easter 3/Easter 4	1
2:19-25	Easter 3/Easter 4	6
2:21-25	Easter 2/Easter 3	1
3:8-15	Trinity 5/Pentecost 6	1
3:15-17	Epiphany 3	5
3:15-18a	Easter 5/Easter 6	6
4:3-7	Advent 4	5
4:7-11	Sunday after Ascension/Easter 7	1
4:12-19	Sunday after New Year	1
4:12-17; 5:6-11	Sunday after Ascension/Easter 7	6
5:1-5	Trinity 5/Pentecost 6	5
5:6-11	Trinity 3/Pentecost 4	1

2 Peter

1:3-11	Advent 2	2
	Septuagesima	3
1:16-19	Transfiguration	6
1:16-21	Transfiguration	1
	Sexagesima	3
2:1-11	Trinity 27/Last Pentecost	5
3:3-14	Trinity 26/Pentecost 27	1
3:8-14	Advent 2	7
3:14-18	Transfiguration	4

1 John

1:1-4	Advent 4	2
	Christmas Day	3
1:5-10	Epiphany 4	3
1:5—2:2	Easter 2/Easter 3	7
	Trinity 20/Pentecost 21	4

2:3-11	Easter 3/Easter 4	4
2:12-17	Lent 2	2
2:24-29	Trinity 18/Pentecost 19	5
3:1,2	Easter 3/Easter 4	7
3:1-5	Christmas Day	2
3:1-6	Epiphany	3
3:1-9	Trinity 16/Pentecost 17	4
3:13-18	Trinity 2/Pentecost 3	1
3:18-24	Easter 4/Easter 5	7
3:19-24	Easter 5/Easter 6	4
	Sunday after Ascension/Easter 7	3
4:1-6	Easter 1/Easter 2	3
4:1-11	Easter 5/Easter 6	7
	Trinity 8/Pentecost 7	4
4:7-17	Epiphany 5	3
4:9-14	Easter 3/Easter 4	2
4:9-16	Christmas Day	4
4:13-21	Sunday after Ascension/Easter 7	7
4:16-21	Trinity 1/Pentecost 2	1
5:1-6	Easter 1/Easter 2	7
5:4-12	Easter 1/Easter 2	1
5:11-15	Easter 5/Easter 6	5

2 John

6-11	Trinity 17/Pentecost 18	5

3 John

1-12	Epiphany	5

Revelation

1:4-8	Advent 1	3
1:4b-8	Trinity 27/Last Pentecost	7
1:4-18	Easter 1/Easter 2	8
2:1-5	Easter 2/Easter 3	3
2:8-11	Trinity 26/Pentecost 27	2
3:1-6	Easter 3/Easter 4	3
3:7-11	Easter 4/Easter 5	3
3:7-13	Trinity 24/Pentecost 25	4
3:14-22	Easter 5/Easter 6	3
5:8-14	Lent 4	4

5:11-14	Easter 2/Easter 3	8
7:9-17	Easter 3/Easter 4	8
	Trinity 25/Pentecost 26	5
	Trinity 26/Pentecost 27	3
	Trinity 27/Last Pentecost	2
12:7-12	Good Friday	5
14:6-7	Reformation	1
19:6-10	Maundy Thursday	5
19:11-16	Ascension	5
21:1-5	Easter 4/Easter 5	8
21:1-7	Trinity 27/Last Pentecost	3
21:10-14,22,23	Easter 5/Easter 6	8
22:6-11	Trinity 26/Pentecost 27	5
22:12-14,16,17,20	Sunday after Ascension/Easter 7	8
22:12-21	Trinity 27/Last Pentecost	4

1 Historic
2 Eisenach
3 Thomasius
4 Synodical Conf.
5 Soll
6 ILCW - A
7 ILCW-B
8 ILCW-C

CHURCH YEAR INDEX

Advent 1

Ps 24	4
Is 2:1-5	6
Is 61:1-3	3
Is 62:10-12	5
Is 63:16b-17; 64:1-8	7
Jr 31:31-34	1,2
Jr 33:14-16	8
Mt 11:25-30	4
Mt 21:1-9	1
Mt 24:37-44	6
Mk 13:33-37	7
Lk 1:68-79	2,3
Lk 17:20-25	4
Lk 19:29-40	5
Lk 21:25-36	8
Ro 1:16-20	4
Ro 13:11-14	1,6
1 Cor 1:3-9	7
Eph 5:6-14	5
1 Th 3:9-13	8
He 10:19-25	2
Re 1:4-8	3

Advent 2

Dt 18:15-22	4
Is 11:1-10	6
Is 40:1-11	7
Zph 1:7-18	5
Mal 3:1-4	8
Mal 4:1-6	1,2,3
Mt 3:1-12	6
Mk 1:1-8	7
Mk 13:1-8	5
Lk 1:67-80	4
Lk 3:1-6	8
Lk 17:20-30	2,3
Lk 17:26-37	4
Lk 21:25-36	1
Ro 15:4-13	1,6
2 Cor 10:7-18	5
Php 1:3-11	8
1 Tm 6:11-16	3
2 Tm 3:10-17	4
2 Pe 1:3-11	2
2 Pe 3:8-14	7

Advent 3

Is 35:1-10	6
Is 40:1-8	1,2
Is 50:1-10	3
Is 56:1-7	5
Is 61	4
Is 61:1-3,10,11	7
Zph 3:14-18a	8
Mt 3:1-11	2
Mt 3:1-12	3,4
Mt 11:2-10	1
Mt 11:2-11	6
Lk 3:3-14	4
Lk 3:7-18	8
Lk 7:18-26	5
Jn 1:6-8,19-28	7
Ro 2:12-16	3
1 Cor 4:1-5	1
1 Cor 9:16-23	4
Php 4:4-7	8
1 Th 5:16-24	7
2 Tm 2:3-15	5
2 Tm 4:5-8	2
Jas 5:7-10	6

Advent 4

Dt 18:15-19	1,2
2 Sm 7:8-11,16	7

1 Historic
2 Eisenach
3 Thomasius
4 Synodical Conf.
5 Soll
6 ILCW - A
7 ILCW - B
8 ILCW - C

Is 2:2-5	3
Is 7:10-14	6
Hg 2:7-10	4
Mic 5:2-4	8
Zch 6:12-15	5
Mt 1:18-25	6
Mk 6:17-29	4
Lk 1:26-38	7
Lk 1:39-45	8
Lk 1:46-55	3
Lk 1:56-66	5
Jn 1:15-18	2
Jn 1:19-28	1
Jn 1:29-34	4
Ro 1:1-7	6
Ro 16:25-27	7
1 Cor 1:26-29	3
Php 4:4-7	1
1 Tm 2:1-6	4
He 10:5-10	8
1 Pe 4:3-7	5
1 Jn 1:1-4	2

Christmas Eve

Is 9:2-7	6,7,8
Tt 2:11-14	6,7,8
Lk 2:1-20	6,7,8

Christmas Dawn

Is 52:7-10	6,7,8
He 1:1-9	6,7,8
Jn 1:1-14	6,7,8

Christmas Day

Is 9:2-7	1,4,6
Is 9:6,7	2,3
Is 52:7-10	7
Is 62:10-12	6,7,8
Eze 17:22-24	5
Mic 5:1-3	3
Zch 2:10-13	4
Mt 1:18-23	2
Mt 1:18-25	4
Lk 1:26-38	5
Lk 1:46-55	4
Lk 2:1-14	1
Lk 2:1-20	3,6,7,8
Jn 1:1-14	3,4
Jn 1:1-18	7
Jn 1:15-18	4
1 Tm 3:16	5
Tt 2:11-14	1,6
Tt 3:4-7	6,7,8
He 1:1-6	3
He 1:1-9	7
He 1:1-12	4
1 Jn 1:1-4	3
1 Jn 3:1-5	2
1 Jn 4:9-16	4

Sunday after Christmas

Is 28:14-19	4
Is 43:16-20	5
Is 45:22-25	7
Is 63:7-9	6
Is 63:7-16	1,2
Is 63:7-17	3
Jr 31:10-13	8
Mt 2:13-15,19-23	6
Lk 2:22-32	3,4
Lk 2:25-32	2
Lk 2:25-40	7
Lk 2:33-40	1
Lk 2:41-52	8
Lk 9:57-62	4
Jn 10:31-42	5
Ac 18:24-28	5
2 Cor 5:1-9	2
Ga 4:1-7	1
Ga 4:4-7	6

Col 3:12-21	7
2 Tm 4:3-8	3
He 2:10-18	8
1 Pe 2:1-10	4

New Year's Day

Nu 6:22-27	6,7,8
Jos 24:14-18	1
Ps 90	2
Ps 121	4
Is 60:17-22	5
Lm 3:22-32	3
Lk 2:21	1,6,7,8
Lk 4:16-21	2
Lk 12:1-3	5
Lk 12:4-9	4
Lk 13:1-9	4
Lk 13:6-9	3
Ro 1:1-7	6,7,8
Ro 8:24-32	2
Ga 3:23-29	1
Php 4:8-17	5
Col 2:6-15	4
He 13:8	3

Sunday after New Year (Second Sunday after Christmas)

Gn 27:22-46	5
1 Sm 2:1-10	1
Ps 73:23-28	2,3
Is 61:10—62:3	6,7,8
Lm 3:22-32	4
Mt 2:13-23	1
Mt 9:9-13	4
Mt 16:1-4	2
Mk 6:20-29	3
Lk 5:27-32	5
Lk 13:18-24	4
Jn 1:1-18	6,7,8
Ac 19:1-7	3
Ro 3:21-26	4
Ro 9:1-8	5
Eph 1:3-6,15-18	6,7,8
Jas 4:13-17	2
1 Pe 4:12-19	1

Epiphany

Is 2:2-5	1,2
Is 49:1-9	3
Is 60:1-6	1,6,7,8
Is 60:1-11	4
Zch 14:8-11	5
Mt 2:1-12	1,6,7,8
Mt 3:13-17	2,3
Mt 4:12-17	4
Mt 13:10-17	5
Lk 4:16-21	4
Ac 8:26-39	4
2 Cor 4:3-6	2
Eph 3:2-12	6,7,8
1 Jn 3:1-6	3
3 Jn 1-12	5

Epiphany 1

Dt 6:1-9	3
Ps 78:1-7	4
Ps 122	2
Ec 12:1-7	1
Is 42:1-7	6,7,8
Mal 1:6-11	5
Mt 3:13-17	6
Mt 10:32-39	4
Mk 1:4-11	7
Lk 2:41-52	1
Lk 3:15-17,21,22	8
Lk 12:51-59	5
Jn 1:35-42	2
Jn 1:36-51	3
Jn 6:28-40	4
Ac 10:34-38	6,7,8

Ro 10:8-18	4
Ro 10:12-21	3
Ro 12:1-5	1
Ro 14:13-23	5
2 Cor 6:14—7:1	2

Epiphany 2

Gn 46:28-34	5
1 Sm 3:1-10	7
Ps 104:24-35	4
Is 8:20-22	3
Is 49:1-6	6
Is 61:1-6	1,2
Is 62:1-5	8
Mt 8:19-22	5
Mt 12:56-50	4
Lk 4:14-22	3
Jn 1:29-41	6
Jn 1:35-42	4
Jn 1:43-51	2,7
Jn 2:1-11	1,8
Ro 10:1-12	3
Ro 12:6-16	1
1 Cor 1:1-9	6
1 Cor 2:6-16	2
1 Cor 6:12-20	7
1 Cor 12:1-11	8
Eph 5:22-33	4
Tt 2:1-10	5

Epiphany 3

Nu 24:10-17	3
2 Kgs 5:1-19	1,2
Job 1:1-22	5
Is 9:1-4	6
Is 61:1-6	8
Dn 6:10-23	4
Jon 3:1-5,10	7
Mt 4:12-23	6
Mt 8:1-13	1
Mt 11:25-30	3
Mk 1:14-20	7
Mk 1:40-45	5
Lk 4:14-21	8
Lk 4:38-44	4
Jn 4:1-14	4
Jn 4:5-14	2
Ro 1:13-20	2
Ro 5:1-5	3
Ro 8:24-30	4
Ro 12:17-21	1
1 Cor 1:10-17	6
1 Cor 7:29-31	7
1 Cor 12:12-21,26,27	8
1 Pe 3:15-17	5

Epiphany 4

Ex 14:21-31	1
Dt 18:15-20	7
1 Kgs 19:9-18	4
Job 2:1-13	5
Ps 93	2
Is 51:1-12	3
Jr 1:4-10	8
Mic 6:1-8	6
Mt 5:1-12	6
Mt 8:23-27	1
Mt 14:22-33	4
Mk 1:21-28	7
Mk 6:45-56	5
Lk 4:21-32	8
Jn 4:15-26	4
Jn 4:31-42	2
Jn 8:12-16	3
Ro 7:7-16	2
Ro 13:8-10	1
1 Cor 1:10-17	5
1 Cor 1:26-31	6
1 Cor 3:1-11	4
1 Cor 8:1-13	7

1 Cor 12:27—13:13	8
1 Jn 1:5-10	3

Epiphany 5

Gn 11:1-9	4
Job 7:1-7	7
Is 6:1-8	8
Is 48:5-9a	6
Jr 18:1-10	3
Eze 33:10-16	1,2
Hg 1:2-14	5
Mt 5:13-20	6
Mt 7:24-29	2
Mt 13:24-30	1
Mt 13:31-35	4
Mk 1:29-39	7
Mk 4:26-32	4
Mk 6:1-6	5
Lk 5:1-11	8
Jn 6:26-35	3
Ro 8:1-9	2
1 Cor 2:1-5	6
1 Cor 9:16-23	7
1 Cor 14:12b-20	8
Ga 3:5-14	5
Col 2:16-23	4
Col 3:12-17	1
1 Jn 4:7-17	3

Epiphany 6

Dt 30:15-20	6
2 Kgs 5:1-14	7
Jr 17:5-8	8
Mt 5:20-37	6
Mk 1:40-45	7
Lk 6:17-26	8
1 Cor 2:6-13	6
1 Cor 9:24-27	7
1 Cor 15:12,16-20	8

Epiphany 7

Gn 45:3-8a,15	8
Dt 19:1,2,17,18	6
Is 43:18-25	7
Mt 5:38-48	6
Mk 2:1-12	7
Lk 6:27-38	8
1 Cor 3:10,11,16-23	6
1 Cor 15:35-38a,42-50	8
2 Cor 1:18-22	7

Epiphany 8

Is 49:13-18	6
Jr 7:1-7	8
Ho 2:14-16,19,20	7
Mt 6:24-34	6
Mk 2:18-22	7
Lk 6:39-49	8
1 Cor 4:1-13	6
1 Cor 15:51-58	8
2 Cor 3:1b-6	7

Transfiguration

Gn 28:10-22	4
Ex 3:1-6	1,2,3
Ex 24:12,15-18	6
Ex 40:34-38	5
Dt 34:1-12	8
2 Kgs 2:1-12c	7
Mt 17:1-9	1,6
Mk 9:2-9	7
Mk 9:2-13	4
Lk 7:1-10	3
Lk 9:28-36	5,8
Jn 4:27-42	4
Jn 5:39-47	2
2 Cor 3:12-18	2
2 Cor 3:12—4:2	7
2 Cor 4:1-10	5
2 Cor 4:3-6	8

1 Pe 1:3-21	3
2 Pe 1:16-19	6
2 Pe 1:16-21	1
2 Pe 3:14-18	4

Septuagesima

Dt 34:1-12	5
Jr 9:23-24	1,2
Jr 31:31-34	4
Dn 4:31-34	3
Dn 5:17-30	3
Mt 5:17-29	4
Mt 20:1-16	1
Lk 6:20-35	5
Lk 10:38-42	2,4
Jn 7:14-17	3
1 Cor 9:24—10:5	1
2 Cor 13:5-14	5
Eph 1:3-14	4
Php 1:27—2:4	2
2 Pe 1:3-11	3

Sexagesima

Ex 32:15-35	5
1 Sm 17:42-51	4
Is 25:1-9	3
Am 8:11,12	1,2
Mt 13:1-9,18-23	5
Mt 16:13-20	4
Mt 17:1-9	3
Lk 8:4-15	1
Jn 8:25-36	4
Jn 11:20-27	2
Ac 16:24-35	4
2 Cor 1:3-7	5
2 Cor 3:12-18	3
2 Cor 11:19—12:9	1
Php 1:12-21	2
2 Pe 1:16-21	3

Quinquagesima

Jr 8:4-9	1,2
Jr 8:19-22	3
Jon 3:1-9	5
Jon 3:10—4:11	4
Mt 16:21-23	4
Mt 20:17-28	4
Mk 8:27-38	3
Mk 9:30-32	5
Mk 10:32-45	3
Lk 18:31-43	1
Jn 11:47-57	2
1 Cor 1:18-24	3
1 Cor 1:21-31	2
1 Cor 13	1
He 12:18-29	5
He 13:12-21	4

Ash Wednesday

Jl 2:12-19	1,6,7,8
Mt 6:1-6,16-21	6,7,8
Mt 6:16-21	1
2 Cor 5:20b—6:2	6,7,8

Lent 1

Gn 2:7-9,15-17; 3:1-7	6
Gn 3:1-15	4
Gn 22:1-14	1,2,7
Nu 20:1-13	5
Dt 26:5-10	8
Jr 2:17-19	3
Jr 3:22-23	3
Mt 4:1-11	1,6
Mt 11:20-24	3
Mt 16:21-26	2
Mt 26:36-46	5
Mk 1:12-15	7
Lk 4:1-13	8
Lk 4:1-15	4
Jn 15:9-17	4

1 Historic
2 Eisenach
3 Thomasius
4 Synodical Conf.
5 Soll
6 ILCW - A
7 ILCW - B
8 ILCW - C

Ro 3:27-31	4
Ro 5:12,17-19	6
Ro 8:31-39	7
Ro 10:8b-13	8
2 Cor 6:1-10	1
He 1:13—2:10	5
He 4:15,16	2
He 12:14-17	3

Lent 2

Gn 12:1-8	6
Gn 22	4
Gn 28:10-17	7
Ex 14:13-21	3
Ex 33:17-23	2
Ex 33:17-25	1
Lv 20:6-8	5
Is 52:7-17	3
Jr 26:8-15	8
Mt 15:21-28	1
Mk 7:24-30	5
Mk 8:31-38	7
Lk 10:17-20	2
Lk 13:31-35	8
Jn 4:5-26	6
Jn 8:21-30	3
Jn 12:20-26	4
Jn 15:18-25	4
Ro 4:1-5,13-17	6
Ro 5:1-11	7
1 Cor 1:18-25	4
Php 3:17—4:1	8
Col 2:1-5	5
1 Th 4:1-7	1
He 2:10-15	3
1 Jn 2:12-17	2

Lent 3

Gn 22	3
Ex 3:1-8a,10-15	8
Ex 20:1-17	7
Ps 25	4
Is 42:14-21	6
Is 49:22-26	5
Jr 26:1-15	1,2
Mt 12:22-29	5
Mk 10:35-45	4
Lk 9:51-56	2
Lk 11:14-28	1
Lk 13:1-9	8
Jn 2:13-22	7
Jn 2:13-25	4
Jn 9:13-17,34-39	6
Jn 10:24-33	3
Ro 5:17—6:2	5
1 Cor 1:22-25	7
1 Cor 10:1-13	8
Ga 2:17-21	4
Eph 5:1-9	1
Eph 5:8-14	6
He 5:1-10	3
1 Pe 1:13-16	2

Lent 4

Gn 41:25-45	5
Nu 21:4-9	7
Dt 7:6-11	4
Is 12:1-6	8
Is 42:1-8	3
Is 52:7-10	1,2
Ho 5:15—6:2	6
Mt 20:17-28	6
Lk 9:10-17	5
Lk 15:1-3,11-32	8
Jn 3:14-21	7
Jn 6:1-15	1
Jn 6:47-57	2
Jn 11:46-57	4
Jn 11:47-57	3
Jn 17:1-6	4

Ro 8:1-10	6
1 Cor 1:18-31	8
2 Cor 7:4-10	2
Ga 4:21-31	1
Eph 2:4-10	7
He 10:1-14	3
1 Pe 1:10-16	5
Re 5:8-14	4

Passion Sunday (Lent 5)

Gn 14:8-20	4
Lv 16:29-34	5
Nu 21:4-9	1,2,3
Is 43:16-21	8
Jr 31:31-34	7
Eze 37:1-3,11-14	6
Mt 23:34-39	4
Lk 13:31-35	5
Lk 20:9-19	8
Jn 8:46-59	1
Jn 11:47-53	6
Jn 12:20-33	7
Jn 12:23-33	3
Jn 12:27-36	4
Jn 13:31-35	2
Ro 8:11-19	6
Eph 2:1-10	4
Php 3:8-14	8
He 3:1-6	5
He 4:14-16	3
He 5:7-9	7
He 7:24-27	3
He 9:11-15	1
1 Pe 1:17-25	2

Palm Sunday

Dt 32:36-39	8
Ps 8	4
Is 45:22-25	5
Is 50:4-9a	6
Zch 9:8-12	1,2,3
Zch 9:9,10	7
Mt 21:1-9	1
Mt 27:11-54	6
Mk 11:1-10	5
Mk 15:1-39	7
Lk 23:1-45	8
Jn 12:1-8	2
Jn 12:1-11	4
Jn 12:1-19	3
Jn 12:12-19	4
2 Cor 4:11-18	5
Php 2:5-11	1,6,7,8
Php 2:12-18	4
He 12:1-6	2,3

Maundy Thursday

Ex 12:1-14	1,3,4,6
Ex 24:3-11	7
Lv 16:15-22	5
Ps 111	2
Jr 31:31-34	8
Mt 26:17-30	4
Mk 14:12-26	7
Lk 22:7-20	4,8
Lk 22:14-20	2
Lk 22:14-23	3
Jn 13:1-15	1
Jn 13:1-17,34	3,6
Jn 13:16-20	5
1 Cor 10:14-21	4
1 Cor 10:16,17	2,3,7
1 Cor 11:23-26	6
1 Cor 11:23-32	1
1 Cor 11:28-32	3
He 10:15-39	8
Re 19:6-10	5

Good Friday

Ps 22:1-11	2
Is 52:13—53:12	1,6,7,8

1 Historic 2 Eisenach 3 Thomasius 4 Synodical Conf. 5 Soll 6 ILCW - A 7 ILCW - B 8 ILCW - C

Is 53	4
Is 53:1-7	1,3
Zch 13:6-9	5
Mt 27:29-56	3
Lk 23:26-38	5
Lk 23:39-46	2
Lk 23:39-53	4
Jn 18:1—19:42	1
Jn 19:17-30	6,7,8
2 Cor 5:14-21	2,3,4
He 4:14-16; 5:7-9	6,7,8
He 10:19-23	3
Re 12:7-12	5

Easter Sunday/Easter 1

Ex 15:1-11	8
Job 19:22-27	3
Job 19:23-27	4
Ps 118:14-24	2
Is 25:1-8	1
Is 25:6-9	7
Is 53:8-12	3
Jon 2:1-10	5
Mt 28:1-8	3
Mt 28:1-10	2,4
Mk 16:1-8	1,7
Lk 24:1-11	8
Lk 24:1-12	4
Jn 20:1-9	6
Jn 20:1-10	5
Ac 10:34-43	6
Ac 13:26-39	4
1 Cor 5:6-8	1
1 Cor 15:1-11	8
1 Cor 15:12-20	2
1 Cor 15:19-28	7
1 Cor 15:20-28	5
Col 3:1-4	6
1 Pe 1:3-9	3

Easter 1/Easter 2

Gn 32:22-31	1,2,3
Jos 3:9-17	5
2 Sm 12:1-10	4
Mt 12:38-42	4
Lk 11:29-36	5
Jn 6:65-71	3
Jn 20:19-31	1,6,7,8
Jn 21:1-14	4
Jn 21:15-19	2
Jn 21:15-24	3
Ac 2:14a,22-32	6
Ac 3:13-15,17-26	7
Ac 5:12,17-32	8
2 Cor 2:5-11	5
Eph 2:11-18	4
1 Pe 1:3-9	2,6
1 Pe 1:22-25	3
1 Jn 4:1-6	3
1 Jn 5:1-6	7
1 Jn 5:4-12	1
Re 1:9-19	8

Easter 2/Easter 3

Ps 23	2,4
Is 40:6-11	5
Eze 34:11-16	1,3
Eze 34:23-31	3
Lk 24:13-35	6
Lk 24:36-49	7
Jn 10:1-11	4
Jn 10:11-16	1
Jn 10:17-21	4
Jn 12:37-45	5
Jn 14:1-6	2
Jn 21:1-14	3,8
Ac 2:14a,36-47	6
Ac 4:8-12	7
Ac 9:1-20	8
Ro 4:23—5:11	5

1 Historic
2 Eisenach
3 Thomasius
4 Synodical Conf.
5 Soll
6 ILCW - A
7 ILCW - B
8 ILCW - C

Eph 2:4-10	2
He 4:1-13	4
1 Pe 1:17-21	6
1 Pe 2:21-25	1
1 Jn 1:1—2:2	7
Re 2:1-5	3
Re 5:11-14	8

Easter 3/Easter 4

2 Kgs 20:1-11	5
Ps 100	4
Is 40:26-31	1,2
Is 61:10-11	3
Mt 9:14-17	5
Mk 2:18-22	4
Jn 10:1-10	6
Jn 10:1-11	3
Jn 10:11-18	7
Jn 10:22-30	8
Jn 11:1-16	4
Jn 12:20-26	2
Jn 16:16-23	1
Ac 4:23-33	7
Ac 6:1-9; 7:2a, 51-60	6
Ac 13:15-16a, 26-33	8
Php 3:13-16	5
1 Pe 2:11-20	1
1 Pe 2:19-25	6
1 Jn 2:3-11	4
1 Jn 3:1,2	7
1 Jn 4:9-14	2
Re 3:1-6	3
Re 7:9-16	8

Easter 4/Easter 5

Jdg 7:15-22	5
Ps 98	2
Is 5:1-7	3
Is 49:1-15	1
Jr 15:15-21	4
Jn 5:19-29	4
Jn 6:60-69	2
Jn 11:17-27	4
Jn 13:31-35	8
Jn 14:1-12	6
Jn 15:1-8	7
Jn 15:1-11	3
Jn 16:5-15	1
Jn 21:20-25	5
Ac 8:26-40	7
Ac 13:44-52	8
Ac 17:1-15	6
1 Cor 14:20-26	5
Eph 2:19-22	4
2 Tm 2:8-13	2
Jas 1:16-21	1
1 Pe 2:4-10	6
1 Jn 3:18-24	7
Re 3:7-11	3
Re 21:1-5	8

Easter 5/Easter 6

Gn 18:16-33	4
1 Kgs 3:5-15	5
Is 54:7-13	3
Is 55:6-11	1,2
Mt 7:7-12	5
Lk 11:5-13	2
Lk 18:1-18	4
Jn 11:28-45	4
Jn 14:13-21	3
Jn 14:15-21	6
Jn 14:23-29	8
Jn 15:9-17	7
Jn 16:23-30	1
Ac 11:19-30	7
Ac 14:8-18	8
Ac 17:22-31	6
1 Tm 2:1-6	2
Jas 1:22-27	1

1 Pe 3:15-22	6
1 Jn 3:19-24	4
1 Jn 4:1-11	7
1 Jn 5:11-15	5
Re 3:14-22	3
Re 21:10-14, 22,23	8

Ascension

Gn 5:21-24	1
Ps 47	4
Ps 68:15-20	5
Ps 110	2,3
Mt 16:24-28	5
Mk 16:14-20	1
Lk 24:44-53	6,7,8
Lk 24:50-53	2,3,4
Jn 17:17-26	4
Ac 1:1-11	1,6,7,8
Eph 1:15-23	3
Eph 1:16-23	6,7,8
Eph 4:7-16	4
Col 3:1-4	2
Re 19:11-16	5

Sunday after Ascension/Easter 7

Gn 45:1-15	5
Ps 42	2
Is 32:14-20	1
Is 55	4
Is 65:1-2	3
Lk 9:51-56	5
Lk 11:5-13	4
Jn 7:33-39	2
Jn 8:12-20	4
Jn 14:1-12	3
Jn 15:26—16:4	1
Jn 17:1-11	6
Jn 17:11b-19	7
Jn 17:20-26	8
Ac 1:8-14	6
Ac 1:15-26	7
Ac 13:1-12	5
Ac 16:6-10	8
2 Cor 5:1-10	4
Eph 1:15-23	2
1 Pe 4:7-11	1
1 Pe 4:12-17; 5:6-11	6
1 Jn 3:19-24	3
1 Jn 4:13-21	7
Re 22:12-17,20	8

Pentecost

Gn 11:1-9	8
Is 32:14-18	5
Is 44:1-6	3
Eze 36:22-28	1,2,4
Eze 37:1-14	7
Jl 2:28,29	6
Mt 10:1-15	5
Jn 6:60-71	4
Jn 7:37-39a	7
Jn 7:37-39	3
Jn 14:15-21	2,4
Jn 14:23-31	1
Jn 15:26,27; 16:4b-11	8
Jn 16:5-11	6
Ac 2:1-13	1
Ac 2:1-21	6
Ac 2: 22-36	7
Ac 2:37-47	8
1 Cor 2:6-16	4
2 Cor 1:18-24	5
Eph 2:10-22	2
He 8:8-11	3

Trinity Sunday/Pentecost 1

Nu 6:22-27	2,3,4
Dt 4:32-34,39,40	6
Dt 6:4-9	7
Pr 8:22-31	8

1 Historic
2 Eisenach
3 Thomasius
4 Synodical Conf.
5 Soll
6 ILCW - A
7 ILCW-B
8 ILCW-C

Is 6:1-6	1
Is 6:1-8	2
Is 6:3-7	3
Jr 10:1-16	5
Mt 3:13-17	4
Mt 28:16-20	2,4,6
Mt 28:18-20	3
Lk 3:21-33	5
Jn 3:1-15	1
Jn 3:1-17	7
Jn 16:12-15	8
Ro 5:1-5	8
Ro 8:14-17	7
Ro 11:33-36	1
1 Cor 12:4-13	3
2 Cor 13:11-14	2,6
Eph 1:3-14	2
2 Tm 1:7-14	5
1 Pe 1:1-9	4

Trinity 1/Pentecost 2

Gn 12:1-4	3
Dt 5:12-15	7
Dt 5:22-33	5
Dt 6:4-13	1,2
Dt 11:18-21,26-28	6
1 Kgs 8:41-43	8
Pr 11:23-31	4
Mt 7:21-29	6
Mt 13:31-35	2
Mt 19:16-26	4
Mk 2:23-28	7
Mk 4:26-29	3
Lk 7:1-10	8
Lk 16:19-31	1
Jn 6:47-58	5
Jn 15:1-8	4
Ac 2:42-47	3
Ac 4:32-35	2
Ro 3:21-25a,27,28	6
Ro 8:1-11	4
2 Cor 4:5-12	7
Ga 1:1-10	8
2 Tm 2:19-26	5
1 Jn 4:16-21	1

Trinity 2/Pentecost 3

Gn 3:9-15	7
Gn 15:1-6	3
Jdg 2:1,2	4
1 Kgs 17:17-24	8
Pr 9:1-10	1,2
Dn 1:1-21	5
Ho 5:15—6:6	6
Mt 9:9-13	2,3,6
Mt 11:16-24	4
Mk 3:20-35	7
Lk 7:11-17	8
Lk 14:16-24	1
Jn 7:40-53	5
Jn 8:1-11	4
Ac 3:1-10	3
Ro 4:18-25	6
Ro 10:1-15	2
2 Cor 4:13-18	7
Ga 1:11-24	8
He 13:1-9	4
Jas 2:1-13	5
1 Jn 3:13-18	1

Trinity 3/Pentecost 4

Gn 17:1-9	3
Ex 19:2-8	6
2 Sm 11:6—12:10,13-15	8
2 Chr 33:9-16	4
Is 4:2-6	5
Is 12:1-6	1,2
Eze 17:22-24	7
Mt 5:1-6	3
Mt 9:35—10:8	6

Mk 4:26-34	7
Mk 10:13-16	4
Lk 7:36-50	8
Lk 15:1-10	1
Lk 15:11-32	2,4
Lk 18:15-17	5
Ac 3:1-16	2
Ac 4:1-12	3
Ro 5:6-11	6
2 Cor 5:1-10	7
Ga 2:11-21	8
1 Tm 1:8-17	4
1 Tm 4:6-11	5
1 Pe 5:6-11	1

Trinity 4/Pentecost 5

Gn 18:20-33	3
Job 38:1-11	7
Is 12:1-6	4
Is 43:8-13	5
Is 65:17-19,24,25	1,2
Jr 20:7-13	6
Zch 12:7-10	8
Mt 5:7-12	3
Mt 5:13-16	2
Mt 7:1-6	4
Mt 10:24-33	6
Mk 4:35-41	7
Mk 11:27-33	5
Lk 6:36-42	1
Lk 9:18-24	8
Lk 17:1-10	4
Ac 4:1-12	2
Ac 6:8-15	5
Ac 7:54—8:3	4
Ac 8:26-38	3
Ro 5:12-15	6
Ro 8:18-23	1
2 Cor 5:14-21	7
Ga 3:23-29	8

Trinity 5/Pentecost 6

Gn 19:15-26	3
Ex 3:1-15	4
1 Sm 3:1—4:1a	5
1 Kgs 19:14-21	8
Jr 28:5-9	6
Lm 3:22-32	1,2
Lm 3:22-33	7
Mt 7:24-29	3
Mt 10:34-42	6
Mk 5:21-24a,35-43	7
Lk 5:1-11	1
Lk 9:18-26	2
Lk 9:51-62	8
Lk 10:1-15	5
Jn 1:43-51	4
Jn 21:15-19	4
Ac 5:34-42	2
Ac 9:1-19	3
Ac 9:1-22	4
Ro 6:1b-11	6
2 Cor 8:1-9	7
Ga 5:1,13-25	8
1 Pe 3:8-15	1
1 Pe 5:1-5	5

Trinity 6/Pentecost 7

Gn 4:3-16	4
Gn 25:7-10	3
Jos 24:14-28	5
Ru 1:1-17	1
Ps 1	2
Is 66:10-14	8
Eze 2:1-5	7
Zch 9:9-12	6
Mt 5:20-26	1
Mt 11:25-30	6
Mt 15:1-9	4
Mt 18:1-14	4
Mt 19:16-26	3

1 Historic
2 Eisenach
3 Thomasius
4 Synodical Conf.
5 Soll
6 ILCW - A
7 ILCW - B
8 ILCW - C

Mt 21:28-32	2
Mk 6:1-6	7
Mk 9:33-37	5
Lk 10:1-12,16	8
Ac 8:26-39	2
Ac 14:8-18	3
Ro 6:3-11	1
Ro 6:12-18	4
Ro 7:15-25a	6
2 Cor 12:7-10	7
Ga 6:1-10,14-16	8
1 Tm 5:17-25	5

Trinity 7/Pentecost 8

Gn 28:10-22	3
Gn 41:45-47	5
Dt 30:9-14	8
1 Kgs 17:1-6	4
Is 55:10,11	6
Is 62:6-12	1,2
Am 7:10-15	7
Mt 13:1-9	6
Mt 13:44-46	3
Mt 15:10-20	4
Mt 18:15-22	4
Mk 4:26-29	2
Mk 6:7-13	7
Mk 7:14-23	5
Mk 8:1-9	1
Lk 10:25-37	8
Ac 16:22-33	3
Ro 6:19-23	1
Ro 8:18-25	6
Eph 1:3-14	7
Eph 4:29-32	4
Col 1:1-14	8
1 Tm 6:6-12	2
He 12:12-17	5

Trinity 8/Pentecost 9

Gn 18:1-10a	8
Ex 3:1-14	3
Ps 119:121-128	5
Is 44:6-8	6
Jr 23:1-6	7
Jr 23:16-29	1,2
Jr 23:21-32	4
Mt 5:33-37	5
Mt 7:15-23	1
Mt 12:46-50	2
Mt 13:24-30	6
Mk 6:30-34	7
Mk 8:34-38	3
Lk 10:38-42	8
Jn 5:30-38	4
Jn 7:14-24	4
Ac 16:12-15	3
Ac 16:16-32	2
Ro 8:12-17	1
Ro 8:26,27	6
2 Cor 6:14—7:1	5
Eph 2:13-22	7
Col 1:21-28	8
1 Jn 4:1-6	4

Trinity 9/Pentecost 10

Gn 18:20-32	8
Ex 17:1-7	3
Ex 24:3-11	7
Ex 32:1-14	4
Jos 4:1-18	5
1 Kgs 3:5-12	6
Pr 16:1-9	1,2
Mt 12:44-46	2
Mt 13:44-52	6
Mt 14:22-34	3
Mk 12:38-44	4
Lk 5:17-26	5
Lk 11:1-13	8

1 Historic
2 Eisenach
3 Thomasius
4 Synodical Conf.
5 Soll
6 ILCW - A
7 ILCW - B
8 ILCW - C

Lk 16:1-9	1
Jn 5:39-47	4
Jn 6:1-15	7
Ac 17:16-34	2
Ac 24:22-26	3
Ro 8:28-30	6
1 Cor 10:6-13	1
1 Cor 10:29—11:1	5
Eph 4:1-7,11-16	7
Col 2:6-15	8
1 Tm 6:6-10	4

Trinity 10/Pentecost 11

Ex 16:2-15	7
Dt 4:23-31	4
Dt 32:1-9	3
Ec 1:2; 2:18-26	8
Is 55:1-5	6
Jr 7:1-11	1,2
Eze 33:30-33	5
Mt 14:13-21	6
Mt 21:12-22	4
Mt 21:33-46	4
Mt 23:34-39	2,3
Lk 12:13-21	8
Lk 19:41-48	1
Lk 20:9-19	5
Jn 6:24-35	7
Ac 4:8-20	4
Ac 7:54-59	3
Ac 20:17-38	2
Ro 8:35-39	6
1 Cor 12:1-11	1
Eph 4:17-24	7
Col 3:1-11	8
He 5:11—6:10	5

Trinity 11/Pentecost 12

Gn 15:1-6	8
Nu 9:15-23	5
1 Sm 7:5-12	3
1 Kgs 19:4-8	7
1 Kgs 19:9b-18	6
Dn 9:15-18	1
Dn 9:15-19	2
Mic 2:7-13	4
Mt 14:22-33	6
Mt 16:13-20	3
Mk 2:13-17	4
Mk 11:20-26	5
Lk 7:36-50	2
Lk 12:32-40	8
Lk 18:9-14	1
Jn 6:41-51	7
Jn 9:1-7	4
Ac 17:15-34	3
Ro 8:33-39	2
Ro 9:1-8,30-33	6
1 Cor 15:1-10	1
Eph 4:30—5:2	7
2 Tm 4:1-8	4
He 11:1-3,8-16	8
Jas 4:7-17	5

Trinity 12/Pentecost 13

Ex 34:29-35	4
Dt 30:11-20	5
1 Sm 16:1-13	3
Pr 9:1-6	7
Is 29:18-21	1,2
Is 56:1,6-8	6
Jr 23:23-29	8
Mt 9:27-34	4
Mt 13:31-35	3
Mt 15:21-28	6
Mt 19:1-12	5
Mk 7:31-37	1
Lk 12:49-53	8
Jn 6:51-58	7
Jn 8:31-36	2

1 Historic
2 Eisenach
3 Thomasius
4 Synodical Conf.
5 Soll
6 ILCW - A
7 ILCW - B
8 ILCW - C

Jn 9:24-41	4
Ac 16:9-15	2
Ac 19:23-40	3
Ro 9:30—10:8	5
Ro 11:13-15,29-32	6
2 Cor 3:4-11	1
2 Cor 3:12-18	4
Eph 5:15-20	7
He 12:1-13	8

Trinity 13/Pentecost 14

Ex 6:2-8	6
Ex 20:18-24	4
Jos 24:1-2a,14-18	7
2 Sm 12:1-10	3
Pr 2:1-8	5
Is 66:18-23	8
Zch 7:4-10	1,2
Mt 5:13-19	3
Mt 16:13-20	6
Mk 12:28-37	4
Mk 12:41-44	2
Lk 10:23-37	1
Lk 13:22-30	8
Lk 20:41-44	5
Jn 6:60-69	7
Jn 7:25-31	4
Ac 20:17-38	3
Ro 2:11-16	5
Ro 11:33-36	6
Ga 3:15-22	1
Eph 5:21-31	7
He 12:18-24	8
Jas 1:2-12	4
1 Pe 2:1-10	2

Trinity 14/Pentecost 15

Nu 12:1-15	5
Nu 21:4-9	4
Dt 4:1,2,6-8	7
Ps 50:14-23	2
Pr 4:14-23	1,3
Pr 25:6,7	8
Jr 15:15-21	6
Mt 10:16-22	3
Mt 12:9-21	4
Mt 16:21-26	6
Mk 7:1-8,14,15,21-23	7
Lk 6:6-11	5
Lk 7:36-50	4
Lk 14:1,7-14	8
Lk 17:11-19	1
Jn 5:1-14	2
Ro 7:14-25	4
Ro 12:1-8	6
Ga 5:16-24	1
Eph 2:19-22	3
Eph 6:10-20	7
1 Tm 1:12-17	2
He 13:1-8	8
Jas 3:6-18	5

Trinity 15/Pentecost 16

1 Kgs 17:1-16	3
1 Kgs 17:8-16	1,2
1 Kgs 18:21-40	4
Ps 37:12-24	5
Pr 9:8-12	8
Is 35:4-7a	7
Eze 33:7-9	6
Mt 6:24-34	1
Mt 18:15-20	6
Mk 7:31-37	7
Mk 9:14-29	5
Lk 11:5-13	3
Lk 14:12-15	4
Lk 14:25-33	8
Lk 18:1-8	3
Jn 11:1-11	2
Jn 14:7-14	4

Ro 3:1-20	5
Ro 13:1-10	6
2 Cor 9:6-11	4
Ga 5:25—6:10	1
Eph 4:8-16	3
2 Th 3:6-13	2
Phm 10-21	8
Jas 1:17-22,26,27	7

Trinity 16/Pentecost 17

Gn 50:15-21	6
Ex 32:7-14	8
1 Kgs 17:17-24	3
2 Kgs 4:18-37	5
2 Kgs 5:8-19	4
Job 5:17-26	1,2
Is 50:4-10	7
Mt 11:25-30	2
Mt 18:21-35	6
Mt 22:23-33	4
Mt 25:14-30	3
Mk 8:22-26	5
Mk 8:27-35	7
Lk 7:11-17	1
Lk 15:1-10	8
Lk 20:27-40	4
Ro 14:5-9	6
1 Cor 8:1-6	5
Eph 3:13-21	1
1 Th 5:14-24	3
1 Tm 1:12-17	8
He 12:18-24	2
Jas 2:1-5,8-10,14-18	7
1 Jn 3:1-9	4

Trinity 17/Pentecost 18

Nu 27:12-23	5
1 Sm 15:13-26	4
Ps 75:4-7	2
Pr 16:1-9	3
Pr 25:6-13	1
Is 55:6-9	6
Jr 11:18-20	7
Am 8:4-7	8
Mt 12:1-8	2,4
Mt 20:1-16	6
Mk 2:23-28	5
Mk 9:30-37	7
Lk 10:38-42	3
Lk 13:10-17	4
Lk 14:1-11	1
Lk 16:1-13	8
Ac 6:1-7	4
Eph 4:1-6	1
Php 1:3-5,19-27	6
1 Tm 2:1-8	8
He 4:9-13	2
Jas 3:16—4:6	3,7
2 Jn 6-11	5

Trinity 18/Pentecost 19

Nu 11:4-6,10-16,24-29	7
2 Chr 1:7-12	1,2
Ps 138	5
Jr 17:5-10	3
Eze 3:17-21	4
Eze 18:1-4,25-32	6
Am 6:1-7	8
Mt 5:1-12	4
Mt 6:5-15	4
Mt 21:28-32	6
Mt 22:34-46	1
Mk 9:38-50	7
Mk 10:17-27	2
Lk 7:36-50	3
Lk 11:1-4	5
Lk 16:19-31	8
1 Cor 1:4-9	1
2 Cor 7:6-10	3
Php 2 :1-5	6

2 Th 3:1-5	4
1 Tm 6:6-16	8
Jas 2:10-17	2
Jas 4:7-12	7
1 Jn 2:24-29	5

Trinity 19/Pentecost 20

Gn 2:18-24	7
Gn 28:10-17	1
1 Kgs 19:1-18	3
Ps 32:1-7	2
Ps 37:25-40	4
Is 5:1-7	6
Jr 16:16-21	5
Hab 1:1-3; 2:2-4	8
Mt 6:19-23	4
Mt 9:1-8	1
Mt 10:40-42	4
Mt 12:1-13	3
Mt 21:33-43	6
Mk 9:38-50	5
Mk 10:2-16	7
Lk 17:1-10	8
Jn 9:24-41	2
2 Cor 2:14-17	5
Eph 4:22-28	1
Php 3:12-21	6
Col 3:1-10	4
2 Th 3:5-12	3
2 Tm 1:3-14	8
He 2:9-11	7
Jas 5:13-20	2

Trinity 20/Pentecost 21

Ru 1:1-19a	8
1 Kgs 21:17-25	3
2 Kgs 2:6-18	4
Pr 2:1-8	1,2
Is 25:6-9	6
Jr 30:12-17	5
Am 5:6,7,10-15	7
Mt 7:24-29	4
Mt 22:1-10	6
Mt 22:1-14	1
Mk 1:21-28	5
Mk 1:21-28	5
Mk 10:17-27	7
Lk 6:43-49	4
Lk 17:11-19	8
Lk 19:1-5	3
Jn 15:1-8	2
Ro 14:1-9	2
Eph 5:15-21	1
Eph 6:1-9	3
Php 4:10-13,19,20	6
2 Tm 2:8-13	8
He 3:1-6	7
Jas 5:13-20	5
1 Jn 1:5—2:2	4

Trinity 21/Pentecost 22

Gn 32:22-30	8
Gn 37:12-28	5
2 Sm 7:17-29	1,2
Is 30:15-19	3
Is 45:1-7	6
Is 53:10-12	7
Dn 3:19-30	4
Mt 20:29-34	5
Mt 22:15-21	6
Mk 10:13-16	2
Mk 10:35-45	7
Mk 10:46-52	4
Lk 12:15-21	3
Lk 18:1-8a	8
Jn 4:46-54	1
Jn 5:1-9	4
Ro 14:4-12	4
2 Cor 8:1-12	3
2 Cor 10:3-6	5
Eph 6:1-9	2

Eph 6:10-17	1
1 Th 1:1-5a	6
1 Tm 6:3-12	3
2 Tm 3:14—4:5	8
He 4:9-16	7

Trinity 22/Pentecost 23

Gn 50:15-23	4
Lv 19:1,2,15-18	6
Dt 10:12-22	8
Ne 1:1-11	5
Pr 24:14-20	1,2
Jr 31:7-9	7
Zph 3:14-20	3
Mt 18:23-35	1
Mt 22:34-40	6
Mk 5:1-20	5
Mk 10:46-52	7
Lk 8:27-39	4
Lk 9:57-62	2
Lk 10:17-22	3
Lk 14:25-35	4
Lk 18:9-14	8
Ro 4:1-8	4
Php 1:3-11	1
1 Th 1:5b-10	6
2 Tm 4:6-8,16-18	8
He 5:1-10	7
He 7:26—8:2	5
He 13:1-9	2
Jas 5:7-11	3

Trinity 23/Pentecost 24

Ex 34:5-9	8
Dt 6:1-9	7
1 Sm 20:27-42	4
2 Kgs 18:1-8	5
2 Kgs 23:1-3	1
Ps 85:6-13	2
Am 5:18-24	6
Hg 2:1-10	3
Mt 10:24-33	2
Mt 17:24-27	4
Mt 22:15-22	1
Mt 25:1-13	6
Mk 12:28-34	7
Lk 13:23-30	3
Lk 19:1-10	8
Lk 20:20-26	5
Jn 7:1-13	4
Ac 20:26-32	4
Ro 16:17-20	5
Php 3:17-21	1
Col 3:1-4	3
1 Th 4:13,14	6
2 Th 1:1-5,11,12	8
1 Tm 4:4-11	2
He 4:9-13	3
He 7:23-28	7

Trinity 24/Pentecost 25

1 Kgs 17:8-16	7
1 Kgs 17:17-24	1
1 Chr 29:10-13	8
Ps 39	2
Is 54:7-13	4
Is 63:1-9	3
Jr 6:10-16	5
Ho 11:1-4,8,9	6
Mt 9:18-26	1
Mt 24:1-14	3
Mt 25:14-30	6
Mk 8:10-21	5
Mk 8:34-38	4
Mk 12:41-44	7
Lk 20:27-38	8
Jn 10:22-30	4
Jn 10:23-30	2
1 Cor 1:26-31	5
Col 1:9-14	1

1 Historic
2 Eisenach
3 Thomasius
4 Synodical Conf.
5 Soll
6 ILCW - A
7 ILCW - B
8 ILCW - C

1 Th 5:1-11	3,6
1 Th 5:14-24	2
2 Th 2:13—3:5	8
He 9:24-28	7
Re 3:7-13	4

Trinity 25/Pentecost 26

Ex 32:15-20	8
Ex 33:11-17	4
Job 14:1-5	1,2
Is 35:4-10	3
Dn 12:1-3	7
Jl 3:9-21	5
Mal 2:1,2,4-10	6
Mt 13:44-52	4
Mt 16:1-12	4
Mt 23:1-12	6
Mt 24:15-28	1
Mt 24:29-36	5
Mk 13:1-13	7
Lk 21:5-19	8
Jn 5:19-29	2
Jn 11:21-27	3
Ro 8:31-39	4
1 Th 2:8-13	6
1 Th 4:13-18	1
2 Th 2:1-12	3
2 Th 3:6-13	8
He 10:32-39	2
He 12:26-29	7
Re 7:9-17	5

Trinity 26/Pentecost 27

Gn 19:15-29	4
Ps 126	2
Is 52:1-6	8
Jr 26:1-6	6
Eze 34:17-24	5
Dn 7:9-10	7
Dn 7:9-14	1
Mt 24:1-14	6
Mt 24:37-44	5
Mt 25:31-46	1
Mk 13:24-31	7
Lk 16:10-17	4
Lk 19:11-27	2,4,8
Jn 5:19-29	3
1 Cor 15:54-58	8
1 Th 3:7-13	6
He 4:14-16	4
He 12:1,2	7
He 12:18-24	3
2 Pe 3:3-14	1
Re 2:8-11	2
Re 7:9-17	3
Re 22:6-11	5

Trinity 27/Last Pentecost

Nu 14:10-24	5
Ps 126	4
Is 35:3-10	1,2
Is 51:4-6	7
Eze 34:11-16,23,24	6
Mal 3:14-18	8
Mt 25:1-13	1
Mt 25:13-30	4
Mt 25:31-46	6
Mk 13:32-37	7
Lk 12:35-43	2
Lk 12:35-46	3
Lk 12:42-48	8
Lk 13:24-30	5
Lk 22:24-30	4
1 Cor 15:20-28	6
Col 1:13-20	8
1 Th 5:1-11	1
2 Pe 2:1-11	5
Re 1:4b-8	7
Re 7:9-17	2
Re 21:1-7	3
Re 22:12-21	4

Reformation

1 Sm 3:19—4:1a	1
2 Kgs 23:21-27	4
2 Chr 29:12-19	3
Ps 46	2,4
Ps 87:1-3	3
Jr 31:31-34	6,7,8
Hab 2:1-4	5
Mt 23:1-12	4
Lk 7:27-35	4
Lk 11:37-54	5
Jn 2:13-17	2
Jn 2:15-17	3
Jn 8:30-36	3
Jn 8:31-36	1,6,7,8
Ro 3:19-28	6,7,8
1 Cor 3:11-23	2
Ga 1:1-12	5
2 Th 2:7-17	4
He 13:7-9	3
Re 14:6,7	1

Mission Festival

Is 43:1-7	5
Is 62:1-7	6,7,8
Zph 3:8-17	4
Mt 5:13-16	4
Mt 9:35-38	4
Lk 22:31,32	5
Lk 24:44-53	6,7,8
Ac 16:9-15	4
Ro 10:11-17	6,7,8
1 Cor 12:26-31	5

Harvest

Gn 8:15-22	4
Gn 9:1-15	5
Dt 11:8-17	1
Dt 26:1-11	3,6,7,8
Ps 34:1-9	2
Ps 145:15-21	3
Mt 6:1-4	4
Mt 13:24-30	6,7,8
Mt 15:29-39	3
Lk 12:15-21	1,3
Lk 12:24-34	4
Lk 22:35-37	5
Jn 6:24-29	2
Ac 14:11-17	4
2 Cor 8:8-15	5
2 Cor 9:6-11	1,2
2 Cor 9:6-15	3,6,7,8
1 Tm 6:17-19	5

Thanksgiving

Dt 8:1-10	6,7,8
Dt 8:1-20	1
Dt 8:6-18	4
Dt 28:1-10	5
Mt 5:42-48	4
Mt 6:25-34	1
Lk 12:15-21	4
Lk 17:11-19	6,7,8
Jn 6:22-27	5
Ac 17:22-31	4
2 Cor 8:8-15	5
Php 4:6-20	7,8
1 Tm 2:1-4	6
1 Tm 2:1-8	1